THE S
RO
the

with Hen Cloud, Ramshaw, the Five Clouds, Newstones,
Baldstones, Biddulf Moor and the Churnet Valley cliffs plus a
special supplement with **Windgather** and **Castle Naze**

Edited by Geoff Milburn
Compiled by Gary Gibson

with the assistance of the guidebook team of :
Steve Dale, Richard Davis, Nick Dixon, Ian Dunn, Graham Hoey,
Simon Nadin , Andy Popp, Simon Whalley, Malc Baxter, Carl Dawson,
Dave Farrant, Neil Foster, Dave Gregory, Chris Hardy,
Keith Sharples and Ian Smith

The Windgather and Castle Naze Supplement was adapted from
chapters in *Kinder* by Dave and Bill Gregory and Jim Rubery.

First published in 1989 by
The British Mountaineering Council

Reprinted in tradepaperback 2003
Copyright © 2003 by
The British Mountaineering Council
ISBN 0-903908-97-2

CONTENTS

(Line drawings in italics)

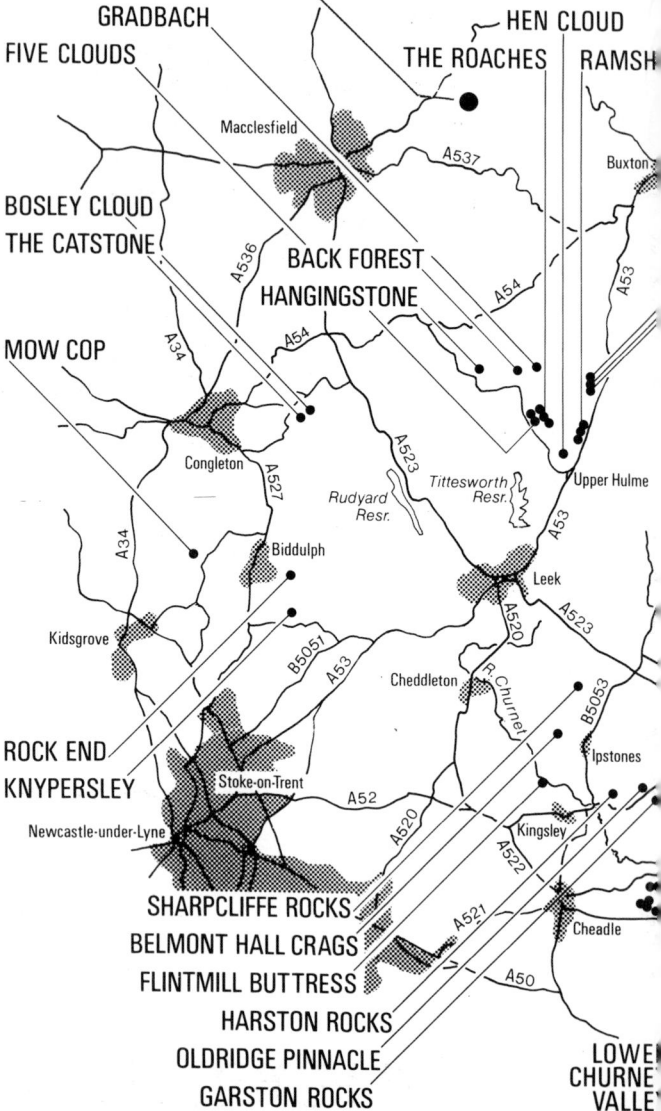

4

(Windgather)

GRADBACH

FIVE CLOUDS

HEN CLOUD
THE ROACHES
RAMSH

BOSLEY CLOUD
THE CATSTONE

BACK FOREST
HANGINGSTONE

MOW COP

ROCK END
KNYPERSLEY

SHARPCLIFFE ROCKS
BELMONT HALL CRAGS
FLINTMILL BUTTRESS
HARSTON ROCKS
OLDRIDGE PINNACLE
GARSTON ROCKS

Macclesfield

Buxton

A537

A536

A34

A54

Congleton

A527

Rudyard
Resr.

A523

Tittesworth
Resr.

Upper Hulme

A53

A54

A53

Leek

A520

A523

Kidsgrove

B5051

A53

Cheddleton

R. Churnet

B5053

Ipstones

Stoke-on-Trent

A52

A520

Kingsley

A522

Newcastle-under-Lyne

A521

Cheadle

A50

Biddulph

LOWE
CHURNE
VALLE

CKS

GIB TORR

BALDSTONES
NEWSTONES

ROCK CLIMBS IN THE PEAK
FOURTH SERIES
1. Stanage Millstone 2. Derwent Gritstone
3.4.5. Peak Limestone 6. Chew Valley
7. Staffordshire

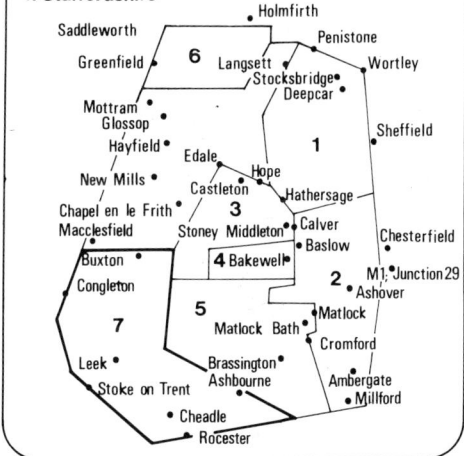

Holmfirth

Saddleworth
Greenfield • 6 Langsett Penistone
Stocksbridge • Wortley
Deepcar

Mottram
Glossop
Hayfield • Edale 1 Sheffield
New Mills • Hope
Castleton Hathersage
Chapel en le Frith 3 Calver
Macclesfield Stoney Middleton • Baslow Chesterfield
Buxton 4 Bakewell 2 M1, Junction 29
Congleton • Ashover
7 5 Matlock
Leek • Matlock Bath Cromford
Stoke on Trent Brassington • Ambergate
Ashbourne Millford
Cheadle
Rocester

River Dove
River Manifold

A515

B5054

Hartington

Wetton

R. Manifold

Ilam
Thorpe

A523
A52

A52

Mayfield
B5023

Ashbourne

0   5   10 km

R. Dove

Rocester

STAFFORDSHIRE

INTRODUCTION

---

*'The best gritstone climbing in Derbyshire,
actually lies in Staffordshire.'*

Paul Nunn, 1970s.

It has been said on many occasions that the diversity of the
Staffordshire Gritstone area is its greatest ally with both
popular and esoteric areas alike joining forces to provide
probably the most likeable and enduring of all the Peak
District regions. From the jungles of the Lower Churnet
Valley in the south to the rugged outcrops of Bosley Cloud
and Mow Cop overlooking the Cheshire plain in the north,
these cliffs will long remain the preserve of the dedicated
enthusiast seeking solitude and atmosphere amongst
modern-day life. Located in the middle are the popular
outcrops of The Roaches, Hen Cloud and Ramshaw Rocks to
which large numbers of climbers flock to test their
aspirations on the best quality gritstone routes and boulder
problems.

This guidebook, the seventh in this particular series and the
third to serve solely this area, attempts to encapsulate all
that is good (and in some circumstances bad!) about the
region, its climbs and its history. Dave Salt's guidebook of
1973 was the first real attempt to categorise all of the climbs
on every cliff, foresaking the routine of chronicalling only the
major crags, and venturing forth to describe many a hidden
gem amongst well-known but hitherto undocumented ones.
This was without doubt a major task but Dave drafted in a
number of well-suited and highly enthusiastic climbers to
make it a great success. As with most guidebooks, this work
was based loosely on other people's attempts to document
certain crags; Peter Bamfield at Bosley Cloud being a prime
example. But, as was the order of the day, many regarded
the outlying crags as minor in comparison to The Roaches
and Hen Cloud and certain crags were not given a deserved
billing. Today, thanks to the work of Dave, they demand as
much attention as the larger crags.

The next guidebook to the area brought another amazing
step forward that was to transform the whole of the British
guidebook scene, at the time rather staid and sterile. Two
main authors, Dave Jones and Nick Longland (backed up by
a veritable host of writers and workers), were to set the
scene alight with an interesting, readable and extremely

likeable work, far detached from the rather droll guidebook writing of the day. Jones's particular style, based loosely on North American (particularly Boulder Canyon) guidebooks, rightly brought wide acclaim as the humorous side of its writing was brought out; a side that has been attempted by many a guidebook writer since but rarely as successfully or as with as much aplomb. There can be no greater accolade. Now this, the next guidebook on the throne of Staffordshire Gritstone, brings new ideas. Colour photographs have, since 1983, become normal amidst present day guidebooks and now this edition is the first to show the area in its full glory. Climbers clad in all manner of colourful garb adorn the pages of this guidebook depicting the intricacies of the day or the routes of the moment; like any trend they are demanded by the public.

This guidebook also sees the first attempt to chronicle the history of the routes more closely than ever before. A vast amount of work has gone into unearthing first and second ascent dates, and interesting anecdotes, to propagate a new dimension to the area's climbing. Gritstone, especially in Staffordshire, has always been taken at a leisurely pace and many climbers of the past have failed to record their first ascents fully or relied on other climbers to do their work for them. Therefore it has been impossible to label every climb with a first ascent date or first ascensionists; perhaps time, another edition or popular demand will decide their outcome. However, these pages now depict Staffordshire gritstone climbing as never before. Whilst the esoteric crags have mainly been the preserve of the enthusiast or local climber, the larger crags form a story akin to that of the many other gritstone areas. Such greats as James Puttrell, Stanley Jeffcoat, 'Fred' Pigott, Peter Harding, Joe Brown and Don Whillans preceded modern day athletes such as John Allen, Jonny Woodward or Simon Nadin in the hall of fame. There is no doubt that Staffordshire Gritstone will continue to draw the leading climbers of the day to push standards forth like never before and that someone will be there in the future to record their exploits in yet another edition of the guidebook.

Gary Gibson, January 1988.

ACKNOWLEDGEMENTS

The foundations for this particular guidebook were formed years ago in the previous editions. Their editors are owed a great debt by the new breed of climber; John Laycock, Fergus Graham, Allan Allsopp, Eric Byne, Wilf White, John Smith, Nick Longland, Dave Jones, Steve Dale and Brian Dale have made valuable contributions to Staffordshire gritstone climbing over the years. One name in particular amongst these editors, Dave Salt, is owed probably the greatest debt of all. Dave unearthed many esoteric gems whilst working amongst the Matto Grasso of The Churnet Valley and was largely responsible for bringing such popular crags as Ramshaw Rocks, The Five Clouds and Baldstones, plus many more, to the attention of the climbing world. Upon his very hard work, this opus and the previous volume were largely based.

New writers now take their place alongside these famous names as the nucleus of a new guidebook team; Nick Dixon, Simon Nadin, Andy Popp, Richard Davies, Ian 'Squawk' Dunn, Simon Whalley and Steve Dale all deserve credit for their work on certain areas. All were also helpful in proof-reading and making comments on grading and one could not wish for a better bunch of lads.

The diagrams were, as always, the sole preserve of Phil Gibson who kindly agreed to the use of his superb 'old' drawings which were used in the last guidebook. Thankfully, Phil added two more essential drawings to the list and was largely responsible for planning the reductions and sorting out the route lines and numbers; no mean task. Keith Sharples also pitched in under stress and helped out with a number of excellent and highly functional maps.

The Executive was the engine behind the wheels in driving this guidebook from its conception to its conclusion and so remains the main reason for such guidebooks appearing on the shelves in the first place. Their work is totally voluntary and should not go unnoticed; Malc Baxter, Mike Browell, Dave Farrant, Neil Foster, Dave Gregory, Chris Hardy, Graham Hoey, Geoff Milburn, Keith Sharples and Ian Smith deserve great credit for their time spent making this 'machine' work.

The names of the photographers appear in the photographic list and are thus credited.

The historical side of the Staffordshire Gritstone area

provided the sternest test of all which nearly had me, in particular, floundering. It would seem that first ascent details for gritstone were never intended to be taken seriously and as a result many of the old routes never had such details recorded. Whilst unearthing as much of this information as possible some amusing hours were had by the editor reading other people's notes and letters whilst also sifting out the relevent facts. Nat Allen provided many old guidebooks from which to make notes and aid the searching and to him I am greatly indebted for his never waning enthusiasm. Vivienne Smith, whilst in extremis, provided the goods with a superb, articulate and well-researched history which should give another angle from which to look at the development of the Staffordshire Gritstone crags.

On a personal note I would also like to thank my wife Hazel for being that ever-so-bit tolerant and for Dill the dog, a constant companion on many a lonesome walk through the wilderness, in search of that elusive route description or the new 'crag x'.

To all of these invaluable helpers I feel indebted and as it is usual to dedicate a guidebook to someone, I feel it should be dedicated to them all for their enthusiasm and loving of these superb Staffordshire Gritstone outcrops.

Gary Gibson, December 1987.

After quite a long stint serving on the guidebook Executive, Gary felt that he needed a change of scene and finally resigned at the end of December 1978. Both Gary and his brother Phil have done a great deal of work to enhance the last two Staffordshire Area guidebooks

THE CRAG ENVIRONMENT

It is no overstatement to say that the future of the sport depends upon a sympathetic understanding of the environment, an appreciation of the pressure placed upon it from many quarters and a genuine desire to preserve all that is good for future generations. It is, therefore, with some sense of urgency that we have included this section on the crag environment and trust that its message will not be lost on the thousands of climbers who will seek recreation on the gritstone edges, conglomerate outcrops and quarries contained in this particular volume.

INCREASING POPULARITY

The crags described in this guide contain some of the most popular and heavily used rock in the country. Ten years ago the hardest routes of the day retained a certain aura and early ascensionists proceeded with caution and respect. Today, owing to a number of reasons, none less than the increased publicity of new routes in the magazines, new lines are well-known and their reputations relatively short-lived. Crags which were a few years ago approached by narrow tracks are now often served by wide areas of trampled and denuded moorland. The day of the secret buttress and quiet Sunday afternoon is long gone (except in the esoteric depths of the Churnet) and in its place are usually crowds, queues and human pressure. The crags and surrounding moorland can no longer be expected to withstand, unaided, a human invasion on this scale. Owing to the popularity of our sport we are now in danger of hastening the demise of the very environment we seek to enjoy.

GEOLOGY

The area is one of contrasting rock formation and as a direct result of this the topography is varied.

To the north of Leek, The Roaches forms a pronounced physical feature which lies at the southern end of the Goldsitch syncline. This syncline trends north-to-south and farther to the north it becomes part of the Goyt syncline which extends northwards towards the Stockport area. The synclinal structure of The Roaches can be clearly seen from the vicinity of The Mermaid Inn when one looks over towards The Roaches. The Goldsitch syncline pitches towards the north with the result that the folded rocks in the south dip to the north. As a result the beds in The Roaches area form a distinct V-shaped outcrop on a geological map. The rocks forming this area (being primarily Namurian, Millstone Grit, beds with some Lowest Westphalian, Coal Measures) are all in the core of the Goldsitch syncline. To the west of these Carboniferous rocks the Triassic series of the Cheshire Plain occur. The junction between these two sets of rocks is probably faulted and runs approximately north-to-south. To the east of the Goldsitch syncline the Namurian gives way to the underlying Avonian (Carboniferous Limestone) of the Derbyshire Dome. South-east of Leek, Carboniferous rocks give rise to the younger Triassic beds which overlie the other series unconformably.

The Namurian rocks to the north of Leek give rise to the typical moorland scenery. The rocks are mainly the result of marine sedimentation and comprise sandstones, gritstones and shale beds. The sandstones and gritstones are much more resistant to erosion than the shales and so they form pronounced escarpments facing southwards. The shale bands lie between the sandstone and gritstone beds and they often contain marine fossils which make correlation easier.

The Roaches, Hen Cloud and Ramshaw Rocks consist of The Roaches Gritstone. This is about 45m to 60m thick and it is a coarse to gravelly gritsone, frequently felspathic and purplish in colour. It is often thickly bedded and has various sedimentary structures such as ripple marking and current bedding which give information as to the conditions which prevailed at the time when the rock was formed. The Roaches Gritstone forms a pronounced outcrop on which most of the climbs described are found.

The gritstones accumulated in shallow water and the shale bands were formed in deeper water conditions – thus during Namurian times there was considerable variation in the depth of the sea. Namurian conditions were different from those which prevailed in Avonian times when clear water gave rise to thick limestone deposits.

Ludchurch is an imposing feature which trends approximately north-west to south-east. It is about 10m deep in places and is probably the result of some slight faulting in the area. Several smaller features of a similar nature occur nearby in the vicinity of Black Brook, although these are too small to provide any such impressive situations.

To the south of Leek the countryside becomes less rugged, with substantial soil-cover and fewer exposures. In the Churnet Valley, in the neighbourhood of Alton, there are to be found several cliff faces which illustrate the nature of the Triassic Series. The rocks are red in colour, being heavily stained with iron oxides, and show few traces of fossils. The chief rock-types are sandstones with thick conglomerate beds at higher horizons. These conglomerates contain pebbles of quartz which are up to 15cm in diameter; the infamous 'Bunter Pebble'.

The Triassic rocks were formed in shallow-water lakes and seas which formed from time to time in a vast desert which covered most of the English Midlands during Triassic times. The thicker coarser beds were the result of flooding and the pebbles are rounded as a result of transportation by water. The northern boundary of the Triassic occurs just north of Alton and is unconformable upon carboniferous rocks below. In more recent times, man's quarrying activities have been responsible for much of the debris lying below some of the crags. A number of fine walls in this guidebook are man-made; man's impact upon the landscape has been uncompromising, unplanned and fortuitously has given scenery quite magnificent in scale. It is interesting that the Peak District National Park, set up to protect and conserve this landscape, has chosen a millstone as its symbol.

VEGETATION

The vegetation around these crags is fragile and incapable of coping with the pressure of thousands of climbers, walkers and other visitors. The turf which once grew at the foot of The Great Slab on The Roaches Upper Tier has long since disappeared, although grass remains in places such as on less popular crags and buttresses. Replacing it is a sandy mixture which brings tears to the eyes as dust storms blow up on a windy day. Paths leading to the crags have been enlarged by the pounding of millions of pairs of feet, some as gullies and others as super-highways. Once the protective layers of vegetation are eroded, wind and rain quickly carve away the soil and within a very short period of time, paths become unusable. Although climbers can do little to protect this aspect of the environment they should be aware of the reasons for footpath diversion and car parking restrictions. Similarly, care should be taken at the top of the routes. Think about this when climbing a route choked with dust and sand which washes down each time it rains. Sand below the crag may not in itself be a bad thing; it provides a softer landing.

It should be pointed out that under the 1981 Wildlife and Countryside Act it is illegal to pick wild flowers.

BIRD LIFE

Hardly any of the moorland areas around these crags are now managed as grouse moors but the legacy of this activity lives on. However, other birdlife is of interest to naturalists. The birds of prey and ravens which gave their name to many Peak District buttresses have now largely disappeared, harried by egg collectors, shot by gamekeepers and poisoned by agricultural pesticides. In recent years, however, the breeding populations are growing and spreading, returning to ancestral nesting sites especially in the less-frequented areas. A wide berth especially during the nesting season — March to June — should be a matter of course. Disturbing birds from a nest can cause eggs to chill or unattended chicks to die. The rarer species are protected by law making it an offence to cause any disturbance.

LITTER

Climbers should remember that while they are using the crags they are also acting as custodians for a generation; soon they will pass them on and, we hope, in a fit state. Increasingly the biological diversity is finding itself in competition with many undesirable bits and pieces including broken glass, tins, scrap food, plastics and human excrement. This is inexcusable. None has a place here, as those who have inadvertently fallen into the latter will agree. All rubbish should be removed from the crag and taken to the nearest litter bin, or taken home. The crags have already survived for several million years; surely we cannot break them in a century?

CONFLICT OF INTERESTS

Other groups of people are interested in the same area of the landscape for different reasons. Ornithologists and other naturalists share the high places with walkers, who also enjoy the open spaces and freedom. All have an equal right to their recreation and it is good that we have entered the Eighties without a serious conflict of interests. Co-existence must continue to be the theme for the future.

PROTECTION

On the crags themselves minor conflicts have arisen and died down. It is now generally accepted that **ON NATURAL GRITSTONE NO PEGS OR BOLTS ARE PLACED**; it goes without saying that hammer and pegs etc., need not to be taken to any gritstone cliff. Those which have been placed in a less-enlightened era have largely rusted away, been removed or forgotten and the vast majority of recent routes have shown a high ethical standard. It must, however, be taken into consideration that many of the harder routes were initially, and sometimes on subsequent ascents, climbed after intimate knowledge, usually in the form of top-rope practice. This is a major factor, since while the first ascensionist has made an attempt at an objective grade, an on-sight ascent has not yet been achieved and the grade could be open to some variation.

LAND OWNERSHIP

Every piece of land covered in this guidebook has an owner. Some are private landowners who make their living from the land, some are public authorities which manage the land for a specific purpose, others are societies and groups of people who own the land to protect their own interests. Most of the crags described in this book are within The Peak District National Park. This designation gives a high priority to the conservation of the landscape, and to the provision of facilities and opportunities for public recreation. It does not in itself provide any rights of access to the countryside, but legislation does allow local authorities to negotiate access agreements to specific areas of land. The Peak Park have negotiated more access land than any other local authority in England and Wales. A number of crags are owned or managed by either the National Trust or the Nature Conservancy Council. While it is true that, in some ways, these bodies see things differently to climbers it is equally true that they have shown a very enlightened attitude to climbing and have been willing to agree access to a number of botanically sensitive areas.

Where access agreements exist there are provisions for suspension of the right to go on the land when periods of drought result in a high fire-risk. Fires can spread rapidly and cause severe long-term damage. It is essential that every care is taken to avoid the possibility of starting a fire — cigarettes and camping stoves are the most obvious dangers. The argument has been successfully made that climbers who spend all day on a particular section of cliff are very effective fire-watchers rather than fire-risks. The passing walker who leaves his fire to smoulder behind him is more likely to be the culprit. It is hoped that climbers as a whole will accept the responsibilities that negotiated access agreements place upon them with understanding. Camping is NOT allowed at any of the crags within this guidebook; there is always an obligation to obtain the landowner's permission. There are, in many cases, a number of camp-sites within the region.

ACCESS

There is no legal right of access to climb on any of the crags in this guidebook but at most of them climbers have long enjoyed a traditional freedom to climb. On the others, unless a problem is indicated in the crag notes, a request for permission is usually granted. It is as well to be aware that technically, unless there is a right of access, a climber is trespassing – a civil wrong against the ownership of the property, not a criminal offence. Landowners are within their rights to request a trespasser to leave. As the number of climbers has increased in the past decade, so too has the concern of landowners who are often worried about liability, vandalism and protection of their livelihood. The Landowner's Liability Act, passed in 1984, has gone a long way to solving the former problem, but fears of the other problems are still real and, sadly, often justified. Simple things such as damaged walls, or gates left open, can lead to considerable problems for the farmer; time is wasted on rounding up strayed stock or making repairs and income is lost. It is vital for the present generation of climbers to recognise that climbing is only possible because of the continuing tolerance and goodwill of the landowner. Providing that we continue to show a responsible attitude to the land, and especially other users of the land, we shall probably continue to enjoy our freedom.

Occasionally, conflicts will arise. When this happens it is imperative that individual views and political allegiances should be put aside in the short-term, in the interest of the long-term security of our traditional climbing grounds. **Too many hours of patient negotiation have been put in jeopardy by the selfishness and bad manners of a few climbers.** Major confrontations should be avoided at all costs. If there is an access problem to any crag in this volume, then it affects climbers nationally, and the British

Mountaineering Council should be advised (see address at end of Classification section). Many minor access problems have been amicably settled by the anonymous work of guidebook writers and local club members, but the major issues are best tackled at national level. Whatever the size of the problem, the guiding rule should be NOT to assume right of access. Details of any particular access agreement are given before each crag description.

> THE INCLUSION OF A CRAG OR THE ROUTES
> UPON IT IN THIS GUIDEBOOK DOES NOT
> MEAN THAT ANY MEMBER OF THE PUBLIC
> HAS THE RIGHT OF ACCESS TO THE CRAG OR
> THE RIGHT TO CLIMB ON IT.

TECHNICAL NOTES

CLASSIFICATION

Adjectival Grades
These are subjective assessments of the overall difficulty of a route and the seriousness involved in doing it. They take into consideration the quality of the rock, the exposure, quantity of protection, technical difficulty, strenuousness and sustained nature of the route. They assume that climbers carry a comprehensive range of modern protection devices. The grades are: Moderate, Difficult, Very Difficult, Hard Very Difficult, Severe, Hard Severe, Very Severe, Hard Very Severe and Extremely Severe. The Extremely Severe grade is open-ended and is indicated by E1, E2, E3, E4, E5, E6, E7, E8 etc.

Technical Grades
The technical grade is an objective asessment of the cumulative difficulty of a pitch and, as such, considers the strenuousness and sustained nature of the climbing up to and after the hardest move. There is no definite relationship between the technical grade and the adjectival grade although climbs of a given adjectival grade are likely to cover a limited range of technical grades. Technical grades have mostly been given to climbs in or above the Very Severe category. The grades used are 4a, 4b, 4c, 5a, 5b, 5c, 6a, 6b, 6c, 7a etc; the system being open ended. **The climbs are graded for on-sight leads but some of the**

harder routes have not been led without some prior knowledge. The symbol † has been used after the technical grade to indicate routes where the grade and/or description is in doubt, either because the first ascent has not been authenticated or the climb has had insufficient ascents to arrive at a consensus grade.

Route Quality
A star system is used to indicate the quality of routes; only the most outstanding climbs are given three stars.

First Ascent Lists
This is the first volume to attempt to chronicle the history of climbing on the Staffordshire Gritstone outcrops. It is an intricate story which will inevitably take much unravelling and is not wholly possible at the first attempt. It is hoped that future editions will carry a more accurate picture and to this end further first ascent details would be greatly appreciated. Please send them to the BMC at the address below.

New Routes
Descriptions of all new routes should be sent direct to the BMC, (New Routes), Crawford House, Precinct Centre, Booth Street East, Manchester, M13 9RZ. Second-hand information from magazines or new routes books is often insufficient.

MOUNTAIN RESCUE and FIRST AID

Dial 999 and ask for POLICE
Rescue equipment is kept at the Mountain Rescue Post, The Mill, Upper Hulme.

FIRST AID in case of ACCIDENT

1. IF SPINAL INJURIES or HEAD INJURIES are suspected DO NOT MOVE THE PATIENT without skilled help, except to maintain breathing.

2. IF BREATHING HAS STOPPED, clear airways and commence artificial respiration. DO NOT STOP UNTIL EXPERT OPINION DIAGNOSES DEATH.

3. STOP BLEEDING by applying direct pressure.

4. SUMMON HELP.

THE GRITSTONE AREA

'The short gritstone routes of Britain bear more significance to me than an ascent of Everest or of The Eiger North Wall in Winter. This is because these small crags were never thought of as ultimate. In the conquest of the impossible one can only encounter a great insufficiency. There is no elite climb that will not eventually be visited by circuses. There is a pleasure in a small climb, in a drop of water or an obscure boulder never visited before.'

Pat Ament, Mountain Magazine, 1986.

HISTORY

by Vivienne Smith

While enthusiasts for Staffordshire would argue that its gritstone has qualities unsurpassed anywhere else, the area often appears a forgotten backwater of Peak District climbing. In common with the Eastern Edges innovations in technique and method have often been quietly pioneered and tested to the full here before being transferred to other areas. The earliest pioneers often 'cut their teeth' on the harsh unforgiving edges before continuing their exploits further afield. The 'rock masters' have also seen fit to leave their own stamp of approval on these crags.

It therefore comes as no surprise to learn that E.A. Baker, J.W. Puttrell and other members of the Kyndwyr Club explored the area and were probably the first to exploit its potential. The group enjoyed the gullies, the chimneys and the odd face-climb on Hen Cloud and Roach End, one of which was described as 'a tussle with gloves on', but they were less impressed with Ramshaw Rocks which Baker described as 'a gross succession of ghoulish faces, bovine and porcine heads, and half-finished monsters springing from the parent rock'. An interest in Raven Rock seems to have been somewhat overshadowed by Rock Hall, a cottage built into the cliff and famous for its less than law-abiding inhabitants, the moss-trooper 'Bowyer of the Rocks' and his daughter Bess. Here sheltered smugglers and deserters, amongst others, along with a beautiful girl reputed to be Bess's daughter who had a haunting voice that, it is said, can still be heard among the rocks on a summer evening.

Staffordshire Gritstone Area.

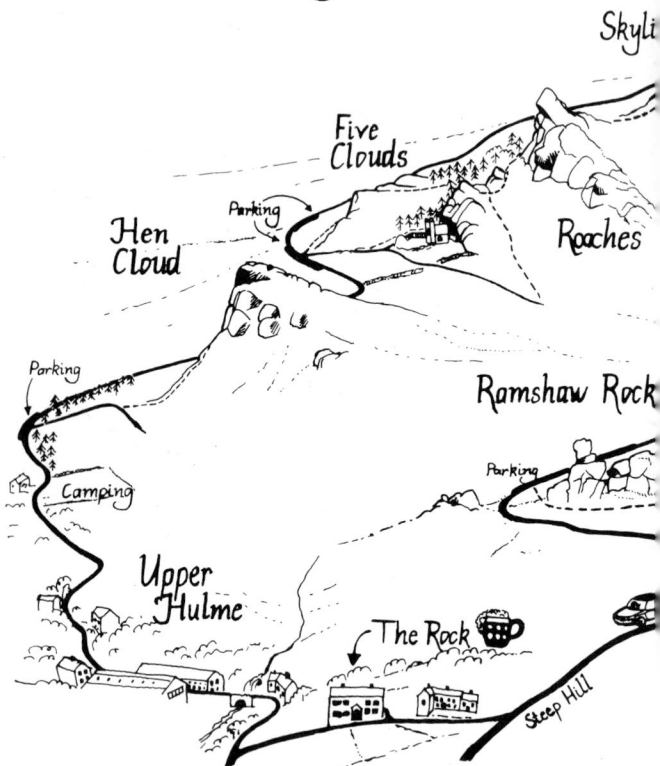

Skyli

Five Clouds

Hen Cloud

Parking

Roaches

Parking

Ramshaw Rock

Camping

Parking

Upper Hulme

The Rock

Steep Hill

Legend has it that the girl was carried away by strange men and the disconsolate Bess was left alone to die. 'Doxy's Pool', supposedly named after this daughter, provided an enticing attraction to three members of the club one hot summer's day on a walk from Ludchurch to Rock Hall. A plunge into its apparently clear waters left them, like many

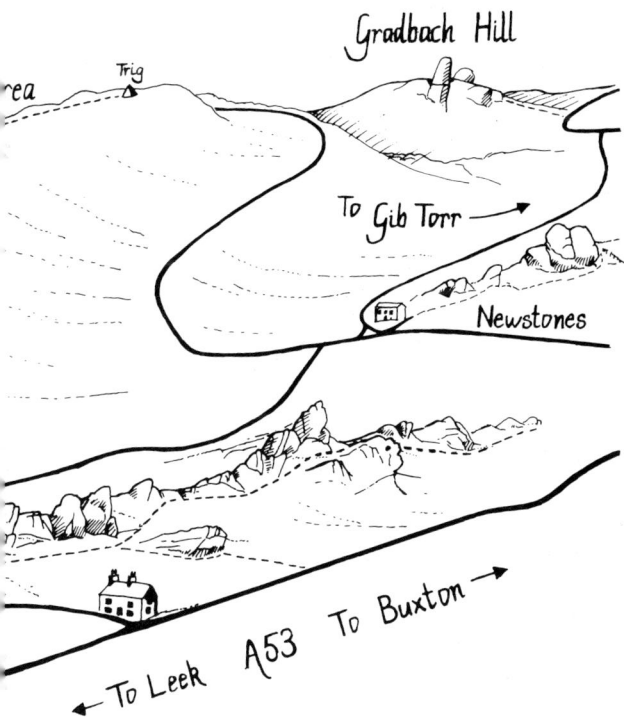

since, not refreshed and clean but brown and bearing an unpleasant smell from the decaying peat disturbed from the pool bottom.

Not long afterwards John Laycock began to explore the Peak District and was attracted to Hen Cloud. Late one afternoon he and A.R. Thompson tackled a route (later known as *Central Climb*) with several stances and three awkward pitches that his second couldn't follow. He therefore sat on a ledge whilst Thompson went for help in the form of a chauffeur and a rope. Undaunted, Laycock continued his adventurous style on various gritstone edges along with Siegfried Herford and the powerfully built Stanley Jeffcoat. They began to rely more on friction and balance, and were aided in this by less-cumbersome clothing. By 1913 they had climbed *Great Chimney* on Hen Cloud, *Raven Rock Gully* near Rock Hall and *Jeffcoat's Chimney* at The Roaches. Sadly the war brought an end to the careers of many of these dedicated and enthusiastic pioneers of the sport who had begun to appreciate the value of rock climbing for its own virtues rather than as a prelude and training for 'greater' things.

A new era dawned after the war with young enthusiasts such as Morley Wood, Fred Pigott and Harry Kelly. With the introduction of rubbers or gym shoes and the shoulder belay this hard team of the Rucksack Club began to push standards not only in the Peak District but also in Wales and the Lake District. They found the Upper Tier of The Roaches almost untouched and Pigott was able to climb *Bachelor's Buttress* and the bold *Black and Tans*, a misnomer for a group of lacrosse players who had been encouraged to fill some empty beds on an Easter meet. Amongst several routes *Crack and Corner* was notable for the use of a shoulder on the top pitch until the removal of a clod of grass revealed a useful jug, and *The Girdle Traverse*, a style of climb in keeping with the times. Fergus Graham's much needed 'Recent Developments on Gritstone', published in 1924, confirmed all the existing routes and was a great help to future explorers including Lindlay Henshaw. However one of the most notable achievements of the period was Ivan Waller's ascent of *Bengal Buttress*, an exposed and delicate route with little protection, very much in Ivan's style. His boldness impressed the climbers he was with, although the man himself remained modest and diffident.

While some people found they had time, though little money, to pursue their rock-climbing hobby during the depression years, access became particulalrly difficult in some areas. Most notable, perhaps, was Hen Cloud which was patrolled by armed gamekeepers and was also the site of an open-air zoo. At about that time Harry Scarlett was able to rediscover The Five Clouds although his stumble over the edge resulted in a broken rib and a bitten tongue.

The end of the Second World War heralded a new phase in rock climbing development. Access problems were somewhat relaxed, aided by the mass-trespass and the move towards National Parks, a reflection of the changing attitude towards these open spaces. Gear also saw major advances with the introduction of nylon ropes, vibram soles, slings and karabiners. With more protection and safer belaying techniques, climbers had more confidence to 'break' new ground and use new techniques. This was particularly exemplified by members of the Valkyrie Club who pioneered jamming. Peter Harding attempted *Valkyrie*, and having been unable to climb the obvious corner, was spurred on by Bowden Black to 'come over the flake Peter, there's a good foothold at the bottom... and you might be able to step across the side of the buttress'. At the hard move he had to stop and request a penknife in order to clean out the only fingerholds which were choked with soil and moss.

Joe Brown visited the impressive Staffordshire outcrops early on in his career finding the classic *Saul's Crack* which marked a new standard of achievement, reinforced the following year by stunning leads on Froggatt. Working towards the production of the 1951 guidebook (Volume 3 of Climbs on Gritstone) Brown, often accompanied by Whillans, produced other classic routes including *Dorothy's Dilemma*, and *Valkyrie Direct*. Between 1951 and 1955 the pair were able to pick off all the obvious major cracks to produce a whole series of classics. *The Sloth*, by Whillans, remains a route for many to aspire to today while at the same time pioneering a new type of climb; the overhang. Having won the toss for the lead he stepped from Brown's shoulders onto the wall and went up to the roof to arrange the now customary sling. In his book, Portrait of a Mountaineer, Whillans recalls:

> *'What I intended doing was to ease myself into the gap between the flake on the roof and the ceiling itself. Very gingerly I worked my way inside and along it. The crowd below were enjoying the spectacle! I reached to the crack and got a jam in. By this time I was committed. I jammed my way along the crack until only the heel of my foot was left on it. Now I reached out over the lip of the overhang for a hold above it and my foot came off. I quickly pulled*

> *up, jammed a foot in the crack, whipped a
> runner on in case anything unaccustomed
> happened and pulled over the overhang. I was
> up.'*

Whillans's infamous wit was demonstrated to an admiring
Eric Byne who upon asking, perhaps foolishly, 'was it hard'
was told 'not if you use your loaf'!

This ability to jam was also used to the full on *Teck Crack*,
named after the commemorative plaque laid by the Duchess
of Teck at the top of the route. *Delstree*, on Hen Cloud,
provided strenuous and delicate climbing for Brown. It is
hard to imagine now the number of opportunities open to
such climbers with so much virgin rock. However it was not
until many years later (1964) and many impressive routes in
the Peak, Wales and the Lakes, that Brown led the
outstanding *Ramshaw Crack* albeit with some aid. Nat Allen
was able to describe the route and the techniques used as
follows:

> *'At full stretch a finger jam can be made and
> then a pull up to better jams, the feet can be
> got into the crack, up, then a chockstone can be
> threaded which was used for aid. The crack
> then becomes a bit too wide but eventually he
> got his flat hand and bent arm jammed to get
> his feet in and up.'*

After such phenomenal activity it is not surprising that a lull
followed during the early Sixties, despite some activity from
Clive Shaw with *Bulwark* on Hen Cloud, at the time a very
serious lead. Time was needed for others to attain and
consolidate this new standard. Many of the routes that
followed were of high quality as new possibilities were
realised. Thus Tony Nicholls and the Black and Tans Club
were able to produce routes such as *Encouragement* and
Chicken, while Graham West climbed the devious *Wallaby*.
Perhaps the best routes of this period fell to Mike Simpkins
in the form of *Elegy*, 'one of the finest slab climbs on grit'.
Originally climbed using tension from a side-runner, the
ascent was impressive because of the prospect of a major
fall from the unprotected slab. A route that should not be
underestimated even today.

1957 saw the formation of the North Staffordshire Mountaineering Club which, along with various offshoots, was to dominate the area's development for a couple of decades. The initial assault had been in the early-Sixties by Clive Shaw. This was followed by Dave Salt and Colin Foord's ascent of the mauling *Hank's Horror* on the Skyline. Foord also climbed the two quality lines of *Tower Eliminate* and *Hypothesis*. On the latter he fell during a top-rope inspection before making the first ascent. Meanwhile Bob Hassall was pioneering some obvious lines on Hen Cloud and Foord forced the steep crackline of *High Tensile Crack*. Salt, however, had to resort to aid (later removed by John Allen) on the top part of *The Bitter End*. Activity was also stimulated by the publication in successive years of paperback guidebooks, one by John Smith of the Alpha Club and the other by the North Staffs. M.C. Salt, its author, had wagered a pound that everything possible had now been done, thus spurring many to attempt to disprove the statement. It was John Amies who led the relatively minor *Sifta's Quid*, but was unable to extract the money from Salt.

However these were not the only groups to be active in the area. The Five Clouds were to become the province of Martin Boysen following Bob Downes' visit (resulting in *Crabbie's Crack*) in the Fifties. Boysen began in 1968 with ascents of *Boysen's Delight* and *Rubberneck*. This latter route had, however, been climbed the previous year by the Barley brothers, Tony and Robin. More impressive, perhaps, was *Flower Power Arête* named after the clothing worn on the day, and much in keeping with the era, though using pre-placed protection. John Yates also began working on routes in the area, pioneering climbing on the Nth Cloud, later to be known as Roach End Crag. Yates made some notable contributions during his brief spell of activity especially *The Death Knell* a particularly bold lead on The Lower Tier from which he picked himself out of the rhododendron bushes on at least one occasion, and the extremely delicate and underrated *Up the Swanee*, probably the hardest route of the period.

This period was notable for the popularity of aid-climbing, especially on limestone, but pegs did appear on gritstone as well. Prominent amongst these was that hammered into *The Swan* by John Gosling (who wasn't averse to using aid for progress on gritstone). This was later to be eliminated by Ron Fawcett and Geoff Birtles in 1977. Whether such aid was ever really necessary remains a matter of some dispute.

The imminent publication of Dave Salt's guidebook in 1973 (unlike many other later guidebooks) did not herald a frenzy of activity as many of the climbers diverted their attentions into other sports. However the editor and the rest of the club worked hard to produce an accurate and much needed volume, highlighting the hitherto neglected crags of Ramshaw Rocks, the Baldstones, Newstones, Gib Torr, Gradbach Hill and Back Forest. Many of these areas had been climbed on by various small groups who saw little reason to record their exploits on problems. A change of attitude towards such routes was aided by this new guidebook.

The publication of the guidebook marked a change as a new breed of young climbers began to search out new routes, tending to look to crags other than The Roaches themselves. John Allen, along with Steve Bancroft, was not to miss out Staffordshire from his whirlwind of impressive routes in the Peak District and elsewhere, though it is fair to say that his scrutiny of these crags was not as thorough as on the eastern edges. Beginning with a free ascent of *Foord's Folly*, Allen went on to lead *Safety Net* on The Skyline and *Caricature* on Hen Cloud; the latter being as impressive as his earlier ascent of *Profit of Doom* on Curbar. Similarly significant, yet not quite as hard, were Bancroft's high-quality routes, *Comedian*, *Corinthian* and *Chameleon*.

At about the same time, 1975/6, the Woodward brothers, Jonny and Andrew, emerged in something of a blaze of self-generated publicity. As local boys working independently, they astonished the establishment with their boldness, both in deed and word. Andrew, the elder of the two, claimed an impressive route *The Ascent of Man* using many more recently established techniques such as heavy wire-brushing and several top-roped ascents. Although their boldness and somewhat dubious tactics sowed doubt in the minds of many at that time, one can now not fail to be impressed by many of their ascents; they pushed standards in the area which were by now starting to lag behind. *Wings of Unreason* is no longer 'the hardest route in the world' but along with *Track of the Cat* and *Piece of Mind* rank highly amongst their routes from 1977. The same year

saw controversy arise between Jonny Woodward and Martin
Boysen, who had continued his affair with Ramshaw with
routes such as *Gumshoe* and *Old Fogey*. The disagreement
was over *Traveller in Time/Jumbo* on Ramshaw which both
climbers claimed but neither was able to prove his case. The
fact that Jonny and Martin were both capable of the grade
does little to solve the dilemma. Boysen's case rested on the
argument that the route was 'unbrushed, green and crumbly'
before he inspected it. Given the Woodwards style it seems
unlikely that they would have tackled such a route without
prior inspection yet, they, for their part, argued that they had
left it unbrushed because they 'thought it would only be
HVS'.

Jonny was to concentrate his efforts in the area for the next
few years and to add to his tally of routes. These included
National Acrobat, as yet unrepeated, the direct version of
Caesarian and *Antithesis*. A fairly hard team had been trying
Antithesis when Jonny arrived to complete, much to the
surprise and chagrin of onlookers, an on-sight lead.
Confirmation of his ability, if needed, came in the form of
Beau Geste at Froggatt in 1982.

Meanwhile more 'reserved' climbers were able to find some
good lines. Phil Burke was to lead *Schoolies*, *Gillted* and,
some time later, *Crystal Grazer* whilst Gabe Regan was to
free *Ramshaw Crack* and lead the lovely *Smear Test*.
Another raider, this time from abroad, was Ray Jardine who
had been searching the Peak District for suitable roof cracks.
He did not find anything to suit until spying *Ray's Roof*
which took three days of work and impressed the natives
with a series of 'jams, stacks and hooks'. With no second
ascent before the 1981 guidebook, the route gained notoriety
for its American grade of 5.11c; it continues to repel many
would-be aspirants.

Others were also keen to climb new routes in the area with
the added incentive of their achievements appearing in the
Crags magazine new routes section. Nick Longland, Dave
Jones, Ian Johnson, Al Simpson and others, operating as
off-shoots from the North Staffordshire Mountaineering
Club, and in friendly rivalry, were able to fill many gaps and
produce some modern classics. Prominent amongst these
were *Kicking Bird*, *The Tower of Bizarre Delights*, *Icarus
Allsorts*, *Chalkstorm* and *Slowhand*. Jones' ascent of
Appaloosa Sunset was notable for perseverance against

unusual odds. The route had been seen during winter months but rain showers forced retreat on the first attempt. However, by the following day, Ian Johnson had made a skyhook specifically for the ascent and success was assured. It is perhaps interesting to note *Babbacombe Lee*, next to Hangman's Crack, named after an infamous criminal for whom the gallows door failed to open on three successive attempts and who was therefore set free. *Borstal Breakout*, on Hen Cloud, by Jim Moran encouraged and stimulated competition intense enough to necessitate time being taken off work in order to bag a line. Longland worked on *Tierdrop* for a long time before circumstances resulted in a substantial weight loss and success. Another problem during 1979 was caused by the occupant of Rock Hall Cottage who took to threatening climbers on the Lower Tier with his axe, hence John Codling's *Eugene's Axe*.

A young and enthusiastic member of the North Staffs. team was Gary Gibson who had begun his new route activity in 1978 and continued to leave his mark on all the crags in the area as well as farther afield. Pointing out plums from so many routes is no easy task but of worth in the earlier period were *Licence to Run* with one rest, *Carrion* and the hazardous route *The Thin Air*.

By now a new guidebook seemed vital but production was fraught with problems. Various groups and individuals had been operating in the area with no real knowledge of each other and with somewhat parochial attitudes. Many had not recorded their activity but had given names to certain problems. Thus *Elephant's Ear* was known as *The Brunel* by the Staffordshire group. Such problems were ironed out one interesting evening when Nick Longland had arranged to meet Tony Barley at Newstones. However, they were joined by teams from Altrincham (the All-stars), Pex Hill, Buxton, Yorkshire and Stoke who set to climbing everything possible while the editor rushed around attempting to record all the route names and comments. A fine evening was had by all.

The resulting guidebook brought the Staffordshire crags into line with the other gritstone areas and thus into the Eighties and the advent of sticky boots and tights. However, its publication did not lead to great activity in the area. Indeed some crags are greener today than eight years ago; although this could be due to a series of bad summers. Staffordshire has remained mainly the preserve of locals.

Gibson continued to find numerous routes including *Fast Piping*, *Cool Fool* and *The Stone Loach* on Hen Cloud and *Live Bait* on The Roaches. Simon Nadin began his climbing career on Baldstones and with Richard Davies often at hand, the 'Buxton stick-men', began to put up many routes of quality, several of which have not yet had a second ascent. Simon in particular has quietly pushed Staffordshire standards at the same pace, if not faster, than some other areas. *Master of Reality*, *Barriers in Time* and *Thing on a Spring*, which heralded the 7a grade on something other than a boulder problem, were climbed when the weather was cool and friction at its best; they remain outstanding. *Paralogism* reflects in its style, and its name, modern gritstone techniques although climbing routes in a snowstorm, as with *Against the Grain*, may not.

Equally impressive are Nick Dixon's bold climbs on The Roaches. He began with *Clive Coolhead...* and followed over the following couple of years with solo ascents, after top-roping, of *A Fist Full of Crystals* (in mistake for Crystal Grazer), *Catastrophe Internationale* and *Judge Dread* on Roach End. *Doug*, climbed in 1986, stands as probably the hardest overall route on Staffordshire Gritstone, and possibly on the whole of the Dark Peak Gritstone.

Local groups were unable to keep all the new possibilities to themselves and various visitors were able to see a line, often having been drawn to the area to climb more established routes. Thus Johnny Dawes and others found gaps to be filled whilst even John Allen returned to put up fine routes such as *Starlight and Storm* and *Licence to Lust*.

Most of the well-known climbers have left their mark on Staffordshire Gritstone but it has largely remained the domain of local activists, especially in recent years. New standards and techniques have been pioneered here by a few dedicated and talented climbers so that it may once again be possible to consider that everything worthwhile has been done. However such statements are all too quickly proved false! Some good weather and the impetus of new blood and a new guidebook may see the area leading the way on gritstone, yet it is tempting to think that it might remain something of a backwater, somewhere to get away from the worst of the crowds and enjoy the outstanding qualities that good grit has to offer.

THE ROACHES

O.S. ref. SK 007621 to 002633

by Nick Dixon, Simon Nadin and Graham Hoey

SITUATION and CHARACTER

Situated approximately 16km south-west of Buxton and 6km north-east of Leek, The Roaches escarpment is one of the most impressive outcrops in the country. Set amongst dramatic landscape at a height of almost 500m above sea-level and affording magnificent views of the outlying countryside, there can be no more impressive a situation in which to climb in the entire Peak District. From The Upper Tier on a clear day, the panorama is outstanding; Bosley Cloud, Jodrell Bank, Cannock Chase, the Welsh mountains and, reputedly, even the boys *in situ* on Pen Trwyn (!), on The Great Orme, are all visible.

The escarpment is at its greatest at its south-eastern end where two tiers of rock thrust powerfully outwards from the edge of the moor. The Lower Tier is less extensive than The Upper Tier yet both present a series of large buttresses separated by open slabs. The buttress fronts are at the same angle as the slabs offering climbs of a bold and technical, rather than strenuous, nature; for example Chalkstorm and Hawkwing. In fact, with The Skyline Area, The Lower Tier contains some of the finest slab climbing in The Peak District. In contrast the steeper side-walls of the buttresses are taken by routes for those strong in the arm and more accustomed to the comfort of protection; Hunky Dory and Licence to Run being prime examples. Generally the rock on The Lower Tier is clean and free from vegetation but because of its close proximity to the trees, can be lichenous and slow to dry after periods of bad weather. In addition, some of the gloomier bays and chimneys retain an emerald plumage well into the summer months as a result of drainage. The Upper Tier on the other hand is much more open, seldom accumulating any lichen and consequently dries very quickly after rain. In form it is similar to, though bigger than, The Lower Tier with a preponderance of overhangs offering exciting alternatives to the routes below. On both tiers the rock is sound, but it is sandier on the upper and some of the flakes, particularly those on the overhangs, should be used with care: even those which have been glued back on! Two types of hold predominate:

sloping breaks and sharp flakes. In addition, the massive jointing has produced classic cracks of all dimensions. Pebbles are best treated with care and **it is hoped that routes climbed using pebbles will not be abseiled down.** The largest range of grades is to be found on The Upper Tier where, with the exception of the roof routes, the majority of climbs are to be found in the middle to lower grades. On The Lower Tier there are fewer easy routes and the best climbs are in the middle to higher grades.

At weekends the popular routes are often booked well in advance but other excellent climbs can be found either side of the main areas; for example The Skyline Area and The Five Clouds are well-worth a visit.

APPROACHES and ACCESS
From Leek, follow the A53 Buxton road. After approximately 5km the road dips slightly before climbing steeply towards Ramshaw Rocks. About 150m up the hill turn left at the signpost to 'Ye Olde Rock Inn'. Bear left again, where the road forks, to drop into the hamlet of Upper Hulme. Continuing through the village, the road emerges into open country with Hen Cloud first on the right and The Roaches beyond it. Parking is available on either side of the road but forgetting to leave room for the various refreshments vans may be regretted later!

If approaching from the north, follow the A53 southwards from Buxton. One kilometre after Ramshaw Rocks turn right past 'Ye Olde Rock Inn' and then take a very sharp right turn to enter Upper Hulme and a junction with the Leek approach. For those people without transport the PMT X23 Hanley-to-Sheffield bus stops at the southern approach to Upper Hulme from where a brisk twenty-minute walk leads to the crag.

From the parking area, a wide track sweeps round below Rock Hall Cottage and up a flight of stone steps leading through The Lower Tier and giving access to The Upper Tier. Except for Rock Hall Cottage, The Roaches is owned by The Peak District National Park Authority. However, there is an agreement between the BMC and the owners of Rockhall Cottage that climbing on the Lower Tier be restricted to between the hours of 9 a.m. and 9 p.m. and for climbers to respect the privacy of the cottage. In addition, climbers are requested to keep to the approaches described in the guide and **not** to take short-cuts across the moors (e.g. from The Skyline Area or The Upper Tier to Roach End or The Five Clouds) in order to preserve the moorland habitat.

THE LOWER TIER
by Nick Dixon

> 'At what is now the hard move Peter paused for several minutes because the face was mossy and the only fingerholds were choked with soil and moss. He shouted for Veronica to pass him his penknife which was lowered down on a rope. He scratched the moss away, closed the knife, put it in his pocket and continued without more ado. I followed and found it rather easier than I though it would be but then I did have a rope above me.'

Bowden Black, talking about the first ascent of Valkyrie.

LEFT-HAND SECTION

This is the compact cluster of buttresses left of The Lower Tier steps. Perhaps the ferocity of the climbing in this area has deprived it of popularity; nevertheless, it is these bluffs that give the greatest density of quality hard climbing at The Roaches. Typically overhanging starts lead to precarious slabs so that strong arms and deft footwork are great assets.

THE CLIMBS on this section are described from RIGHT to LEFT starting at the steps, the first buttress being 15m to their left.

1 Fred's Cafe 10m VS 5a
An unsatisfactory climb up the rightward-slanting crack at the right side of the buttress, finishing leftwards up flakes.

(1978)

2 Doug 12m E8 6c   *†
Start as for A Fist Full of Crystals. Pull left over the overhang and immediately climb up the right-hand side of the front face of the buttress to finish up the hanging scoop. Technical and insecure moves on even less secure pebbles; a harrowing solo.

(1986)

3 A Fist Full of Crystals 12m E6 6b   ***

The beauty of inventive movement, balance and fear make this route uniquely memorable. Start as for Fred's Cafe. Pull left onto the lip of the overhang and traverse left to the small central groove. Climb this and either step left onto a finishing foothold or continue direct.   (1984)

4 Crystal Grazer 10m E5 6a   **

Start as for A Fist Full of Crystals. Foot-traverse left along the lip of the overhang until on the left side of the small central groove. A move up gains the obvious jug.   (1982)

5 Pindles Numb 11m E4 6b   *

A way into the hanging groove right of Lightning Crack. Start from the decaying holly tree just left of Crystal Grazer and climb easily out to the good hand-rail at the lip. Follow this left, with increasing difficulty, until a tiring move allows the groove to be gained.   (1984)

6 Lightning Crack 20m HVS 5b,4c   *

Three metres left of the holly is an undercut layback finger-crack.
1. 8m. Climb the crack, after a puzzling entry, to reach a tree.
2. 12m. Move up behind the tree to a triangular wall. Climb this to a sloping ledge and either finish direct, or better and harder, by a leftward-rising hand-pod.   (1960)

The short roof crack between Lightning Crack and Teck Crack has been climbed at E3 6a, reputedly by Joe Brown. Another variation swings out right to climb the short hanging arête at the same grade.

7 Teck Crack 26m HVS 4a,5b   ***

Awesome laybacking on the second pitch of this route allows some very spectacular ground to be covered. A Joe Brown classic; where the Duchess failed, Brown laybacked and jammed!
1. 11m. Climb the tree and boulder-filled gully 3m left of Lightning Crack, then creep left to the base of the crack.
2. 15m. Commit yourself fully and the crack will succumb. Finish up the continuation crack to a historic bolt and seat belay.   (1958)

The next routes tackle the overhanging base-wall below the second pitch of Teck Crack. This wall gives some of the best extended bouldering at The Roaches. All of these routes can be finished by the second pitch of Teck Crack or by scrambling off to the right.

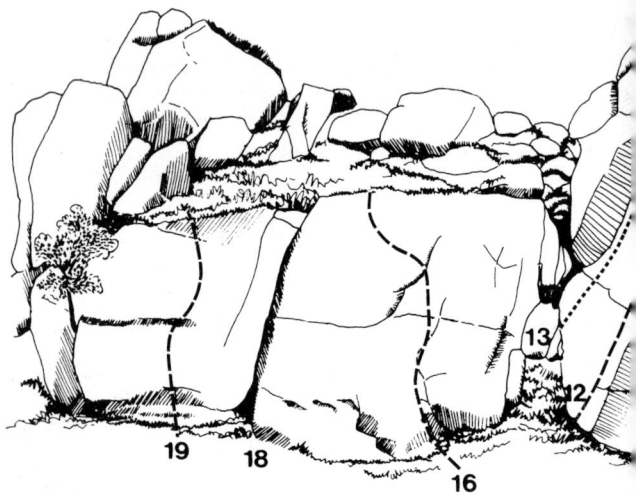

Lower Tier Left-hand

8 The Dignity of Labour 7m E3 6b
Start on a flat boulder at the right-hand end of the
base-wall. Move left onto the wall and make dynamic
moves up to an intimidating mantelshelf finish. (1983)

9 Teck Crack Direct Start 5m E1 6b   *
Start below the main pitch of Teck Crack. Lunge rightwards
on sloping holds until the line of a poorly-defined crack
leads to the tree. Alternatively, gain the crack direct: **The
Super-direct**, 6c. (1983)

Philip Gibson.

10 Inertia Reel 7m E4 6c   *
Powerful moves breach the overhanging prow 5m left of
Teck Crack Direct Start, first by a fingertip undercut, then by
dynamic moves. These moves feel less steep than the route!
(1986)

11 Ant Lives 8m E4 6c
Mantelshelf the wall 3m left and make a technical
hand-traverse rightwards to finish by the top move of
Inertia Reel.   (1987)

The following routes go the full height of the crag!

11a Sunday at Chapel 9m E6 6c   ****†**
Start as for Ant Lives but instead of traversing right, carry on up the right side of the overhanging arête by very sustained 'slapping'. At present a side runner is necessary in the base of the crack of Ackit.   (1988)

12 Barriers in Time 16m E6 6b   *******
The arête right of Ackit, climbed on its left side. One of the greatest additions of the Eighties, combining technical excellence with grace. Climb the scalloped wall to gain protection in the horizontal break. Boldly climb the upper arête, then move left to finish up Ackit.   (1983)

13 Ackit 15m HVS 5b   *****
The layback crack in the right wall of the gully leads to a welcome rest before the bulge and difficult headwall are tackled.   (1958/1967)

The gully left of Ackit is not recommended for a summer ascent but it can prove good sport in a hard winter!

14 The Aspirant 8m E3 5c
Opposite Ackit is a short wall with a small rounded flake-hold in its centre; climb the wall and exit left from just above the flake. A fine little route.   (1978)

15 Days of Future Passed 9m E3 6b   *****
Make powerful moves up the blunt arête left again and finish by a degrading mantelshelf.   (1974)

16 The Ascent of Man 10m E3 6a   *******
Varied climbing centred on the flake in the middle of the buttress. Make a difficult move to exit from the small cave and move up to the flake. Exit left along the tricky ramp to a less-tricky exit. An independent right-hand start followed by a direct finish is very worthwhile at the same grade. This has been labelled **Ascent of Women**.   (1974)

17 Bareback Rider 8m E3 6b   *****
This route follows the arête left of The Ascent of Man on its left-hand side. Either hand-traverse the arête into the top of Slippery Jim or mantelshelf onto the slab.   (1980)

18 Slippery Jim 7m HVS 5a
Recommended for its historic origins if nothing else. Climb the corner-crack, the name becoming appropriate near the top.   (1958)

Right: Descending the flake of **Valkyrie** (p41), Peter Harding and Bowdon Black's great route on the Roaches Lower Tier. This is one of the finest VSs on gritstone (perhaps HVS for those less than 5ft 9in because of a reach on the final slabs). Photo: Richard Davis

Above: J.Perry on the final hard section of **Kicking Bird** (p43) where it joins the 6a traverse of Smear Test. Photo Rob Barnett

Right: Gary Gibson reaches the hand traverse of Hawkwing (E1,5b) during an ascent of **Carrion** (p45) the buttress's E3,5c Direct line. Photo: Hazel Gibson

Above: Simon Nadin on the first ascent of his E6, 7a testpiece **Thing on a Spring** (p43) – the crowning gem of the Roaches Lower Tier. Photo: Richard Davis

Right: The exposed final pitch of **Black and Tans** (p60), generally considered the finest Severe on the Roaches. Photo: Rob Barnett

Above: Lucien Cottle shows fine slab technique on **Wings of Unreason** (p91), one of the attractions of the intriguing Far Skyline cliffs. Photo: Allen Williams

Left: Dynamism is the order on the three star **Safety Net** (p77) on Roaches Skyline. Dean Hammond strikes a suitably urgent attitude . Photo: Lee Hammond

19 Catastrophe Internationale 8m E5 6c   ***
Pure pebble-climbing which represents the state of the art.
Left of Slippery Jim is a cigar-shaped pod. From the right
end of this, make committing moves directly to the top.
(1985)

20 Snap, Crackle and Andy Popp 7m E1 5c
Climb the left extremity of the wall, 1m right of a holly.
(1986)

21 National Hero 12m E2 5c
Just left is a cave with a prow above. Somewhat artificially
climb out of the right side of the cave and go up the
prominent flake.
(1978)

22 Burrito Deluxe 5m E3 5c   †
Start on the grassy ledge just left of the prow. Climb the
wall left of the arête. Dirty.
(1979)

Amongst loam and wallabies, the woods to the left yield
some good problems to those with a wire brush and a bent
for magical woods.

RIGHT-HAND SECTION

The area right of the steps is less compact and contains
more middle and lower-grade delights. The routes are often
long and varied, having a rich taste of tradition. They are
described from LEFT to RIGHT with the first starting
immediately right of the upper flight of steps.

23 Yong Arête 7m HVD   *
The arête just right of the steps gives a good varied outing.
(1957-1968)

24 Poisonous Python 8m HVS 5b   *
The curving crack in the steep slab gives some surprisingly
hard climbing.
(1978)

25 Yong 9m HVD   *
The corner crack 3m right of Yong Arête is climbed on jams.
(1957-1968)

26 Something Better Change 10m E2 5b
The slab right of Yong should have given a fine problem
requiring finesse and precision. However the chipping of
holds has replaced this with a very mediocre route. Climb
the slab directly; unprotected. A side-runner in Yong
reduces the grade to HVS.
(1978)

Left: Lee Hammond leads the celebrated 5b overhang testpiece **Wombat** (p69) at the left
end of the Roaches Upper Tier. Photo: Hammond Collection

Just right, and at a slightly higher level, is a square-cut buttress.

27 Wisecrack 8m VS 4b   *
The slanting crack in the left-hand face.   (1957-1968)

28 Hypothesis 10m HVS 5b   **
The cracked left arête of the buttress is enjoyable, but only just protectable.   (1963)

29 Earthbound 12m E6 6b   **
A sequence of first ascent improvements has provided a hard and serious route. Climb the steep slab right of Hypothesis with a crux section at 7m. A runner 5m up Hypothesis can be placed *en route* and reduces the grade to E4.   (1984)

Down and to the right again is **BENGAL BUTTRESS** *which is a much larger buttress with an undercut base and a twisting crack in its left face.*

30 Cannonball Crack 11m S 4a
Slither up the crack in the left-hand face to a precarious move left onto a boulder and so to the top.   (pre-1913)

31 Graffiti 15m E1 5b
Right of Cannonball Crack. Start at the base of an arête. Climb this until a move left gains a leaning corner which is climbed to the crack above. Finish direct.   (1978)

32 Dorothy's Dilemma 18m HVS 5a   **
Start as for Graffiti but climb the exposed arête for its entirety.   (1951)

33 Bengal Buttress 30m HVS 4c   **
A route which takes a meandering but logical line up the front face of the buttress. Start at the lowest point of the left arête. Move up to a grassy ledge, then go right and up to a break, runners. Move up to gain an airy position on the right arête where a trying move leads to the top of Raven Rock Gully. Step left onto the face and go up a short crack. An inspired product of the Thirties, being exposed, delicate and having disheartening protection.   (1930)

34 Schoolies 22m E3 5c   *
A direct line up the front of Bengal Buttress. Climb the centre of the lower roof using a long reach, then climb the easier wall to join Bengal Buttress at its traverse. Continue straight up the wall and finish as for Bengal Buttress to

reach the summit. An easier 5b alternative moves diagonally left from the half-height break to join Dorothy's Dilemma.

(1978)

35 Crack of Gloom 23m E2 5b   *
Strenuously follow the frightening crack in the left wall of Raven Rock Gully, exiting left round the chockstone in fine position. An exit right avoiding the crux is also possible.

(1958)

36 Raven Rock Gully Left-hand 20m VS 4b
Cracks and grooves in the left corner. Exit direct through the skylight. (1969)

37 Raven Rock Gully 20m D   *
A popular but filthy climb! Follow the flakes in the back of the gully and squirm through the manhole. (1901)

38 Swinger 20m VS 4c
The crack in the right wall of Raven Rock Gully can be used as a direct start to Via Dolorosa or a route in its own right.

(1968-1973)

39 Sidewinder 25m E4 5b,6a   *
1. 7m. From the foot of Swinger, hand-traverse right to climb a shallow groove in the blunt arête. Belay on the slab below the left-hand side of the great overhang.
2. 18m. Climb the left side of the huge roof via the protruding flake, then make a long reach to gain a vertical flake on the wall. Finish up the arête. (1979)

39a Cold Bone Forgotten 6m E3 6b   †
The lower roof left of Via Dolorosa using a side runner in the tree at the level of the roof. (1988)

40 Via Dolorosa 33m VS 4b,-,4c   ***
Start at the foot of the buttress left of a cave.
1. 8m. Ascend a narrow polished slab (hard), then move up left through the polished holly to reach a ledge. This point can also be gained by a horizontal traverse from the left at a slightly easier standard.
2. 10m. Traverse left to the rib and follow a short crack, then a slab round to the left. Belay at a block by the arête.
3. 15m. Traverse boldly up and right to a hidden flake. Climb this and the short corner, then move right round the arête and go up to the top just right of the arête. (1913-1924)

41 Valkyrie Direct 30m HVS 5a   **

From the first belay of Via Dolorosa, climb cracks leading to
the right end of the huge roof. Pull over to the foot of the
Valkyrie flake, then step left and follow the wide crack and
arête above.   (1951)

42 Matinee 23m HVS 5a,5b   ***

A must for those with a masochistic bent, this is the
unbroken fissure which splits the side-face of Raven Rock.
1. 15m. Climb the crack on glorious jams. Crevasse belay.
2. 8m. Continue up the widening crack to tackle the
punishing final bulge and belly-flop finale.   (1951)

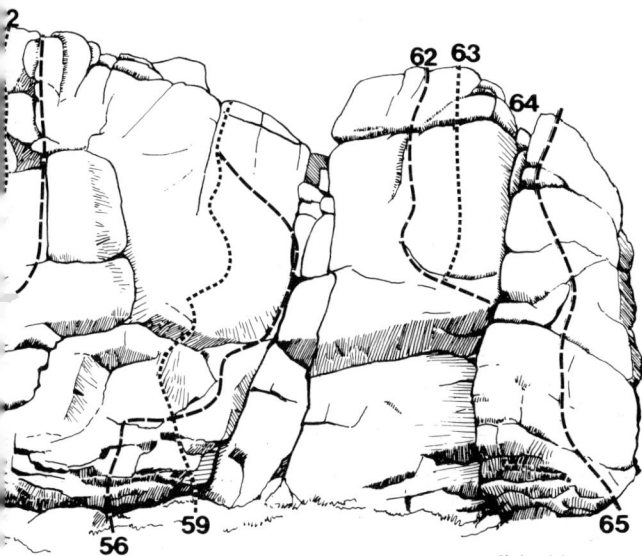

Philip Gibson.

Raven Rock

43 Valkyrie 38m VS 4b,4c   ***
A grit classic, justifiably popular with some intriguing moves in stunning positions. Start 6m right of Matinee in the huge corner.
1. 15m. Follow the corner to the foot of a wide crack. Traverse left to belay at the large triangular flake.
2. 23m. Climb up over the flake and descend it. Step awkwardly left onto the exposed front face where an intimidating balance move brings easy climbing to hand. Continue up the 'forehead' to the top. A memorable trip where good rope-work will increase the enjoyment for both leader and second.   (1946)

44 Licence to Run 22m E4 5c   **
A superb direct finish to Valkyrie starting at that route's first
belay at the crevasse. From the belay, move right to a
layback flake and follow this until moves right gain another
flake leading to the top. Protection is good but difficult to
place.   (1980/1980)

45 Licence to Lust 22m E4 6a   *
Climb the wall right of Licence to Run to join it at its second
and smaller flake. Step left and climb a thin crack to the top.
                                                              (1987)

46 Eugene's Axe 20m E2 5c
Right of Valkyrie's start, a slab props up a perpendicular
wall. Climb the right arête of the slab to a junction with
Pebbledash (the corner below). Step left to below incipient
creases and move up these to holds leading right to pockets.
Finish slightly left.   (1980)

47 Pebbledash 21m HVS 5a,4b   *
1. 12m. Four metres right of the start of Valkyrie is a short
corner. Climb this, then make an insecure move into the
huge corner on the left.
2. 9m. Climb the wide corner-crack to the top or, better,
break out left to climb a flake to the top.   (1969)

48 Secrets of Dance 20m E4 6a
From the initial groove on Pebbledash, climb the crack to a
sloping ramp leading rightwards to the top.   (1984)

49 The Swan 24m E3 5c   ***
Good natural holds allow this route to cross some
impressive ground. Start up Pebbledash but follow the
right-hand bow-shaped crack and place some high
runners. Traverse right with your feet just above a small
overlap to gain good fingerholds. A long reach gains a
rounded break and an even more rounded crack leading to
the top.   (1969/1977)

50 Up the Swanee 22m E4 5c   *
As for The Swan but use the handholds as footholds for the
traverse; delicate.   (1970)

51 Against the Grain 20m E5 6c   ***†
Very hard moves high on the wall with a moderately safe
fall-out zone, make this a rare gritstone route at this grade.
Start as for The Swan. From the top of the bow-shaped

cracks (runner also in Secrets of Dance), step left and climb directly by fingery moves to gain the ramp of Secrets of Dance. Finish up this. (1986)

52 Thing on a Spring 20m E6 7a   ***†
Less sustained but more technical than Against the Grain, taking the wall above The Swan. From the bow-shaped cracks, move diagonally rightwards to the top via a series of frustrating pulls on pebbles which usually result in airborne retreat. Protection is available in the final crack of Up the Swanee. (1986)

53 Swan Bank 20m E4 5c
From 6m up The Mincer, make a move left on a flake before going up to meet and finish as for The Swan. Serious. (1980)

54 The Mincer 20m HVS 5b   **
Twelve metres right of Valkyrie's corner is an obvious crack running rightwards through some stepped overlaps. Climb the shallow groove and move right to the crack. Tigers can start direct. Follow the crack to the nose, shuffle rightwards and grunt through the roof on undercut jams to a welcome respite. All that is left is the wider continuation fissure.
(1951)

55 Smear Test 11m E3 6a   **
A popular introduction to the region's harder slab-climbing. Start at the large resting ledge on The Mincer's final crack. After the placement of a runner on the chockstone, traverse horizontally right across the slab to finish up a bottomless crack. An independent start can be made by moving left from the top of Pincer's initial groove into The Mincer. (1977)

56 Pincer 20m HVS 5a   **
Four metres right of The Mincer's start, and below its final crack, is a groove. Start a further 2m right. Climb leftwards to gain the groove (crux). Traverse back right and climb up to a horizontal crack which is followed rightwards into the gully. Climb this for 4m, then traverse left across the slab to finish up a good crack. (1957-1968)

57 Kicking Bird 19m E4 6a   *
Start 1m right of Pincer. Ascend the bulge direct to join Pincer, then pull awkwardly over the small roof onto the slab. Step left into The Mincer and follow it to the large ledge. Step right, as for Smear Test, then move up to a vague finger-ramp. Pull back left to finish. (1978)

58 Bloodstone 19m E5 6b   *
Follow Kicking Bird to the standing position above the small
roof; (place a side-runner in The Mincer). Climb the slab
just right of The Mincer to join Kicking Bird up which the
route finishes.   (1983)

59 Bloodspeed 19m E6 6b   **
As for Kicking Bird to the standing position on the slab
above the small roof. With protection in The Mincer and in
the crack under the roof to the right, traverse right, then go
up the slab to either join the final crack of Smear Test or
climb the slab to its right.   (1984)

60 Guano Gully 13m HS 4b
The gully to the right of Pincer contains a jammed boulder
which is passed to the left.   (1927)

61 Mousey's Mistake 15m E1 5a
Pass the jammed boulder on the right then climb the left
side of the slab above, left of the flake of Elegy.   (1978)

*The next two routes share a common start; an unpleasant
crack 5m right of Guano Gully.*

62 Elegy 16m E2 5c   ***
An absorbing route of the utmost class. Follow the crack
until above the roof. Pull left and follow the flake in the
centre of the slab until it peters out. Boldly climb the slab
above to the top.   (1960/1969)

**63 Clive Coolhead Realises the Excitement of Knowing You
May Be the Author of Your Own Death is More Intense Than
Orgasm** 15m E5 6b   **
Pull out of the crack as for Elegy and immediately tackle the
holdless slab above. Runners low down in The Bulger and
on the flake of Elegy provide the grade.   (1983)

64 The Bulger 13m VS 4c
The unpleasant crack is climbed direct and proves more
interesting than first imagined.   (1951)

Right of The Bulger is a bouldering roof well-endowed with
good holds which can provide continuing sport even during
light rain.

65 Fledgelings Climb 13m S   *
Start 2m right of the bouldering roof on the left wall of a
recess. Trend leftwards across this wall to finish up the arête
right of The Bulger.   (1927)

66 Little Chimney 9m M
The chimney in the left-hand corner of the recess. (pre-1951)

67 Battery Crack 10m HS 4a
The wide crack out of the sentry-box. Finish up the next
route.
(1968-1973)

68 Lucas Chimney 11m S
The evil slot in the right-hand corner of the recess. Painfully
ascend the chimney, then swing desperately left to finish.
(1927)

*The buttress to the right, and just behind Rock Hall Cottage,
has a flat front-face split at two-thirds height by two
parallel slanting cracks.*

69 Hawkwing 21m E1 5b   **
Start just right of Lucas Chimney. Follow a curving crackline
rightwards onto the front face to join Kestrel Crack. Climb
this for 2m, then traverse back left across the front face via
the parallel slanting cracks. Finish up the left arête.
(1963/1978)

70 Carrion 19m E3 5c   *
Climb over the triangular overhang right of Hawkwing to a
junction with that route at a small ledge. Continue straight
up the centre of the buttress to finish up a short crack
slightly right of centre.
(1980)

71 Poison Gift 19m E3 6a   *
As for Carrion to a ledge 4m below the parallel slanting
cracks. Move up and hand-traverse a thinner, and slightly
lower, break to finish up the left arête.
(1980)

72 Kestrel Crack 20m HS 4a   *
Behind Rock Hall Cottage is a groove with a tree stump at
its base. Climb the groove and step right to enter the crack;
or start more pleasantly round to the right. Climb the crack
past a chockstone to a gruelling chimney-finish.
(1913-1924)

73 Headless Horseman 20m E1 5b
From the chockstone of Kestrel Crack, move out rightwards
to climb the right arête on its left side. Poorly-protected.
(1978)

To the right of Headless Horseman is a smooth wall which
has only been breached by a 7a top-rope problem up the
blunt nose and arête below the small triangular roof.

Lower Tier Right-hand

Right of the smooth wall is a corner with rhododendron bushes at its base.

74 Flimney 18m HVD
Climb a large flake left of the bushes and finish up the crack and corner behind. (1957-1968)

75 The Death Knell 13m E4 5c ***
A superb and often underrated route. Start just right of the bushes at a short arête. Climb the arête and wall above until a step right over the roof brings a crack and the top. (1970)

76 Amaranth 12m E4 5c
A poor route starting up the arête of The Death Knell and finishing to its left up some cracks. (1979)

77 Rhodren 11m HVS 5b
Right again is a great perched flake. Start below the lower left toe of the flake. Climb the groove and move rightwards round the roof to finish up another flake. (1958)

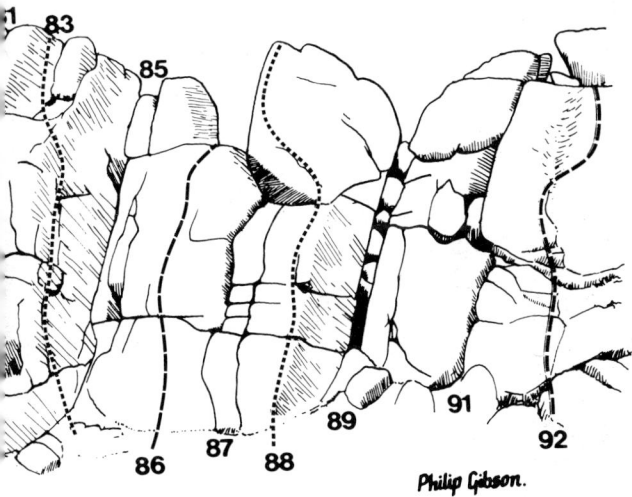

Philip Gibson.

78 Flake Chimney 14m M *
Conquer the flake and climb the chimney on the right.
(pre-1951)

79 Straight Crack 10m S
Bridge against the flake to start the crack behind it and finish
leftwards. (1957-1968)

Right of the great flake is a buttress with an overhang at 3m.

80 Punch 14m E3 6b *
At the left end of the overhang is a short hanging groove.
Pull into this (crux) and climb cracks above. Only for the
gritstone thug. (1957-1968/1978)

81 Choka 12m E1 5c
Start 3m right of Punch below a finger-crack in the roof.
Surmount the roof gymnastically and levitate up the
off-width crack above. (1958)

The next two routes start below the crack in the left wall of the corner to the right.

82 Circuit Breaker 10m E3 6a
Move immediately left to the arête and pull over the bulge. Place protection, then climb the flake in the arête above to a pull over onto the slab. (1980)

83 Hunky Dory 10m E3 5c   **
To the right is a steep wall containing a snaking crack. Climb the crack to a resting ledge on the right. Boldly climb the wall and rib above to an easier-than-it-looks finish. It is also possible to finish left from the top of the crack by way of a 6a mantelshelf. (1975)

84 Fluorescent Stripper 13m E4 6a
An alternative finish to Hunky Dory. From the resting ledge move up and right to climb the featured tower somewhat artificially. (1985)

85 Prow Corner 12m VD   *
The crack in the back of the deep corner on the left side of the slab. Finish up a spectacular 'flying' crack. (1957-1968)

86 Chalkstorm 10m E4 5c   **
Climb the centre of the slab on sloping holds with a small wire at the overlap. Traditionally climbed with a side-runner in Prow Corner which reduces the grade to E1 − E3 depending on how high it is placed. (1977)

87 Prow Cracks 10m D   *
The twin cracks on the right side of the slab are overcome by varied techniques. (1957-1968)

88 Commander Energy 12m E2 5c   **
Right of Prow Cracks is a sharp 'flying' arête above a triangular roof. Climb the rounded right arête of the slab to the roof, pull over and boldly layback the arête. (1975)

89 Rocking Stone Gully 8m VD
The corner right of Commander Energy lives up to its name.

90 Captain Lethargy 8m VD
The crack 2m right. Finish on the left.

91 Sifta's Quid 10m HS 4b   *
Start just to the right. Climb over two large blocks to gain the large bulge which is passed on the right. Entertaining. Squirming through the tunnel beneath the huge boulder provides even more entertainment. (1968)

92 Piece of Mind 11m E6 6b   ***
The first route of its type on gritstone, well ahead of its
time; 6b moves in a position where a fall could be
catastrophic. The blunt arête on the right is ascended to a
finish on the right.   (1977)

93 The Thin Air 9m E5 6a   *
The slab right of Piece of Mind, the substance being a
'rockover' onto the small horizontal vein followed by a long
stretch to finish. Unprotected.   (1980)

94 The Girdle Traverse 80m HVS 5a
A wandering line but pleasant nevertheless. From almost the
top of Bengal Butress, traverse the chockstone and continue
to join Valkyrie at the lip. Reverse this to its stance in the
crevasse, then move right to the corner. Go up a short way,
then move right across the great wall via high-level breaks.
Descend down into The Mincer and continue by a line
almost (but not quite) at the top of the crag into The Bulger
to finish.   (1960)

95 The Underpass 50m E1 5b
A variant on The Girdle Traverse. From the end of the
traverse on Bengal Buttress, reverse the crux of The Crack of
Gloom into the gully and pass rightwards beneath the
chockstone into Raven Rock Gully. Continue the traverse
round under the great overhang to meet Valkyrie Direct.
Awkward moves gain Matinee which is followed almost to
the top. Take the right-hand branch of the crack to finish.
                                                        (1963)

96 The Super Girdle 45m E4 5c,6a,5c   ***
Perhaps a hybrid but nevertheless, marvellous horizontal
movement on the best of gritstone slabs.
1. 22m. Follow The Swan to the end of its traverse, then
continue at the same level to reach The Mincer.
2. 11m. Move out to the crack on Smear Test, arrange gear,
and continue by sustained tiptoeing, slightly downwards into
Guano Gully.
3. 12m. Move out again onto Elegy's slab and traverse quite
boldly in a straight line to meet and finish up The Bulger.
Stepping down to arrange protection in the halfway flake is
strongly advised.   (1980)

THE UPPER TIER
by Simon Nadin

> 'Joe Brown made the second ascent, with
> myself as second, when I was his Gentleman's
> Gentleman. When I was out on the roof he tied
> off the rope to the belay and came down to
> watch me, giving me the shock of my young
> life. When I asked if he was holding the rope
> because of all the slack, up from the deck
> floated the reply " of course I am" .'

> Dennis Gray, talking about The Sloth.

THE CLIMBS are described from RIGHT to LEFT as this
section of the crag is normally approached from the stone
steps splitting The Lower Tier.

*The first climb is situated on a large boulder facing Hen
Cloud, approximately 100m down the hillside from the top
of the steps.*

1 Ou Est Le Spit? 5m E6 6b   †
A bigger problem than first appears, taking the obvious
slipway on the front of the boulder. Survival instinct is
required more than technique for the final crawl.

(1986)

Further extended boulder problems are available here. A line
right of Ou Est Le Spit? gives **Wolfman of the KGB**, E4 6b,
and the prominent left arête direct is **Shelty**, HVS 5c. Thirty
metres left of this boulder is **Dolly Mix, Mix**, HVS 5a, via
small pockets on a wall.

Slightly farther up the hillside beyond Dolly Mix, Mix *is a
compact overhung buttress.*

2 Pepper 7m VS 5a
The overhanging front face leads to a ledge. Move leftwards
to finish up a crack. (1957-1968)

3 Garlic 7m HVS 5a
From a short corner to the left move up before swinging
right onto the ledge of Pepper. Finish over the overhang on
its right-hand side. (1979)

*The next buttress is topped by an impressive overhang just
to the right of which is:*

4 Genetix 11m E3 6a   *

Start just right of a sharp undercut arête and below some flakes in the lower roof. Pull up to the flakes with difficulty and haul over to continue up the right side of the arête and a finish on green sloping holds.   (1979)

5 Calcutta Buttress 11m VS 5a   *

From the left-hand side of the rib, steep pulls lead to a short traverse left, after which a balancy mantelshelf gains an upright position on the break (a slip here may create your own black hole!). Continue rightwards, and then finally, move back left below the roof. The initial roof can be taken direct at 5a.   (1957-1968)

6 Mistral 6m E2 6a

The wall right of the obvious crack leads to a horizontal break beneath the final steep prow. Finish up this on small holds.   (1987)

7 Calcutta Crack 6m S

The crack itself leads to an awkward and tiring finish.
    (1924-1951)

8 Sign of the Times 6m HVS 5b

Use the left arête of the crack to make a difficult move left onto the wall. Finish direct via a short flake.   (1979)

Three metres to the left, an undercut nose provides a 5b problem.

9 Between the Tiles 25m E1 5a

A girdle crossing the buttress at half-height with an awkward section beneath the central prow and a tricky finish rightwards up the scoop.   (1979)

To the left is **BLUSHING BUTTRESS** *which is split by a gully. The smaller right-hand buttress has flakes on its right-hand side.*

10 Sparkle 8m VS 4b

Follow the flakes before making a traverse left to finish. A direct finish is HVS 5a.   (1978)

11 Rib Wall 8m D

From below the small niche, climb up to a large ledge. Continue direct.   (1957-1968)

12 The Rib 8m M

Ascend the right-hand rib of the gully.   (1957-1968)

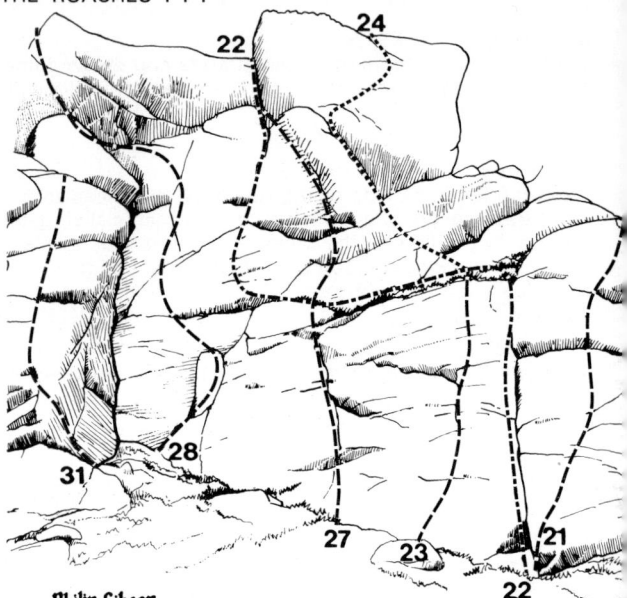

Philip Gibson.

Blushing Buttress

13 Grilled Fingers 9m HVS 4c
The steep left wall of the gully is taken to the right of some
large flakes. Finish direct with long reaches. (1979)

14 Gully Wall 9m VS 4b
The large flakes are followed to an awkward move left onto
the nose of Right-hand Route. (1957-1968)

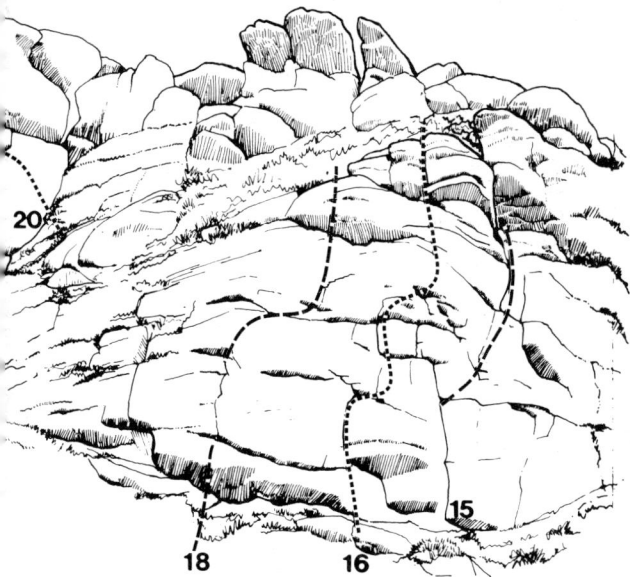

15 Right-hand Route 13m S   **
A very 'pushy' start up the obvious polished layback flake
leads to a small ledge on the right. Continue directly to
attack the protruding nose. Excellent value.   (1924)

16 Left-hand Route 13m VD   *
From 2m left, a layback move leads around the left-hand
end of a roof. Trend slightly right, then follow shallow cracks
before moving round the bulge via a pocket. Delicate moves
then gain a wide crack and finally the top.   (1924)

17 War Wound 11m HVS 5c
A contrived start 1m left of Left-hand Route leads with difficulty past a break to a ledge. Move left along this before ascending the slabby arête. (1978)

18 Scarlet Wall 11m S 4a
Follow the strenuous crack near the left end of the buttress and move right to gain the ledge on War Wound. Step up carefully and exit left. (1924-1949)

19 Aperitif 25m S 4a
A traverse of the buttress from left to right. Start in a cave to the left of Scarlet Wall. Traverse right along the lip to the crack of Scarlet Wall, then hand-traverse into Left-hand Route. Follow this for a few moves until it is possible to reach the ledge on Right-hand Route. Swing right strenuously to reach the gully, then continue right across the next buttress. (1968-1973)

Above Blushing Buttress are three jutting prows. The centre one, by swinging up and over the lip, is a good 5a problem. In fact the keen boulderer can find many other excellent problems in the vicinity.

THE MAIN AREA

From the top of the steps, a dry-stone wall can be seen running towards the crag. Immediately behind this is a short wall and a roof.

20 Hangman's Crack 11m S
The right-hand side of the wall leads to a large black roof flake. Step left to attack the wide crack. Difficult to protect. (1924-1949)

21 Babbacombe Lee 11m E1 5b *
Start just right of the prominent undercut crack of Crack and Corner. Difficult moves up the short wall lead to a ledge. Move up via a short crack and finish boldly over the nose. (1978)

22 Crack and Corner 35m S 4c,-,4a **
1. 12m. The undercut crack itself is frequently a cause for foul language.
2. 8m. Wander left along the ledge and belay at a large block.
3. 15m. The wall above leads, via long pockets, to a ledge on the left. Follow the corner above to a final obstacle: the roof. (1913)

23 Roscoe's Wall 11m HVS 5b   *
The centre of the pink wall 3m to the left. Start with a crafty
heel-hook to gain a small niche. Swing right before making
steep pulls up to a ledge. Alternatively finish direct or to the
left. A good continuation is: (1955)

24 Round Table 11m E1 5a   *
A route of surprising grade for the line taken. Steep and
committing moves lead into the wide crack (large nut or
Friend 4 needed). Swing right across the bulge to an easy
finish.   (1974)

25 Trebia 10m E4 6a   †
Difficult moves up the undercut rib left of the wide crack of
Round Table lead to a niche below the final roof. Take this
direct at a shallow hole.   (1980)

26 Magic Child 7m HVS 5a
The left-hand side of the lower wall contains a thin crack
(Jelly Roll). Start on a flake 1m right of this to gain holds
leading right. Pull up via the large pocket and move left for
3m before moving back right to finish.   (1978)

27 Jelly Roll 23m HS 4a,4a
1. 8m. The thin crack itself leads to a belay at a block.
2. 15m. Climb the wall above, via long pockets, to a move
right into a slanting crack. Follow this to finish as for Crack
and Corner.   (1957-1968)

28 Easy Gully Wall 21m VD
From 3m left of Jelly Roll, climb a blunt rib to reach a block.
Move left onto the steep wall before climbing leftwards to
gain a sandy ledge. Trend rightwards to a short layback
crack and a bulge. Traverse left below the overhang to finish
up a wide crack.   (1957-1968)

29 Destination Venus 24m HVS 5b
A traverse of the lower wall from right to left. From the
ledge on Babbacombe Lee, move into Crack and Corner.
Step down before making difficult moves left into the niche
on Roscoe's Wall. Traverse left passing the large pocket into
Jelly Roll.   (1979)

To the left is the nasty overhanging gully of **Easy Gully**. The
overhanging buttress to the left of this provides some
desperate routes, each one seemingly more improbable than
the last.

30 Bed of Nails 12m E3 5b   *
From the bottom of Easy Gully, move out left across the wall and gain the usually green, slanting crack which will hopefully lead to easier ground. Move left to finish.   (1978)

31 Antithesis 15m E4 6b   ***
The concave wall to the left of Bed of Nails is climbed leftwards towards the exposed lip by an inventive series of finger-changes and heel-hooks. Finish direct. A small wire placed 3m up Bed of Nails helps protect. One final hint; pick your feet up if you fall off!   (1980)

32 Paralogism 15m E7 6c   ***†
A hard and serious roof pitch up the right-hand side of the roof proper. From the short corner, work leftwards across the roof, with difficulty in keeping two points of contact, let alone three! From the flake on the lip, move right before making the final pull over. Small wires in Bed of Nails and behind flakes in the unclimbed roof to the left provide minimal protection.   (1987)

To the left is THE GREAT SLAB.

33 Kelly's Shelf 17m HVD   *
The obvious slanting ledge above the overhang is gained from below. To gain and follow the ledge will normally cause expert and novice alike to abandon the 'no knees rule' and opt for the 'as many points of contact as possible', approach. From the end of the ledge, move into the crack to finish. A HS 4a finish goes over the bulge from the right end of the ledge to follow pockets to the top.   (1924-1949)

34 Kelly's Direct 15m E1 5b   **
From the foot of the slanting ledge of Kelly's Shelf climb a thin crack on the left to a ledge. Gain the obvious flake above and climb it to a large pocket continuing direct on further pockets to the top.   (1968-1973)

35 Right Route 24m VD   **
The classic introductory route for the novice.
1. 15m. Follow well-worn pockets on the right-hand side of the slab passing a short corner-crack to reach a roof. Step delicately left before moving up to reach a belay on the large ledge on the right.
2. 9m. Move up, then make an exposed traverse leftwards to gain a crack. Follow this to the top. A fine climb, though showing signs of wear-and-tear.   (1913)

36 Right Route Right 15m VS 4b
As for Right Route to the roof. Thrutch over this to gain the corner and the top. **Kelly's Connection**, HVS 5a, takes a strenuous traverse-line from the roof to the large pocket on Kelly's Direct. (1957-1968/1957-1968)

37 Central Route 15m VS 4a ✳✳
A bold lead on small holds up the centre of the slab between Right Route and the large triangular flake in the slab to the left, taken by Pedestal Route. Traverse right below the overhang to belay on the large ledge. (1949-1951)

Other lines exist, at either side of Central Route, but these crowd the slab somewhat.

38 99% of Gargoyles Look Like Bob Todd 24m E5 6b †
The handsome hanging groove above Central Route is gained from that route. A shaky flake is used to reach the groove, from where moves left lead to an obvious pocket to finish. (1986)

39 The Sloth 24m HVS 5b ✳✳✳
A milestone in any leader's roof-climbing career. From the top of the pedestal on Pedestal Route, climb the short wall to the 'cheeseblock', then launch out across the roof using adrenalin to the final strenuous pull into the wide crack. Follow this to the top. A direct start to the pedestal together with its front face is 5b. (1954)

40 New Fi'nial 28m E6 6b ✳†
Follow The Sloth to its lip. Swing right along the lip of the overhang via sloping holds, heel-hooks and vast amounts of commitment. Passing the short crack 5m out is the crux. Definitely no verandah! (1985)

41 Loculus Lie 28m E5 6a ✳✳✳†
Bold roof-climbing with outstanding positions, though few may appreciate them. From the 'cheeseblock' on The Sloth, stretch out left to reach thin flakes. Follow these before moving back right to the lip of The Sloth. Traverse left on obvious holds until a blind reach helps gain a cave. Take a deep breath, then pull out on the left to climb the wall on small rugosities. (1983)

42 Pedestal Route 27m HVD ✳✳✳
A route with a good feel of adventure attached to it and requiring a variety of techniques.
1. 12m. Either climb the short ramp leading to the crack forming the right edge of the pedestal or, harder, climb the

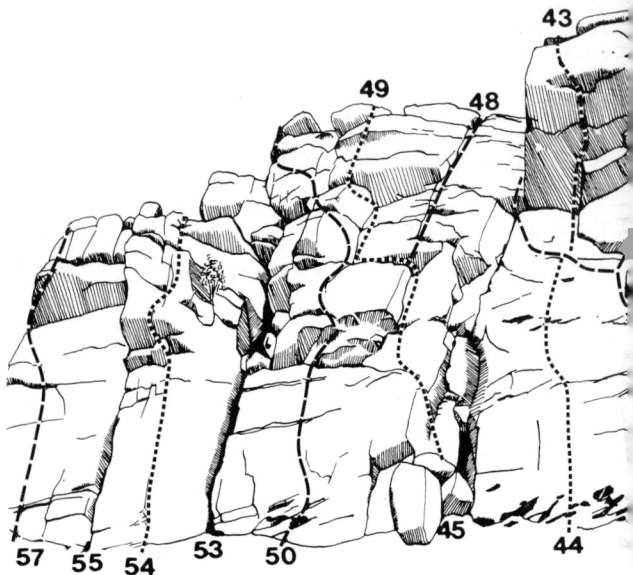

The Great Slab

steep wall direct to the left-hand side. Follow this by
strenuous laybacking to the pedestal top. Belay.
2. 15m. Shuffle left to an awkward mantelshelf onto the
break before moving left again into the corner, possible
belay. Go up to and over the small roof (a strategically
placed nut runner here can prevent the rope from jamming)
and continue up the corner above.   (1913)

43 Painted Rumour 26m E6 6a   ***†
This stunning route takes the centre of the huge roof left of
The Sloth. From the back of the roof beneath the cave, climb
out strenuously via long reaches and a glued flake, until a
welcome rest can be taken in the cave. Finish up the
headwall on rugosities (as for Loculus Lie).   (1985)

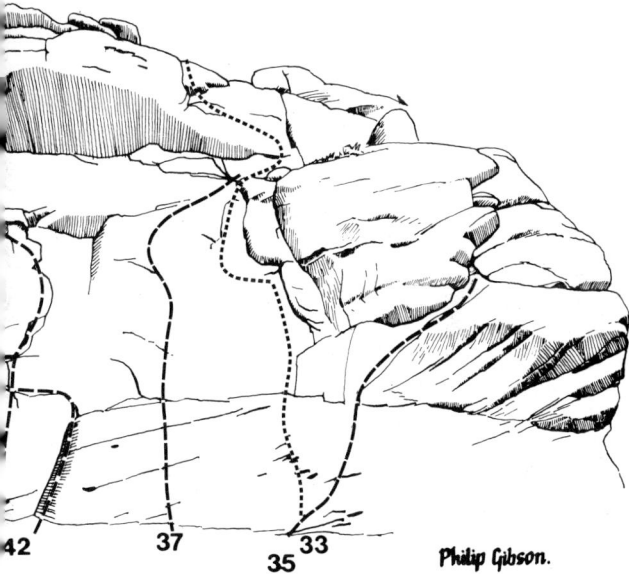

Philip Gibson.

44 Technical Slab 23m HS 4a   *
Start 3m right of the narrowing crack to the left; Hollybush
Crack. Boldly climb the steep slab with long and committing
stretches to reach a horizontal break beneath the roof. Move
left, continue over the small roof, then go up the final
corner.   (1945)

45 Hollybush Crack 26m VS 4a,4b   **
The chimney to the left, complete with hollybush.
1. 12m. Carefully (box advised for gentlemen) bridge up
above the holly until a difficult step right can be made into a
wide crack. Belay a little higher.
2. 14m. Follow the crack round the small overhang and go
up the corner to a thread. Step down to follow the pockets
on an exposed ascending traverse across the right wall.
Finish near the right arête.   (1957-1968)

46 Gillted 30m E4 5c   *
The final trip across the great overhang. From the corner on
the left-hand side of the roof, follow the obvious handrail
running rightwards to its end. Swing blindly round under the
very lip of the overhang to reach the cave. With luck
climbers will extricate themselves from here via a pocket
above and to the right of the cave.   (1979)

47 Diamond Wednesday 26m HVS 5a
Follow Hollybush Crack until above the holly. Continue up
the thin crack on the left to a small triangular roof. A
difficult move round this then leads to easier climbing up
the buttress to reach the top.   (1978)

48 Black Velvet 27m HVD   **
From the bottom of Hollybush Crack, swing left onto a ledge
and move left again into the corner of Black and Tans. Climb
this before continuing directly over the roof and going
up the easier final crack.   (1957-1968)

49 Black and Tans 30m S   ***
1. 12m. Start as for Black Velvet. Follow this to the small
roof but move left onto a ledge. Belay in the corner.
2. 18m. Climb the corner, then move left onto the exposed
nose. Continue in a direct line to the top, via three awkward
mantelshelves. Poorly-protected.   (1913)

Variations;
1a. 12m. The steep wall beneath the corner of Black Velvet
can be climbed on pockets and flake holds to give a harder
start, 5a.
2a. 18m. From the stance, climb the wall on the right and
continue directly over the roof and up the wall above, 5a.

50 Ruby Tuesday 30m E2 5b,4b,5b   **
Has the feel of a big mountain route with both technical and
bold climbing on the first and last pitches.
1. 12m. Start as for Black and Tans Direct but continue
straight up to reach the overhang. Pull over this into a
shallow niche. Delicate and fingery moves out right lead to
the belay ledge on Black and Tans.
2. 6m. Swing round left onto the bulging rib to belay below
cracks on the left.
3. 12m. Climb the cracks above for 3m, then make an
increasingly worrying traverse left to gain the overhung
arête above a chimney. Follow this. A variation on this pitch

has been climbed by pulling through the roof to bisect the traverse midway and continuing direct to the top, E4 6a.

(1970)

51 Hanging Around 24m HVS 5b   *
Climb the bulging wall 3m left of Ruby Tuesday and continue direct via a hanging corner to reach the large cracked roof. Move strenuously right beneath the roof until technical moves help gain the crack above. Follow Jeffcoat's Buttress to finish.   (1974/1978)

52 Jeffcoat's Buttress 27m HS 4c,4a   **
1. 18m. From just right of the obvious chimney, a desperately-smooth start soon leads to easier moves up a short corner left of an overhang. A hard pull, aided by a hidden hold, leads to an awkward traverse right above the large roof. Belay on the ledge beneath two cracks. Modern equipment may give more peace of mind than the ancient metal pipe in the crack.
2. 9m. Follow the cracks above to finish.   (1913)

53 Jeffcoat's Chimney 24m VD   **
A classic climb of considerable character, though the passage of many pairs of boots has left its mark.
1. 18m. Climb the heavily-polished chimney past the cave to arrive at a spacious ledge.
2. 6m. From the left end of the ledge, make a long step right. Go up to a move left at the overlap, then finish more easily.   (1913)

Variations.
1a. 18m. Ascend the left wall of the chimney, then move right to the cave, Severe.
1b. 18m. Follow the chimney for 3m, step right, then go up to where the wall steepens. Move back left into the chimney, Difficult.
2a. 6m. From the right-hand end of the ledge, climb the corner, strong fingers required, to easier ground on the left, 5a.

To the left of Jeffcoat's Chimney, a steep crack cleaves its way through a series of overhangs.

54 Humdinger 18m E1 5b   *
Climb directly up the wall 2m right of the crack to reach the
tiered overhang. Gain a jug out on the lip before making a
frustrating long reach for the beckoning hold above. Pull
round the next bulge on its right and continue direct to the
top.   (1969)

55 Saul's Crack 18m HVS 5a   ***
Direct and sustained with excellent protection. Climb easily
up the crack to gain the obvious niche. Awkward moves
then gain the corner-crack leading to the final roof. Climb it.
                                                          (1947)

56 Something Biblical 18m E2 6a
Climb directly up the wall 2m left of Saul's Crack to the roof.
Pull blindly through using a small flake and continue up the
wall above. Runners are used in Saul's Crack.   (1987)

57 Gypfast 18m E4 5c   ***
This route now sports fewer creaking flakes than it did on
the first ascent but nevertheless, it still gives very exciting
roof climbing. Ascend the slab to reach the left-hand side
of the roof. Follow flakes across right to the widest point
where it is possible to pull over to join Bachelor's Buttress
and finish up the cracked rib. Protection is placed either side
of the roof at this grade.   (1979)

58 Bachelor's Buttress 18m VS 4a,4b   *
1. 9m. Start as for Gypfast, then move diagonally left to a
belay in the gully.
2. 9m. An ascending traverse right leads with difficulty and
exposed positions to the arête. Follow a short crack to finish.
                                                          (1913)

2a. 8m. **Direct Finish**, HVS 4c. Climb directly up the centre of
the wall from midway along the traverse. Straightforward
climbing leads to a surprising finish.

59 Rotunda Gully 15m M
Not really a climb though a crack in the right face of the
buttress to the left gives an alternative HVD finish.

60 Rotunda Buttress 18m VS 4c
Start at a wide crack left of the gully. Follow this for 3m
before moving up and left with some concern to a ledge.
Ascend rightwards, then left to another ledge below an
arête. The steep final wall provides the punch.   (1945)

The final route and probably the poorest on this section of crag is the aptly-named, **True Grot**, VS 5a. Follow the left-hand side of the buttress before finishing up the arête.

On the left of Rotunda Buttress is an easy way down. Ten metres left again the rock reappears once again. The right-hand side consists of an arête with a square overhang at 3m which gives Tealeaf Crack. *Up and to the right is a small diamond-shaped buttress.*

61 A Short Trip to a Transylvanian Brain Surgery 8m S
Climb the front face of the buttress for a three-star name but a no-star route. (1978)

62 Cornflake 8m M
The chimney in the corner. (1957-1968)

63 Tealeaf Crack 12m S   *
Climb up to the square overhang. Move around this on the right to a crack. A difficult move up and a step left gain the pleasant arête above. (1957-1968)

64 Quickbrew 12m E2 5c   *
Gain jugs on the hanging arête bounding the left-hand side of the roof. Pull round this with a difficult transition onto the 'brick edges' on the slab above. (1981)

65 Public Enemy Number One 12m HVS 5a
This route fills a gap by taking the overhang 1m left and finishing directly up the slab above. (1979)

66 Aqua 12m VS 4b
The obvious roof split by a thin crack gives some strenuous and enjoyable moves. Continue in the same line to reach the top. (1954)

67 Central Massive 15m D
Three metres left of Aqua, a large flake protrudes from the face. Climb to this then go direct in the same line to the top. (1945)

68 Wipers 18m VS 4b
Pick a direct line up the wall 2m left of Central Massive to finish up the right arête of the upper wall. (1978)

69 Little Perforations 15m E2 6a   *
Climb the vague pink scoop in the blank-looking wall just to the left. Technical and reachy moves constitute the crux above a faint horizontal break. Finish easily and straight up. (1985)

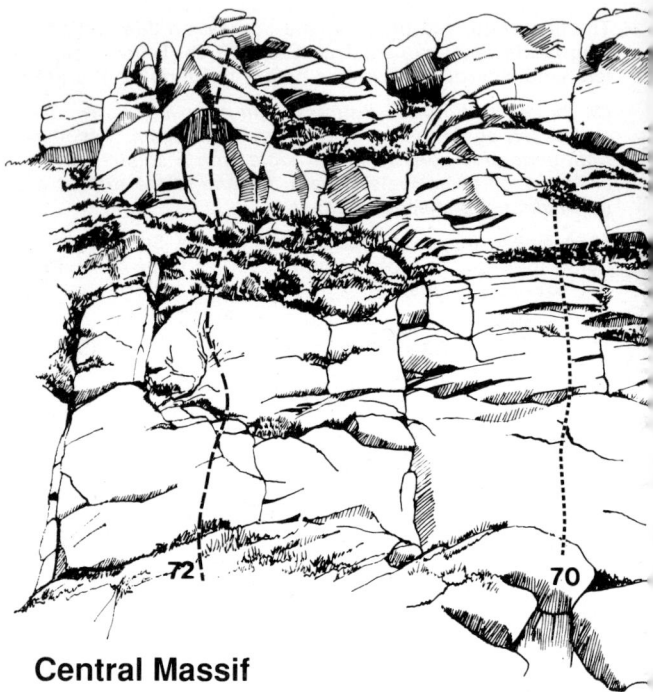

Central Massif

70 Lone Ascent 18m HS 4b
Five metres left of the flake of Central Massive is a good
hold at 3m. Delicate moves or a long stretch lead to the
hold. Swing up and right to follow the wall just to the left of
a crack. Finish up a wide crack.   (1951-1957)

71 Joe Public 18m HS 4a
Start up a groove 3m left or the wall just to the right. From
the break reach a crack above and continue direct.   (1978)

72 A Day at the Seaside 12m VS 4b
A poor route taking the centre of the gardened wall and slab
to the left of Joe Public. Finish over a small triangular roof.
                                                       (1982)

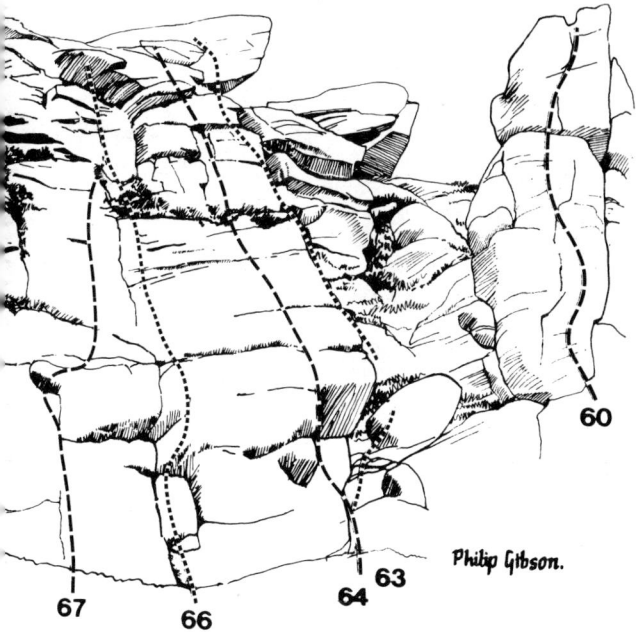

Philip Gibson.

67   66   64 63   60

73 Libra 14m HVS 4c   *
The vague technical crackline on the right side of a wall 15m
to the left of Joe Public. Climb the crack with increasing
interest and delicacy to its top. Wander left and ascend a
small tower on amazing pockets.   (1957-1968)

74 Third Degree Burn 9m E2 5b
Follow the easiest possible line up the centre of the wall left
of Libra avoiding the chimney on the left.   (1978)

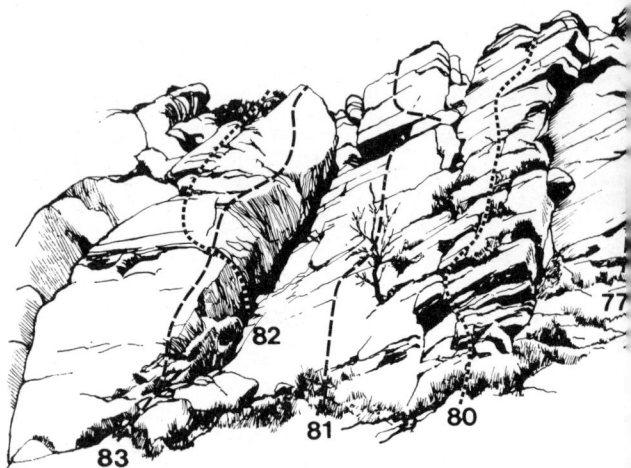

Philip Gibson.

75 Damascus Crack 12m HS 4a   *
The obvious crack 4m to the left is followed with excellent
protection to reach a ledge. The small buttress is climbed
with flaky holds. Alternatively, take a short crack in the tower
over to the left; VS 4b.   (1955)

76 Runner Route 11m S   *
From the corner on the left of the slab and beneath the
holly, pad delicately rightwards across the slab. Mantelshelf
onto the break, then move left to the holly and continue up
the crack behind it.   (1955)

The arête to the left gives **Dawn Piper**, an acute problem at
HVS 5b.

*Across to the left is a corner with a chimney and overhang
above.*

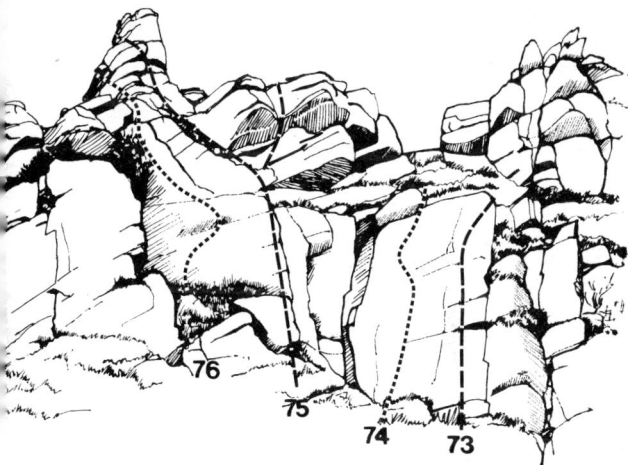

Maud's Garden

77 Broken Slab 12m S
From 2m right of the corner, ascend the wall direct for 7m, then bear right to reach a crack. A difficult move starts the crack which is then followed to the top. A groove to the right of the slab can be taken as an alternative start and a direct finish on the original line proves to be VS 4b.　(1945)

78 Reset Portion of Galley 37 12m S
The corner with a chimney and overhang above. Ascend until forced awkwardly right below the roof. Finish up the crack.　(1958)

79 Coldfinger 15m VS 4b
Climb the obvious arête to the left, stepping out right above the overhangs at the top.　(1978)

80 Contrary Mary 15m VS 4b
Climb the short steep corner just right of the oak tree on the
front face of the buttress before climbing easily up the slabs
to the headwall. This gives a delicate and exciting finish.
(1951-1957)

*The clean slab left again is overlooked by a steep wall. The
right side of this slab is taken direct by* **Lybstep**, *VS 4b.*

81 Maud's Garden 21m VD   *
1. 12m. The centre of the rippled slab requires nimble
footwork in the first few metres to gain the crack above.
Continue to reach a sandy alcove.
2. 9m. From the right-hand side of the ledge, pull up the
chimney above until it is possible to step left onto the
exposed headwall. Good holds then lead up this to the top.
The upper wall can be gained by tackling the overhang
slightly left of centre at 5c.   (1945)

82 Beckermet Slab 15m VD   *
From the foot of the gully left of Maud's Garden, bridge out
to gain the horizontal break on the left wall. Swing onto this
with difficulty then move left to the arête. Gain a ledge
above and finish up the slabby arête.   (1945)

83 The Valve 15m E4 5c   *
The route follows the looming tower above the gully. Start
around the arête to the left of Beckermet Slab. A long reach
gains the ledge on that route, then pull up the short
overhanging wall just right of the arête to the base of the
tower. Move right across the curving ramp-line then break
out leftwards to finish up the arête. Bold.   (1978)

The evil overhung chimney to the left is taken by:

84 Late Night Final 20m HVD
Squirm and curse up the chimney with techniques that defy
description. Continue up the stony gully above. Easier for
the slim.   (1951-1957)

To the left is an obvious large overhang at 5m.

85 West's Wallaby 23m VS 4c   *
This climb skirts the large overhang on its right. Start by
balancing up the slanting crack leading to the large block
wedged under the roof. Swing wildly right round this to
continue along the horizontal break into the gully. Move up,
then left, to finish by slabs.   (1960)

86 Between the Lines 20m E4 6a †
Start 2m right of West's Wallaby. Climb the thin crack and
the arête on its right-hand side to the block. Move off the
block to climb directly up the wall. (1987)

87 Wallaby Direct 20m HVS 5a *
Climb the steep wall from midway along the traverse of
West's Wallaby. Vertical moves up this pass a short crack on
the right. Continue direct. (1960)

88 Walleroo 20m E2 5c **
From the right-hand side of the block on West's Wallaby,
difficult fingery moves lead leftwards through the bulge into
a faint groove; blind. Finish easily up the slabs above. (1960)

89 Live Bait 20m E4 5c *
Two metres to the left is a tiny flake on the wall. With
difficulty, climb past this to reach the break. Move right to
the block and 'explode' leftwards across the roof to its
widest point. An alarming reach then gains easier ground.
(1981)

90 Wombat 20m E2 5b ***
Climb the obvious flake and wall to the left to reach a thread
runner underneath the roof. The roof leans menacingly
above but a flake carries the climber quickly to the lip. Pull
blindly round this on unlikely flat holds with a feeling of
isolation, then continue easily up the slabs above. A runner
placed on an adjacent tree is sometimes used to help reduce
some of the penalties of a fall. (1960)

91 Wrong Way Round 20m E2 5b
A very mediocre climb going round the left-hand side of
the roof. Climb up to follow dirty flakes into a hanging
groove. Step left past the protruding nose on large flakes
before wandering up the arête above. (1980)

92 Capitol Climb 20m HS 4a
Climb the short corner near the left-hand side of the
buttress. Step right between the roofs to gain the protruding
nose, crux. Move round this to follow the crack on its right
then the slab above. (1954)

93 Heather Slab 14m HVD
The centre of the vegetated slab forming the back wall of
the large recess is climbed directly up its centre. Finish just
left of a short wide crack. (1949-1951)

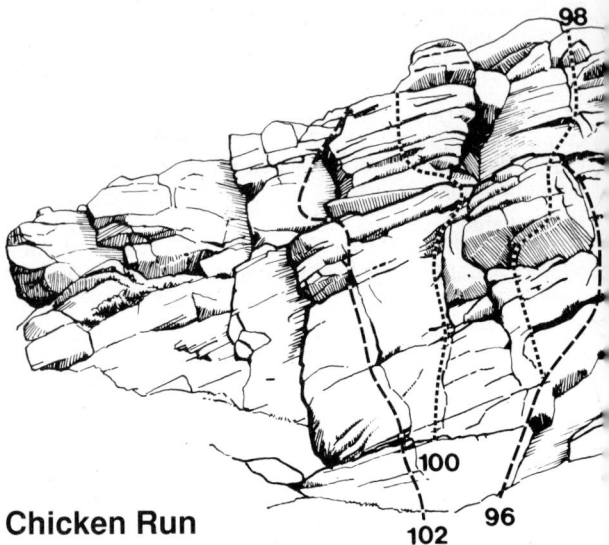

Chicken Run

To the left is a large roof and higher up to the right of this is a triangular wall containing two routes:

94 Crenation 17m E1 5a   *
Climb the rounded arête below the triangular wall to reach a
bulge. Step right round the corner and climb the wall on
hidden holds.   (1978)

95 The Sublime 16m E2 5b   *
As for Crenation to the bulge. Burst over this, then power up
the hanging arête.   (1979)

96 Inverted Staircase 21m D   *
1. 15m. Start below the large roof at the lowest point of the
buttress. Climb rightwards into the groove on the
right-hand side of the overhang. Follow this to the large
ledge on the left or, alternatively, move left onto the arête

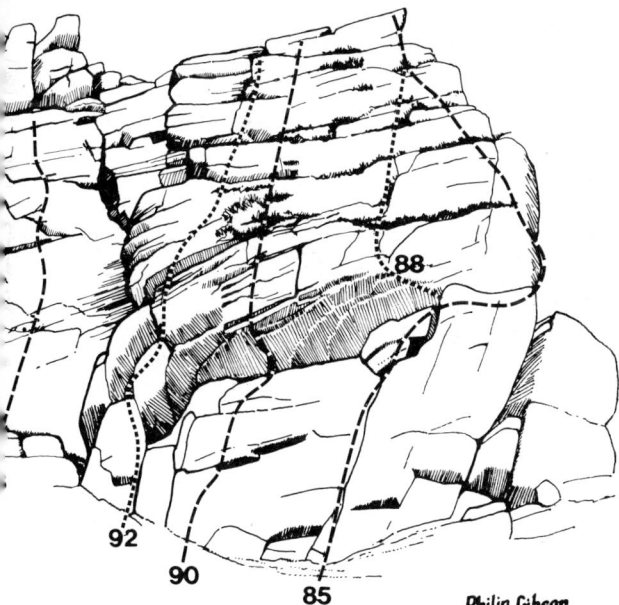

Philip Gibson.

below the ledge.
2. 6m. From the left-hand side of the ledge, wriggle up
through the boulders covering the obvious chimney.   (1931)

97 The Tower of Bizarre Delights 16m E3 5c   *
This route follows the overhanging grooved tower and short
crack above the groove of Inverted Staircase by an intense
and exciting series of moves. Excellent value but with poor
protection until the short crack is reached.   (1978)

98 Simpkin's Overhang 14m E4 5c   **
Originally a top-rope problem; now a route to tire the mind
and body with alarming speed. Climb directly to the flake in
the roof, then reach out along this before cutting loose to
make an impressive hand-traverse right to the end of the
flake. Pull over here and relax! From the back of the sandy
ledge a thin runnel can be climbed; **The Fantasy Finish**, 5b.
                                                      (1979)

99 Perverted Staircase 12m VS 5a
Obscene climbing through the crack splitting the left-hand side of the overhang. Normally the cause for heavy breathing. (1958)

Three metres to the left is a sandy terrace. This is the start for the next three routes:

100 Demon Wall 15m HS 4a,4b
1. 10m. To the left of Perverted Staircase is an undercut sandy corner. Pull over the roof into this before continuing up rightwards to reach a large ledge.
2. 5m. Follow polished holds up the wall left of the chimney with difficulty. (1945)

101 Heartbleed 18m HVS 5b
Climb over the dirty bulge just left of Demon Wall to stand in some sandy pockets. Continue direct up the centre of the face above over a bulge to a shelf. Finish direct. (1978)

102 Fern Crack 18m VD *
1. 12m. Strenuously follow a line of undercut pockets below a crackline until a long flake on the left can be grasped. Continue past a thread and move left onto a ledge. Mantelshelf onto the next sloping ledge; belay. It is also possible to move right to a small notch to finish this pitch.
2. 6m. Walk leftwards round the corner to climb the right wall of the recess on sloping holds. (1931)

103 Freak Out 15m E1 5b
From below the left arête, use pockets to reach a break. Continue around the bulge and climb up to gain the sloping ledge. Finish up the rounded arête above. (1971)

104 Chicken Run 12m VD
Up to the left is a slab with two blocks lying against it. Step up right to a long pocket, then ascend direct following obvious footholds to reach a ledge. From the right side of this, step left and move up precariously to good holds and then the top. (1949-1951)

105 Rooster 12m D
Climb directly up above the blocks to a ledge. Go up again to a jamming crack and so gain the top. (1957-1968)

The final routes on The Upper Tier are the obligatory girdle traverses, three, no less. Being situated on The Great Slab Area, each traverse is rarely climbed as this would normally cause inconvenience to other climbers.

106 The Girdle Traverse 75m S
From Rotunda Gully, traverse right into Hollybush Crack.
Painfully cross the gap past the holly and continue until left
of the ramp on Kelly's Shelf. (Up to this point it is usually
soloed due to its not being more than 5m off the ground!).
Follow Kelly's Shelf to its top, then shuffle down right to join
and finish as for Crack and Corner. (pre-1924)

107 The High Crossing 72m VS 4b   *
Start from Easy Gully and hand-traverse left beneath the
roof to climb Kelly's Shelf with the Buttress Finish. Traverse
left across The Pedestal and so to Hollybush Crack. Swing
around left to join Black and Tans at its stance. Go up, then
move left to Jeffcoat's Buttress below the twin cracks and
descend leftwards into the chimney. Move out left to the top
of Saul's Crack before descending diagonally leftwards to a
ledge on Bachelor's Buttress. Hand-traverse left into the
gully to finish. (1949-1951)

108 The Waistline 60m E1 5b   *
From Rotunda Gully, traverse right beneath Gypfast to Saul's
Crack. Continue right into Jeffcoat's Chimney and cross
rightwards beneath the roof on Hanging Around to swing
into Black and Tans Climb at the stance. Move down into
Hollybush Crack and cross The Great Slab at half-height,
finishing via Kelly's Connection. (1968-1973)

THE SKYLINE AREA

by Andy Popp

> *'Many of these climbs may have been done
> before and left unreported, but of the few that
> we have repeated, some are gritstone classics
> and the contribution of these young lads to the
> area's climbing may well be significant.'*

Crags 8,
on the subject of Jonny and Andrew Woodward, 1978.

THE CLIMBS are described from RIGHT to LEFT starting with
the first buttress which is small and prominently overlapped
and is to be found immediately to the left of the path
bounding the left-hand end of The Upper Tier. It yields
three routes:

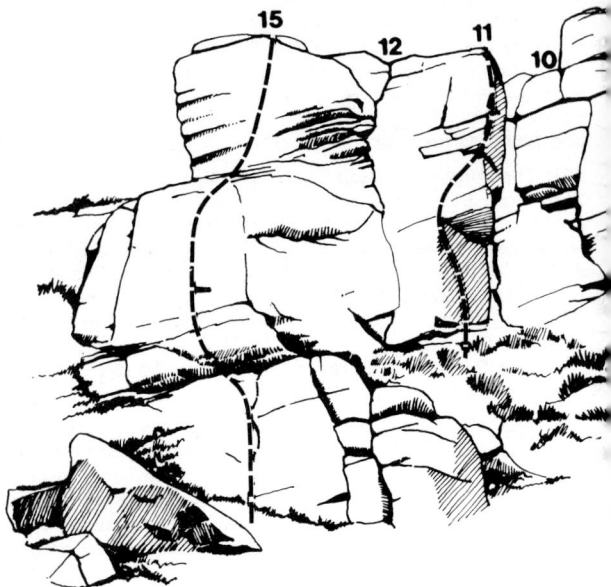

1 The Pugilist 7m HVS 5b *

The crack and groove at the right-hand end of the buttress.
The grade is inherited from sterner times.   (1957-1968)

2 In Passing 8m E1 5c

This takes a crack just left to a step left so that a difficult
pull onto the top slab may be made. Small, difficult and
rather ungainly when actually climbed. A direct start is a
'rollover' at 5c.   (1976)

3 Southpaw 7m S

The next crackline to the left.   (1957-1968)

Left again is a miniscule Very Difficult.

One hundred metres left again is **CONDOR BUTTRESS**, *The
Skyline's first substantial piece of rock. Its many routes,
mostly in the lower grades, are all pleasant and worthwhile.
Begin at its right-hand end for:*

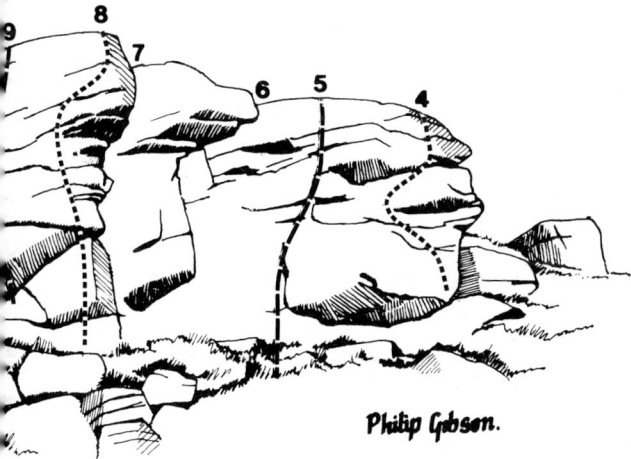

Philip Gibson.

Condor Buttress

4 Lung Cancer 7m S
Start just right of a block to weave through some small
overlaps.   (1977)

5 Chicane 7m VD
An arête, commencing from the block.   (1978)

6 Navy Cut 7m D
A niche to the left. Both entry and exit from this may be
varied according to one's inclinations.   (1957-1968)

7 Bruno Flake 7m S
This corner and flake-crack in a roof to the left afford an
awkward passage.   (1957-1968)

8 Wheeze 8m VS 4c   *
Delicate and airy climbing based on the left arête.   (1976)

9 Tobacco Road 8m VS 4c   *
A direct line, but less finely-positioned than the previous
route, up the wall to its left.   (1957-1968)

10 Time to be Had 8m VD
A cracked wall just out from the next easy corner. (1978)

11 Nosepicker 8m HVS 5b
The left arête of the easy corner with an overhang that must
be by-passed to the left. Do not be deterred by the
unfortunate name. (1976)

12 Condor Chimney 8m VD
A pleasant excursion up the wide chimney to the left.
(1957-1968)

13 Cracked Arête 8m HVD *
Commence a little lower and climb a polished arête to reach
the base of Condor Chimney. Finish up the slab and crack
just to the left. (1951-1957)

14 A.M. Anaesthetic 8m VS 4c
Insecure climbing up a blunt arête to the left. A more
up-to-date counterpart to the following route. (1978)

15 Condor Slab 12m VS 4b **
The classic of the buttress and a bold lead, the impact of
which has been little-softened by modern technology. Start
beneath the centre of the large slab and connect a faint
groove, ledge and hole until one can move right to finish,
alone, up the centre of the buttress. (1957-1968)

16 Chicane Destination 40m VS 4c
A traverse right from the hole of Condor Slab to the finish of
Chicane. Quite an expedition on a crag of The Skyline's
magnitude. (1978)

*Next, after 35m, one encounters a cluster of three
buttresses, known collectively as **THE TRIO**. They yield
several routes of both reasonable size and considerable
quality:*

17 Ralph's Mantelshelves 8m VD
A series of ledges leads left from the right-hand side of the
first buttress. (1951-1957)

18 Lighthouse 10m D *
Ascend directly from the toe of the buttress. (1951-1957)

19 Substance 8m VS 4c
An arête to the left on its steeper left-hand side.
Over-zealously named, perhaps. (1978)

*Next is a dark recess which contains three undistinguished
routes:*

20 Trio Chimney 7m VD
The right-hand corner. (1951-1957)

21 Square Chimney 8m D
The left-hand corner. (1951-1957)

22 Left Twin Crack 10m HS
A groove and then a crack springing from Square Chimney.
(1951-1957)

23 Shortcomings 10m E1 5c *
The buttress to the left contains a fine flake on its right flank
which is gained directly and with some difficulty. People of a
reasonable stature should be able to runner the flake before
the hard move. Those too short will have to go without and
have an extra 'E' point or two. (1978)

24 Safety Net 10m E1 5b ***
To the left is a prominent blunt rib, undercut at its base and
capped by a crack-split overlap. Their combination provides
an excellent means of ascent that is both direct and varied.
(1975)

25 Pebbles on a Wessex Beach 10m E3 6a
To the left of Safety Net is another roof crack which is far
wider and more flared. This crack is gained from (and with a
runner in Safety Net after climbing the short wall below.
(1982)

26 Hank's Horror 8m E1 5b
Around the corner is an exposed sentry-box. From its top,
hard moves lead out right to a wide crack in an airy
position. Seldom climbed. (1963)

It is possible to traverse this small buttress via a half-height
break from either direction; **Central Traverse**, Severe.

A small wall above the previous four routes provides a 5c
problem finish.

27 Letter-box Gully 10m M
Slabs lead to a slot beneath the huge jammed block. Go
through this. (1951-1957)

28 Letter-box Cracks 7m VS 4c
The block above the gully has cracks on either side. They
may be climbed separately or as a pair. (1957-1968)

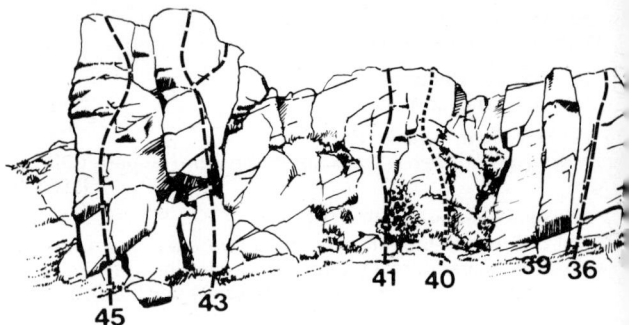

41 40 39 36

45 43

Tower Buttress and The Trio

29 Topaz 10m E2 5b *
To the left, an easy rib leads to a roof from where a crack
and ramp provide difficulties which, though short-lived, are
'involving' whilst they last. (1979)

30 Strain Station 12m E4 5c *
The roof left of Topaz is climbed, either direct or from the
right, to gain a blunt precarious arête. A rest in the cave
above seems most tempting. (1981)

31 Rowan Tree Traverse 15m VD
From 5m up Topaz, ascend leftwards to gain a bilberry
covered ledge and final layback crack. (1951-1957)

32 Middleton's Motion 10m VS 4b
A straighter line. Bisect Rowan Tree Traverse at a small cave
to finish via an obstinate crack. (1957-1968)

33 Spectrum 8m VS 4c *
A pleasant route if only because it is actually better than it
might, at first, appear to be. It takes a faint groove and slab
to gain the final crack of Rowan Tree Traverse. (1977)

34 Bad Sneakers 8m E2 5c
A difficult piece of slab climbing just to the left which
constantly strains to avoid the gully farther left. (1977)

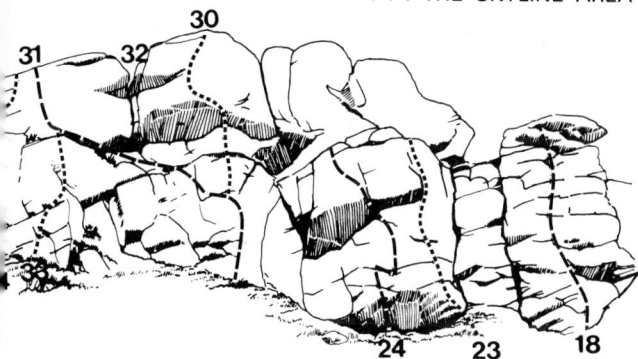

Philip Gibson.

35 Spare Rib 8m S 4a   *
The next rib. Interesting and worthy of attention despite its
enclosed position.   (1977)

36 The Black Pig 8m VS 4c   *
To the left is a chimney, with a thin slanting seam in its right
wall which gives the line. The difficulties increase the earlier
one forsakes the assistance of the chimney.

(1957-1968)

37 Ogden Recess 8m VD
The chimney. Its bowels may be a little loose.   (1957-1968)

38 Ogden Arête 8m S   *
The chimney's left-hand arête is a smart piece of work with
a stern start.   (1957-1968)

39 Ogden 10m D
A crack. Climb it.   (1951-1957)

40 Oversight 10m VD
To the left is a stony gully. Its left arête gives the route.
(1968-1973)

41 Bad Poynt 7m D
Start 3m to the left at a perched block and climb up it to a
slab and crack.   (1978)

A further 10m left is **TOWER BUTTRESS**, *one of The Skyline's steeper bastions.*

42 Thrug 8m VS 4c ✱✱
The right wall of the buttress is split by a steep and blatant crack. Satisfying in a simple muscular manner.   (1957-1968)

43 Perched Block Arête 20m VD ✱
The arête, climbed largely on its right, is followed from its lowest point to the top block from where it becomes necessary to either gain a final chimney on the left or press straight on (VS 4b). Another alternative is to move right in search of a fine layback flake (a finish that holds both unexpected surprises and exposure, HVS 4c).   (1951-1957)

44 Tower Chimney 18m D
The frontal chimney. It is possible to start in another groove, just to the left, which is a little harder.   (1951-1957)

45 Tower Face 15m E1 5b ✱
Start as for the alternative start to Tower Chimney but continue straight up some poor cracks which become increasingly hard to handle. Eventually, moves right lead to a direct finish. Not, by any means, an easy climb.   (1977)

46 Tower Eliminate 15m HVS 5b ✱
Left, around an arête, is a steep disjointed crackline leading to a niche. From the niche, finish either up another crack or, better, out right onto the arête. Strangely gratifying.   (1963)

47 Sorcerer's Apprentice 10m VS 4c
The wall on the left leads to sloping ledges and a crack.
(1978)

Forty-five metres to the left is **CAVE BUTTRESS**. *Its first route is to be found 18m right of the obvious central feature of the cave.*

48 Joiner 9m VD
A fine arête.   (1951-1957)

49 Connector 9m VS 4b
The wall to the left, beginning at a flake. The upper half is disappointing.   (1978)

50 King Swing 7m VS 5a
Begin inside the mouth of the cave and swing out around the jaunty right arête to climb it and slabs to the top.   (1978)

51 Cave Crack 6m HVS 5a   *
The obvious central roof-crack provides marvellous fun and
is a less intimidating introduction to the style of climbing
encountered on climbs such as The Sloth. There are two
alternative starts; the left arête of the initial groove (5b) or a
traverse in below the roof from the left, **The Mousetrap
Start**, 5a.   (1957-1968)

52 Automatix 7m E2 5b   †
From near the start of Stephen, follow roof flakes rightwards
to the finish of Cave Crack. Strenuous and, at the time of
writing, very dirty.   (1981)

53 Stephen 7m VS 5a   *
The crack and tight chimney springing from the left edge of
the cave. Brutal but rewarding.   (1957-1968)

54 Cave Arête 14m S   *
Starting from the lowest point of the buttress, follow the
arête to a ledge. Take to the slab on the left for a while
before finishing back, in a good position, on the arête itself.
A direct finish is possible at 4a.   (1951-1957)

55 Cave Buttress 12m D
Gain the ledge of Cave Arête from a short corner. Go left to
finish up a crack. Poor.   (1951-1957)

Move 65m left for:

56 Capstan's Corner 8m D
The pleasant right edge of the buttress.   (1951-1957)

57 Mistaken Identity 10m VD
To the left is a greasy groove bounded on its left by a slab.
Climb the slab to a roof which can be tackled on both the
right and the left.   (1951-1957)

58 Sally James 10m VS 4c
The left arête of the buttress, a further 10m on. The name
may provoke a few fond memories in those old enough to
remember.   (1979)

Forty-five metres left is **SKYLINE BUTTRESS**, *the edge's
largest face.*

The crack in the side-wall of the buttress gives an
unsatisfactory climb at HVS 5b.

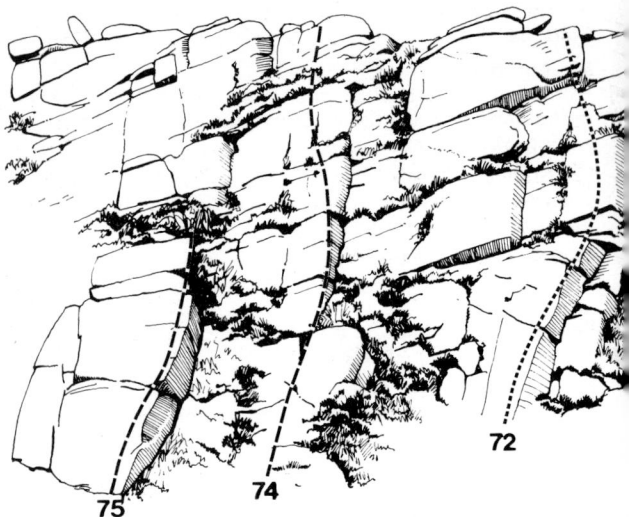

59 Slips 8m E3 6a   *

Starting beneath the right arête of the frontal slab, move up
a delicate little slab to gain a short crack out on the arête. A
difficult move should then land one on easy ground.   (1982)

60 Skytrain 10m E2 5b

A poor route lacking any real definition beyond its initial
crack and that, if obvious, is also painful. A leftward-leaning
crack springs from a slab set in beneath the right arête of
the buttress. Climb this crack to the traverse of Slab and
Arête. Continue as direct as possible somewhere up the slab
above.   (1977)

61 Slab and Arête 18m S   ***

A fine excursion but popular and thus beginning to show its
age. It used to start about 3m left of Skytrain at a polished
and pocketed slab (which is much harder than Severe) but it
may now be necessary to use a corner on the left if the

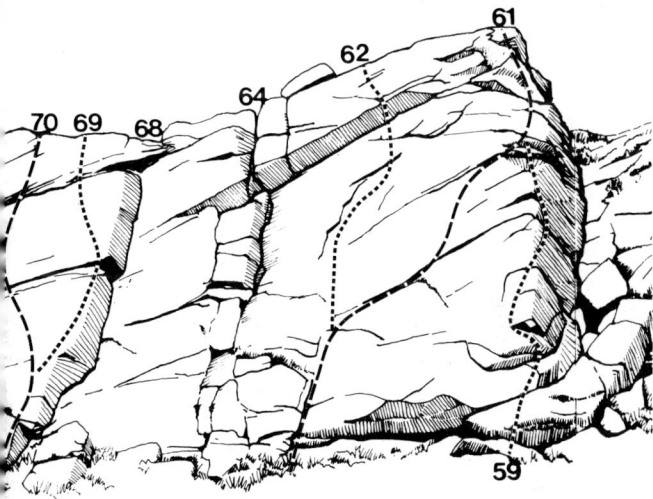

Philip Gibson.

Skyline Buttress

standard is to be maintained. Either start gives access, at
half-height, to a long traverse out right to the finishing
arête.   (1947)

62 Acid Drop 15m E4 5c   ***
Above the traverse of Slab and Arête is a thin arching
overlap. Climb through this to reach a long capping roof
which is surmounted to a wide final crack. The difficulties on
the slab are dependent almost entirely upon reach but the
most improbable roof above can hardly fail to please
anyone.   (1979)

63 Drop Acid 15m E4 6a   *†
Follow a series of thin flakes up the slab just left of the
arching overlap of Acid Drop to reach the roof. Pull over and
finish direct. A side-runner in Abstract protects.   (1987)

64 Karabiner Cracks 12m M
Cracks and a chimney to the left.   (1947)

65 Abstract 12m HVS 5a
Little more than an alternative finish to Karabiner Cracks up
the roof and crack just right of the final chimney.
(1957-1968)

66 Poodle Vindaloo 9m E2 5c
Continues the traverse of Abstract all the way under the roof
to the finish of Slab and Arête. A runner above the lip of the
roof on Abstract is advisable but even with this the route is
difficult to enjoy. (1982)

67 Karabiner Slab 12m VS 4c
A central line on the slab left of the crack. (1957-1968)

68 Karabiner Chimney 12m VD   *
The chimney on the left. Pleasant right to the end. (1947)

69 Enigma Variation 10m E2 5b   **
A lovely route. Start up Mantelshelf Slab but quit it as soon
as possible for the right arête. This too is quitted near the
top for a finish on the slab to the left. Bold but
well-behaved, it plays no dirty tricks. (1977)

70 Mantelshelf Slab 10m HS 4a   *
From the foot of the slab left of the chimney, climb past a
mantelshelf move to a flake and thence to the top. Dainty
and well-scraped. (1947)

71 Bilberry Traverse 35m HS
A mid-height traverse, from the gully bounding the buttress
on the right to Mantelshelf Slab. (1947)

72 Come Girl 13m HS
A series of ribs, 5m left of Mantelshelf Slab, finishing at a
crack. (1968-1973)

73 Go Girl 13m HVD
Vegetated cracks 2m left lead to the finish of Come Girl.
(1968-1973)

*To the left and set at a lower level is the compact square
block of* **THE PINNACLE**.

74 Pinnacle Slab 15m HD
Undistinguished slabs to the right of The Pinnacle itself.
(1951-1957)

75 Pinnacle Arête 6m VS 4b   *
The right arête of The Pinnacle. Utterly sweet. (1947)

76 Split Personality 8m E1 5b
There is some trivial fun to be had on the slab and thin
crack just to the left. (1979)

77 Pinnacle Crack 7m D
The wide crack bounding the left side of The Pinnacle's front
face. (1949-1951)

Thirty metres left is **ALPHA BUTTRESS**. *Near its right-hand
end is a prominent crack and chimney, the start of
Right-hand Route. The first route begins 3m right of this
crack.*

78 Looking for Today 7m HVS 5b
An unhelpful crack leads to a bulge where some effort is
needed to gain a thin but precious flake. Easy ground is now
close at hand. (1976)

79 Right-hand Route 12m S *
Climb the crack then the chimney for a while until a traverse
left leads to the right-most of two flakes in the upper wall.
Continuously interesting. (1951-1957)

80 Definitive Gaze 10m E1 5c
Starting immediately left, move up into a scoop and exit
with difficulty on the left. Carry on, ignoring Wallaby Wall to
the left, to finish left of the flake of Right-hand Route.
(1979)

81 Wallaby Wall 10m S
The next cracks lead to a ledge and then the left-hand of
the two upper flakes. (1951-1957)

82 39th Step 8m E2 6a
The shallow groove and slab 3m to the left, trending slightly
rightwards. A runner in the crack on the left is sensible,
obvious and normal. (1979)

83 Sennapod 7m D
The corner on the left. (1978)

*To the left is a fairly small but commanding slab, bounded
on the right by a prominent arête and divided by a useful
half-height break.*

84 Mantis 8m HVS 5b **
The arête is begun on the right and finished on the left. Very
enjoyable. It can also be started on its left-hand side;
harder. (1977)

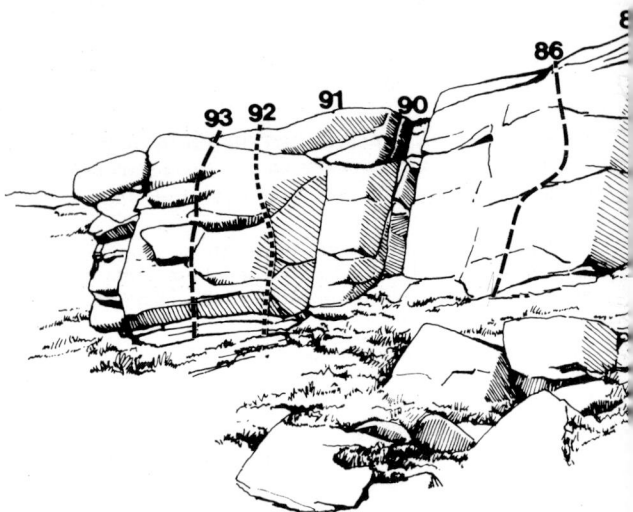

85 Hallow to our Men 8m E4 6b   *
Between Mantis and San Melas, the slab is indented at its
base by a shallow scoop. Difficult climbing on small edges
leads from this to the break, where direction and space is
lost. Finish as you wish.   (1981)

86 San Melas 8m E3 5c   **
The slab, taken centrally after a start slightly to the left.
Whilst never very difficult, the route offers no really positive
straws for which the floundering may grasp.   (1977)

87 Days Gone By 7m S
The right-hand of three close parallel cracks.   (1978)

88 Breakfast Problem 7m VD
The merging left-hand cracks.   (1951-1957)

89 Formative Years 7m E3 6a
The tiny slab set to the left of Breakfast Problem is not for
those who rush to their conclusion.   (1982)

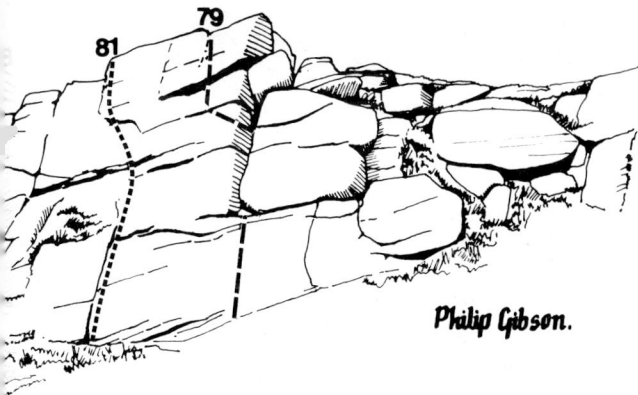

Philip Gibson.

Alpha Buttress

90 Alpha Arête 7m D
To the left is a green corner. This route takes its blocky left
arête.   (1957-1968)

91 Alpha 7m D
The small groove on the left.   (1951-1957)

92 Devotoed 7m VS 5a   *
A 'punchy' crack and sloping finish on the left wall of Alpha.
                                                            (1979)

93 Melaleucion 7m VS 4c   *
Ascend direct through the steep front face.   (1976)

94 Omega 7m VD
Start just left and pull over a bulge for an awkward
mantelshelf on the right.   (1957-1968)

95 Bone Idol 33m VS 4c
A mid-height girdle from Omega to Right-hand Route.
                                                            (1977)

*After Alpha Buttress the edge becomes intermittent and
insignificant until after some 350m the castellated top of the
slabby* **FAR SKYLINE BUTTRESS** *emerges. This buttress has
in its centre a prominent roof about 2m above the ground
and, 9m right of this roof, a short chimney that leans
leftwards.*

96 The Black Ram 11m VD
Starting 4m left of the chimney, climb a thin crack and
square-cut groove to finish up some steep cracks. (1970)

97 Black Ram Arête 11m VS 4c
Start by gaining a small ledge 3m left and 1m up, then go
up and right to a faint crack. Climb this to finish up the left
side of the arête above. (1970)

98 Dangler 11m VS 4b *
From the initial ledge of the previous route, climb up a thin
crack to a bulge. This is surmounted rightwards to a hairline
crack and a slab. (1970)

99 The Chimney 11m S
The blocky chimney just right of the roof is difficult to start.
(1968)

100 Entente Cordiale 12m E3 5c *
Pull direct over the centre of the roof, then step left to climb
a slabby arête to a good ledge. Climb up the centre of the
short, but nonetheless intimidating, slab above. Pleasant
climbing marred by a disjointed line. (1981)

101 Honky Tonk 12m S **
Start in an awkward V-shaped groove just left of the roof.
Stride magnificently rightwards onto the very lip of the roof
and
saunter up the right arête of the slab above. It is possible to
pull over the initial roof at its right arête at 5a but this is out
of keeping with the rest of the route. (1968)

102 Steeplechase Crack 10m VD
A crackline cutting through a square-cut niche. (1970)

103 Dazzler 8m S
A shallow groove with understated twin cracks leads to a
ledge at 9m. A trying move brings easy ground to hand.
(1970)

104 Mudhopper 7m VD
The grassy leftward-slanting groove on the left. (1970)

105 Slither 8m S
Climb the slab and hanging groove 3m left. (1970)

106 Steeplechaser 8m HD
Climb an open corner to an overhang. An excursion out left and then back right sees one safely round this hurdle. (1970)

107 Tree Grooves 7m D
Round the corner and some 2m right of a dead tree is a groove (or climb the slab to its left) leading to another, easier groove. (1970)

108 Tree Corner 7m D
The corner and overhang behind the dead tree. (1970)

109 Chronicle 7m VS 5b
The overlap and slab just right of Flutterbye Grooves. (1979)

110 Flutterbye Grooves 7m S
From the left-hand end of the crag gain 'whispy' cracks from the left or, better and harder, direct. Follow the cracks.
(1968)

111 Microcosm 7m D
A groove on the left moving right onto the front of the buttress at the top. (1979)

112 The Girdle Traverse 30m S
A traverse of variable line that rarely exceeds more than 4m above the ground. (1968-1973)

After perhaps some 100m there are three large boulders on the top of the edge. Here, hidden just beneath the path, is a small but compact square face, easily recognised because of the prominent slanting overlap that runs from bottom right to top left. This gives the line of:

113 Art Nouveau 7m E6 6c ***
The overlap is powerful and complex and can be safeguarded only by pre-placed micro protection or, as per the first ascent, not at all. Superb. (1985)

*Some 100m farther on is the penultimate buttress, the **VERY FAR SKYLINE BUTTRESS**, a small but very compact and deeply undercut block. Few should be able to ignore its magnetic charms.*

114 Mild Thing 7m D   *
Propped up against the right-hand side of the buttress is a
flake. Climb this until it is possible to transfer into cracks on
the slab above. Deserving of attention if only for the name.
(1977)

115 Script for a Tear 7m E6 6c
From the flake of the previous route, step left onto the very
lip of the undercut and ascend direct. Very modern.   (1985)

116 Wild Thing 7m E1 5c   **
The central line of the buttress. A bitter/sweet alliance of a
strenuous roof and a delicate groove... and a little gem at
that!   (1977)

117 Entropy's Jaw 7m E5 6b   ***
Once established over the lip of Wild Thing (crux) a sinuous
seam runs rightwards up the faintest of ribs. This is the line.
The movement required is as beautiful as it is committing.
(1982)

118 Triple Point 7m E1 5c
Once again, pull over the roof of Wild Thing, this time
though to climb the left arête on its right-hand side. A
hideous direct start is possible at 6b.   (1982)

Thirty metres farther left is an arête on a large boulder:

119 Curvature 6m VS 4b
The arête begun on its left. Reclusive.   (1979)

120 Very Connoisseurish 6m E2 6a
Another arête on yet another boulder. Even shyer!   (1970s)

*Fittingly The Skyline reserves its best for last. Walk another
40m and one finds the* **HARD VERY FAR SKYLINE BUTTRESS**
*a fitting conclusion to any cliff. Its boldly sculptured form
and beautifully detailed surface ensure that its original
routes, at least, leave little to be desired.*

121 Prelude to Space 10m HVS 4c   **
The faintly-ledged right arête of the buttress is far from
easy and provides an exciting challenge at the grade. As of
old, the leader simply must not fall.   (1977)

122 Wings of Unreason 11m E4 6b **

Central and direct. A natural line only by virtue of two lonely pockets in an otherwise blank slab. These though are the making of an entire route. Gaining them via an undercut start may be difficult but to leave them requires faith as much as skill.

(1977)

There have recently appeared routes to both the right and left of the previous route. In comparison it is clear that they fall short of the status of line and may, at most, be categorised as gap-fillers. No matter what the quality of the climbing one can only hope that their existence does not blur or spoil the original routes of the slab. Both seek protection in the pockets of the previous route.

123 Counterstroke of Equity 11m E5 6c *

To the right. The harder and better of the pair. (1985)

124 Nature Trail 11m E5 6b

To the left and started direct via an undercut in the roof.

(1985)

125 Track of the Cat 12m E5 6a ***

Based on the left arête of the crag this route's balance of climbing styles makes it perhaps the buttress's best. Begin steeply in an undercut flaky groove to swing right onto the front face beneath the climb's main challenge; a short but perfect 'flyaway' arête. The upper arête can also be climbed on its left-hand side.

(1977)

126 Willow Farm 10m E4 6a **

To the left again the buttress is terminated by a neat little slab capped by a sloping gangway. The right edge of this slab is gained direct and provides the route which is engaging and eccentric in its solution.

(1977)

A girdle, **Inspiration Point**, HVS 5b, from Track of the Cat to Prelude to Space is possible at a little under half-height. *The edge now continues but offers little in the way of routes. However for the boulderer this area is a delight, abounding in numerous uncharted problems of varying grades in a quiet environment.*

THE CUBE   O.S. ref. SK 015629

This small, out of the way, crag lies some 250m immediately behind the buttress containing The Pugilist at the start of The Skyline Area. Whilst having no real home, it just about falls into the category of Skyline crags. It has also been known as Window Buttress and Back End Boulders.

127 The Cube 6m E3 6a   *
The obvious wall on the square, left-hand buttress.   (1986)

128 Jump 6m HVS 6b
The left arête of The Cube.   (1986)

Some fine bouldering also exists on the triangular right-hand buttress. A central line is 5a whilst a left-to-right traverse is 5b.

THE ROACHES AND SKYLINE LIST OF FIRST ASCENTS

by Gary Gibson

1901	**Raven Rock Gully** members of the Kyndwyr Club
1901-1913	**Cannonball Crack**
1913	**Jeffcoat's Chimney, Jeffcoat's Buttress** Stanley Jeffcoat
1922	**Bachelor's Buttress, Black and Tans** A S 'Fred' Pigott
1922	**Pedestal Route Left-hand, Pedestal Route Right-hand, Right Route, Crack and Corner** Morley Wood *'On Crack and Corner the leader took a shoulder from his second who was securely tied on to the block and it looked impossible without this' – Rucksack Club Journal.*
1913-1924	**Via Dolorosa, Kestrel Crack, Upper Tier Girdle**
1924	**Left-hand Route, Right-hand Route** Lindlay Henshaw
1927	**Guano Gully** *Originally named as Dodo's Dilemma but misplaced in the 1957 guidebook, this route has kept the former name.*
1927	**Fledgeling's Climb**
1927	**Lucas Chimney** *'The exit above is painfully tight and the climb cannot be recommended as the pleasantest means of ascent' – Rucksack Club Journal.*

1930	**Bengal Buttress** Ivan Waller

'Some characteristic holes near the left-hand corner mark the start and are followed to a small but good ledge. This is passed in favour of a higher ledge which is followed to the right with increasing respect. The improving angle above deludes one into anticipating some relief, but in actual fact the sharp corner above provides an awkward and exposed finish' – 1951 guidebook.

1931   **Inverted Staircase, Fern Crack** 'Fred' Pigott

1939   **Calcutta Crack** 'Fred' Pigott

1945 May 6   **Karabiner Chimney, Pinnacle Arête** R Desmond-Stevens

1945 May 6   **Karabiner Crack** A Simpson, R Desmond-Stevens

1945 May 6   **Slab and Arête** G Stoneley, R Desmond-Stevens

1945 May 6   **Tower Chimney** A Simpson, R Desmond-Stevens
Originally called Chimney Direct.

1945 May 12   **Bilberry Traverse** R Desmond-Stevens, G Stoneley

1945 June 7   **Central Massive** G Stoneley, R Desmond-Stevens
Originally called Slab Route.

1945   **Demon Wall, Beckermet Slab, Maud's Garden, Broken Slab, Rotunda Buttress, Technical Slab** A Bowden Black

1946 Oct. 6   **Valkyrie** Peter Harding, A Bowden Black

1947   **Mantelshelf Slab** Karabiner Club members

1947   **Saul's Crack** Joe Brown
'The buttress to the right of Bachelor's is split by a fierce-looking crack that was justifiably famous long before its first ascent' – 1951 guidebook.

1949 April 28   **Hangman's Crack** G W S Pigott, C Topping

1949 April 28   **Scarlett Wall, Calcutta Crack** G W S Pigott (solo)

1924-1949   **Kelly's Shelf** Harry Kelly

1924-1949   **Flake Chimney**

1951   **Valkyrie Direct** Joe Brown, Don Whillans

1951   **Dorothy's Dilemma** Joe Brown, Merrick 'Slim' Sorrell, Dorothy Sorrell

1951   **Matinee** Joe Brown, Don Whillans (AL)
'So called from the audience who sat on the boulders and watched the pioneering of Brown and Whillans on their through leads' – 1957 guidebook.

1951	**The Mincer, The Bulger** Joe Brown, Don Whillans *'The Mincer derives its name from the condition of the leader's hands after completing the ascent'* — *1957 guidebook.*
1949-1951	**Little Chimney, Lucas Chimney, Flake Chimney, Calcutta Crack, Central Route, Heather Slab, Chicken Run, High Crossing, Pinnacle Crack**
1951	*Climbs on Gritstone, Volume 3, published.*
1954 Jan.	**The Sloth** Don Whillans, Joe Brown
1954	**Aqua** Joe Brown, Don Whillans
1954	**Capitol Climb** R Handley, Nat Allen
1955 May 25	**Damascus Crack** G W S Pigott, W H Craster
1955	**Roscoe's Wall** Don Roscoe
1955	**Runner Route,** Nat Allen, D Campbell
1951-1957	**Wallaby Wall, Alpha, Breakfast Problem, Mistaken Identity, Cave Arête, Joiner, Ogden, Ralph's Mantelshelves, Cracked Arête, Right-hand Crack, Pinnacle Slab, Capstan's Corner, Rowan Tree Traverse, Square Chimney, Late Night Final, Central Traverse, Lighthouse, Trio Chimney, Left Twin Crack, Letter-box Gully, Perched Block Arête, Cave Buttress, Pinnacle Slab** John and Tony Vereker, Graham Martin and some members from Stafford Mountaineering Club.
1951-1957	**Central Massive, Lone Ascent, Contrary Mary**
1957	*Climbs on Gritstone, Volume 4, Further Developments in the Peak District, published.*
1958	**Crack of Gloom** Joe Brown, Don Whillans
1958	**Teck Crack, Choka** (1 pt.), **Rhodren** Joe Brown *Rhodren was later attributed a point of aid which was certainly not in evidence in earlier descriptions. The first free ascent of Choka is unknown but was certainly achieved soon after the 1973 guidebook.*
1958	**Ackit** Don Whillans *With the right-hand finish.*
1958	**Reset Portion of Galley 37, Perverted Staircase** Geoff Sutton *The former route was named after a printer's error that appeared in the 1957 guidebook.*
1958	**Lightning Crack** Don Whillans, Joe Brown *Incorrectly attributed to Mike Simpkins in 1960.*
1960	**Lower Tier Girdle** Alan Parker, Paul Nunn, Bob Brayshaw

1960	**West's Wallaby** Graham West *Originally named Wallaby.*
1960	**Walleroo** Mike Simpkins
1960	**Wombat** Mike Simpkins *A runner was used in a nearby tree. This is rarely required nowadays.*
1960	**Wallaby Direct** Mike Simpkins *A pre-placed runner was used for protection.*
1960	**Elegy** (1 pt.) Mike Simpkins *Tension was used from a nut in The Bulger to gain the main flake on the slab. Climbed free by John Yates in 1969.*
1963 Sept.	**The Underpass, Hank's Horror** Dave Salt, Colin Foord
1963 Sept.	**Hypothesis, Tower Eliminate** Colin Foord, Dave Salt *Whilst attempting to top-rope Hypothesis Foord slipped but decided to lead the route anyway.*
1967	**Ackit Direct** Tony Barley, Robin Barley
1968	**Sifta's Quid** John Amies *The result of a bet by Dave Salt who claimed that everything that could be done, had been done. Amies never received the pound.*
1957-1968	**Yong Arête, Yong, Wisecrack, The Pincer, Flimney, Straight Crack, Punch** (1 pt.)**, Prow Corner, Prow Cracks, Pepper, Calcutta Buttress, Rib Wall, The Rib, Gully Wall, Jelly Roll, Easy Gully Wall, Kelly's Connection, Right Route Right, Hollybush Crack, Black Velvet, Cornflake, Tealeaf Crack, Libra, Rooster, The Pugilist, Southpaw, Navy Cut, Bruno Flake, Tobacco Road, Condor Chimney, Condor Slab, Letter-box Cracks, Middleton's Motion, The Black Pig, Ogden Recess, Ogden Arête, Thrug, Cave Crack, Stephen, Abstract, Karabiner Slab, Alpha Arête, Omega** *The first free ascent of Punch was made in 1978 by Jonny Woodward (solo).*
1968	*Rock Climbs on The Roaches and Hen Cloud published.*
1969 July	**Humdinger** Mick Guilliard
1969 Oct. 12	**The Swan** (1 pt.) John Gosling, Mike Simpkins *The aid was a peg!* *The first free ascent was made by Ron Fawcett and Geoff Birtles in 1977.*
1969	**Raven Rock Gully Left-hand, Pebbledash** Dave Salt *Even Salt proved his own theory wrong.*
1969	**Elegy** John Yates *First free ascent.*

1969	**Kestrel Crack, Left-hand Start** John Yates *This has now been incorporated into Hawkwing.*
1969	**The Chimney, Honky Tonk, Flutterbye Grooves** Colin Foord
1970 April	**The Black Ram, Black Ram Arête, Dangler, Steeplechase Crack, Dazzler, Mudhopper, Slither, Steeplechaser, Tree Grooves, Tree Corner, The Girdle Traverse of Far Skyline Crag** Steve Dale, Brian Dale
1970 Sept.	**The Death Knell** John Yates, Colin Foord *Rumour has it that Yates slipped off the lower arête to land in the rhododendron bushes below. Bravely he picked himself up to finish the route. Originally it finished left to where Amaranth now finishes. The direct finish was added by Jonny and Andrew Woodward in 1977. For a long time led with a side-runner on a block to the left.*
1971 April	**Up the Swanee** John Yates *A brave and considerably underrated affort.*
1971 June 22	**Ruby Tuesday** Mick Guilliard, John Yates *An unlikely find on The Great Slab Area but now a classic.*
1971	**Freak Out** Steve Dale, Brian Dale
1968-1973	**Swinger, Straight Crack, Aperitif, Kelly's Direct, Waistline, Oversight, Go Girl, Come Girl, Battery Crack**
1973	*The Staffordshire Gritstone Area, Rock Climbs in the Peak, Volume 9, published.*
1974 April	**The Ascent of Man** Andrew Woodward, Jonny Woodward *The first true pebble-route brought raised eyebrows from the notable climbers of the day.*
1974 April	**Days of Future Passed** Andrew Woodward, Jonny Woodward *Later claimed as Pebble-puller.*
1974 May	**Mantis** Andrew Woodward, Jonny Woodward (both solo)
1974 Aug. 17	**Round Table** John Allen, Nick Colton, Steve Bancroft *Also (originally) known as Old Nick.*
1975 March 2	**Safety Net** John Allen, Steve Bancroft, Tom Proctor *A very powerful team who rather surprisingly missed other nearby lines, notably Shortcomings.*

| 1975 Aug. | **Nosepicker** Jonny Woodward (solo) |
| | *Jonny refused to claim the direct version saying that it was an inferior variant to the original which passed the overhang to the left.* |

| 1975 | **Commander Energy** John Allen and party |

| 1975 | **Hunky Dory** Gabriel Regan and party |
| | *Several strong teams had previously failed.* |

| 1976 April | **Melaleucion** Steve Dale, Barry Marsden |
| | *Named after the black and white family cat.* |

| 1976 Aug. | **In Passing, Wheeze** Jonny Woodward (solo) |
| | *Both routes appeared in the 1980 guidebook as being attributed to Al Simpson, named Happy Hooker and Fagash Lil respectively but claimed in 1977.* |

| 1976 Aug. | **Looking for Today** Jonny Woodward (solo) |

| 1976 Sept. | **Enigma Variation** Andrew Woodward, Jonny Woodward |
| | *A little classic.* |

| 1977 May | **Mild Thing, Wild Thing, Prelude to Space** Andrew Woodward, Jonny Woodward |
| | *The latter two routes were reputedly climbed in spring 1974 by John Allen and Steve Bancroft.* |

| 1977 May | **Wings of Unreason** Jonny Woodward, Andrew Woodward |
| | *Claimed to be the hardest route in the world (at HXS/E6 6c) due to the extensive amount of top-roping required before the ascent. 'Magnifying glass for aid'.* |

| 1977 Aug. 28 | **San Melas** Andrew Woodward, Jonny Woodward |
| | *Top-roped first.* |

| 1977 Sept. 3 | **Bone Idol** Jonny Woodward, Andrew Woodward (both solo) |

| 1977 Sept. 11 | **Track of the Cat** Jonny Woodward, Andrew Woodward |
| | *'Top-roped all morning first'.* |

| 1977 Sept. 11 | **Chalkstorm** Ian 'Hotshot' Johnson, Dave Jones |
| | *Top-roped first. 'It has to be harder than Death Knell, hasn't it?* |

| 1977 Oct. 15 | **Piece of Mind** Jonny Woodward, Andrew Woodward |
| | *Top-roped first. An incredibly bold piece of mind!* |

| 1977 | **The Swan** Ron Fawcett, Geoff Birtles |
| | *First free ascent.* |

| 1977 | **Smear Test** Gabriel Regan and party |

| 1977 | **Willow Farm** Chris Hamper (solo) |

| 1977 | **Tower Face** Al Simpson, Dave Jones |

1977	**Bad Sneakers** Dave Jones *Named after Simpson who had been attempting to steal all of Jones' lines.*

1977   **Skytrain** John Peel, Tony Barley

1977   **Spectrum, Spare Rib, Lung Cancer** Jonny Woodward (solo)

1978 April 2   **Punch** Jonny Woodward (solo)
First free ascent. Quite an ascent as the route was done straight from the ground with no falls; it regularly repels people today.

1978 April 3   **Pebbledash, direct start** Dave Wiggin (unseconded)
Now included in Eugene's Axe.

1978 April 5   **Diamond Wednesday** Gary Gibson, Ian Johnson
Probably climbed before.

1978 April 6   **Schoolies** Phil Burke, Gary Gibson
Later climbed direct by John Codling (solo).

1978 April 16   **Something Better Change** Gary Gibson, Fred Crook
Not chipped by the first ascensionists.

1978 April 20   **Sparkle** Gary Gibson (solo)
The direct finish was also climbed.

1978 April 20   **War Wound** Gary Gibson, Dave Jones
Named in honour of a badly gashed knee.

1978 April 23   **Shortcomings, Substance** Gary Gibson (solo)

1978 April 23   **Poisonous Python, Crenation** Gary Gibson, Fred Crook

1978 April 30   **Coldfinger** Gary Gibson, Fred Crook

1978 April   **Dawn Piper** John Codling (solo)

1978 May 4   **Hanging Around** Gary Gibson, Fred Crook
Reportedly climbed before by Steve Bancroft and John Allen in 1974.

1978 May 7   **Fred's Cafe** Gary Gibson, Fred Crook
Fred supplied the coffee and sandwiches.

1978 May 7   **The Man Who Fell to Earth** Dave Wiggin (unseconded)
This route started below Hypothesis, joined it and finish rightwards 3m from the top. It was later straightened out and is now part of Destination Earth.

1978 May 18   **Chicane Destination, Chicane, A.M. Anaesthetic** Gary Gibson (solo)

1978 May 21   **The Aspirant** Gary Gibson (solo)
Top-roped first.

1978 May   **Lybstep** John Dodd

1978 May	**Kicking Bird** Al Simpson, Dave Jones (AL), Nick Longland, Tony Bristlin *Strung together over two evenings. Where Jones failed on the first pitch Simpson used his knees. Most repeat ascensionists follow suit!*
1978 May	**Babbacombe Lee** Dave Jones, Ian Johnson
1978 May	**Time to be Had, Sennapod, Days Gone By, Bad Poynt** Gary Gibson (solo) *All of the routes had most certainly been climbed before but, for some reason were not recorded.*
1978 July 7	**Bed of Nails** Gary Gibson, John Perry
1978 July 7	**National Hero** Gary Gibson, John Perry, Mark 'Ralph' Hewitt
1978 July 13	**Graffiti** Gary Gibson, Mark Hewitt, Derek Beetlestone *The finish had been climbed before as a direct finish to Cannonball Crack.*
1978 July 24	**The Valve, Third Degree Burn** Gary Gibson, Derek Beetlestone *The Valve was top-roped first.*
1978 Aug.	**The Tower of Bizarre Delights** Dave Jones, Bob Cope, Tony Bristlin *Gibson had been trying the line and had come very close two nights previously. Jones' ascent after top-roping was received by Gibson with animosity. Gibson's (second) ascent followed two days later without top-roping.*
1978 Oct. 14	**Headless Horseman** Jonny Woodward
1978	**Mousey's Mistake, Sorcerer's Apprentice** Dave Jones
1978	**Wipers** Gary Gibson, Nick Longland
1978	**Short Trip etc.**
1979 April 5	**Destination Venus** Gary Gibson (solo)
1979 April 19	**Heartbleed** Gary Gibson (solo)
1979 May 14	**Curvature** Gary Gibson (solo)
1979 May 15	**Gypfast** Phil Gibson (unseconded) *A much sought-after line. Al Simpson's attempts had been halted in 1978 by an almighty thunderstorm. Top-roped first.*
1979 June 4	**Between the Tiles** Gary Gibson, Dave Jones
1979 June 4	**Sign of the Times** Dave Jones, Gary Gibson
1979 June 11	**Definitive Gaze** Gary Gibson, Ian Barker *A pebble snapped and Gibson ended up in Barker's arms!*

1979 June 27	**Split Personality** Gary Gibson (solo)	
1979 July 20	**The Sublime** Gary Gibson, John Perry	
	Top-roped first.	
1979 Aug. 9	**Topaz, 39th Step** Gary Gibson, Phil Wilson	
1979 Aug. 20	**Genetix** Gary Gibson (unseconded)	
1979 Sept. 4	**Public Enemy Number One** Gary Gibson, Ian Johnson	
1979 Sept.	**Gillted** Phil Burke, George Cooper	
	Named after Burke's ex-girlfriend.	
1979 Oct.	**Wrong Way Round** Gary Gibson (unseconded)	
1979	**Simpkin's Overhang** Phil Burke (unseconded)	
	Top-roped first. Rumours of chipped holds were completely unfounded.	
1979	**Acid Drop** Jonny Woodward	
1979	**Eugene's Axe** John Codling, Andy Fox, Dave Jones	
	Named in honour of Rock Hall Cottage denizen Doug Moller who had erected a fence around The Lower Tier and fended off all-comers with an axe.	
1979	**Grilled Fingers** Dave Jones (solo)	
1979	**True Grot, The Fantasy Finish** Dave Jones	
1979	**Garlic** Phil Gibson (solo)	
1979	**Chronicle, Microcosm, Inspiration Point** Gary Gibson (solo)	
1979	**Sally James** Nick Longland (solo)	
1980 April 10	**Carrion** Gary Gibson, Derek Beetlestone	
1980 April 13	**The Thin Air** Gary Gibson (solo, with a hanging rope)	
1980 April 30	**Circuit Breaker** Gary Gibson (unseconded)	
1980 May 2	**Amaranth** Gary Gibson (solo with a hanging rope)	
1980 July 7	**Poison Gift** Gary Gibson (unseconded)	
1980 July 12	**Licence to Run** (1 pt.) Gary Gibson, Fred Crook	
	For some reason the route kept its E2 5c grade in the guidebook; this was originally intended as a joke pointed at the authors.	
1980 July 13	**Licence to Run** Pete O'Donovan, Gary Cooper	
	First free ascent.	
1980 Sept.	**Antithesis** Jonny Woodward (unseconded)	
	Originally named Dirty Trick. Climbed in marked contrast to his previous first ascents. Woodward reluctantly took over the lead after Gibson had shown the sequence to everyone but failed to complete the lead.	

1980	**The Super Girdle** John Codling, Dave Jones
1980	**Sidewinder** Phil Burke, Bob Toogood *The first pitch was climbed by Gary Gibson in 1979.*
1980	**Bareback Rider, Burrito Deluxe** Dave Jones
1981 Feb. 14	**Trebia** Gary Gibson (unseconded)
1981 April 14	**Swan Bank** Gary Gibson, Derek Beetlestone, Mark Hewitt
1981	*Staffordshire Area guidebook, Rock Climbs in the Peak, Volume 6, published.*
1981 May 2	**Live Bait** Gary Gibson (unseconded) *Top-roped first.*
1981 July 8	**Hallow to Our Men** Gary Gibson (solo) *After three days of attempts on this. Gibson celebrated with:*
1981 July 8	**Automatix** Gary Gibson (solo) *On-sight!*
1981 Aug. 23	**Strain Station** Gary Gibson, Hazel Carnes (the future Mrs Gibson) *Top-roped first.*
1981 Aug. 23	**Entente Cordiale** Gary Gibson, Hazel Carnes
1981	**Quickbrew** Fred Crook, Ian Barker
1982 April 3	**Pebbles on a Wessex Beach** Gary Gibson (unseconded)
1982 April	**Entropy's Jaw** Andrew Woodward (solo)
1982 May 3	**Slips** Gary Gibson (unseconded)
1982 July	**Formative Years** Howard Tingle (solo) *Top-roped first.*
1982 Aug. 3	**Triple Point** Jonny Woodward (solo) *The direct start was added in 1983 by Nick Dixon (solo).*
1982 Sept. 25	**Poodle Vindaloo** Jonny Woodward (solo)
1982	**Crystal Grazer** Phil Burke (solo) *Top-roped first.*
1982	**A Day at the Seaside** Fred Crook, Ken Crook
1983 June 22	**Loculus Lie** Simon Nadin, Richard Davies *Top-roped first. An early start was made to avoid sweaty hands and to study for exams the following day.*
1983 Sept. 22	**Bloodstone** Simon Nadin (unseconded)

1983 Sept. 25   **A Fist Full of Crystals** Nick Dixon (solo)
Top-roped first. Climbed in mistake for Crystal Grazer. Named from a top-rope ascent by Jonny Woodward who commented:
'Undoubtedly the hardest piece of climbing on The Roaches. It has three desperate moves involving an unlikely toe-jam move, a weird high sort of bridge and an all out crystal move. There are no runners and a fall would land you painfully in a holly tree. It will take me quite a time to pluck up the courage to lead it!'

1983 Oct. 20   **Barriers in Time** Simon Nadin (unseconded)
Top-roped first.

1983   **Clive Coolhead etc...** Nick Dixon, Steve Lowe
Rumours of high side-runners and previous top-roping were completely unfounded. In fact, Dixon had tried to top-rope the pitch a few days previously but failed.

1983   **The Dignity of Labour** Nick Dixon (solo)
On-sight!

1984 April 12   **Destination Earth** Simon Nadin (unseconded)
A fall from the crux, whilst soloing, persuaded Simon to put a rope on and lead the route.

1984 May 27   **Secrets of Dance** Simon Nadin (unseconded)
Simon's first sortie onto this wall and not the last!

1984 Sept. 25   **Bloodspeed** Simon Nadin (unseconded)

1984 Oct. 13   **Pindles Numb** Nick Dixon (solo)
The name refers to the effects of a fall into the holly tree.

1985 May 5   **Script for a Tear** Simon Nadin (solo)
Top-roped first. Originally named The Jester.

1985 July 13   **New Fi'Nial** Simon Nadin, Richard Davies, Gary Cooper

1985 Sept.   **Catastrophe Internationale** Nick Dixon (solo)
Top-roped first. Climbed on a BMC international meet.

1985 Oct. 13   **Painted Rumour** Simon Nadin, Martin Veale
A loose flake was glued back to the roof!

1985 Nov. 3   **Nature Trail** Simon Nadin (unseconded)

1985 Nov. 18   **Art Nouveau** Simon Nadin (solo)
A superb find.

1985 Dec. 27   **Counterstroke of Equity** Richard Davies (unseconded)
Top-roped first. Stolen whilst Simon Nadin was sampling his first ('and last!') taste of Scottish winter climbing.

1985   **Fluorescent Stripper** Nick Dixon, Andi Lovatt

1985	**Little Perforations** Gary Cooper, Fred Crook *Climbed in 1978 as a variation on Wipers by Gary* *Gibson but not recorded in the 1981 guidebook.*
1986 Feb.	**Ou Est Le Spit?** Nick Dixon, Simon Nadin *One of Britain's shortest E6 routes.*
1986 March	**Inertia Reel** Jonny Dawes (solo) *A long-standing problem which finally fell after* *cleaning. Early ascensionists made use of heather (now* *deceased) to finish.*
1986 March	**The Cube** Nick Dixon, Allen Williams, Simon Oaker, Simon Whalley
1986 March	**Jump** Simon Whalley (solo)
1986 April	**Doug** Nick Dixon (solo) *Only soloed after some optimistically glued pebbles* *had been pulled off during a top-roped ascent.*
1986 June 12	**Thing on a Spring** Simon Nadin (unseconded) *Success after numerous failures, most ending in* *airborne retreat.*
1986 July 17	**99% of Gargoyles Look Like Bob Todd** Simon Nadin (unseconded)
1986	**Between the Lines** Gary Cooper, Fred Crook
1987 Feb. 17	**Paralogism** Simon Nadin (unseconded) *Top-roped first. The hardest gritstone roof climb in* *Britain?*
1987 March 30	**Shelty, Wolfman of the KGB** John Allen (solo)
1987 March 30	**Dolly Mix, Mix** John Allen, Martin Veale, Sarah Kent *'Obviously a classic'.*
1987 April	**Ant Lives** Nick Dixon (solo)
1987 July 3	**Licence to Lust** John Allen, Dave Barrell, Mark Stokes *The finish had been climbed previously by a few* *parties.*
1987 Sept 23	**Drop Acid** John Allen, Rob Allen, Steve Bancroft
1987	**Something Biblical, Mistral** Gary Cooper, Fred Crook
1987	**Snap, Crackle and Andy Popp** Fred Crook, Gary Cooper
1988 Feb	**Sunday at Chapel** N Dixon, A Williams, G Cole, I Dunn, C Dunn
1988 May	**Cold Bone Forgotten** P Mitchell, P Evans

THE FIVE CLOUDS

O.S. ref. SK 001625

by Gary Gibson

> *'Simpson tried the top slab/arête a few times*
> *and hit the air, but a fourth go saw him work*
> *out a system of moves for the difficult middle*
> *section; after that he didn't dare fall off.*
> *Subsequent parties have felt it should be 6a.'*

Dave Jones, writing about Icarus Allsorts
in Crags Magazine, 1979.

SITUATION and CHARACTER
The five bluffs that form The Five Clouds lie approximately
500m north-west of The Roaches Lower Tier midway
between Upper Hulme and Roach End and 50m up the slope
above the minor road between these two points. They are
easily recognisable from The Upper Tier as five grassy
'humps' on the skyline.
The isolated nature of The Five Clouds lends a unique
atmosphere to these buttresses, seldom found elsewhere on
gritstone. Superb views of surrounding scenery coupled with
the best rock in the area and some fine lines gives all of the
routes an almost magnetic appeal. Having said this, the cliffs
are rarely visited, never overcrowded and provide a
welcome break from the masses that often frequent the
main crags. The central, Third Cloud is the largest and
provides the best routes, whilst the Second and Fourth give
extended bouldering and the First and Fifth smaller
problems of varying difficulties. As previously mentioned,
the rock is immaculate, though sometimes green after long
periods of bad weather or neglect.

APPROACHES and ACCESS
The normal approach is from The Roaches lay-by. Turn
immediately left after the gate and a brisk 800m walk brings
the buttresses into view. Approach from The Roaches Upper
Tier is via a well-worn path from its northern end whilst
other, more direct approaches are to be discouraged due to
erosion problems.
Access is not a problem though in view of the nearby
cottages noise should be kept to a minimum and litter
should not be left.

THE CLIMBS are described as one normally approaches from The Roaches' lay-by i.e. from RIGHT to LEFT.

THE FIRST CLOUD

The first outcrop approached lies just beyond a small quarry. Minor problems exist here though a large square block, 'footed' by a cave, gives some excellent slab climbing akin to nearby mini-classics. They remain unnamed and ungraded for enthusiasts to discover for themselves.

THE SECOND CLOUD

The second 'hump' is more pronounced and contains a large block split centrally by a leaning fissure.

1 Marxist Undertones 8m VS 5b
Just right of the fissure. Undercut past a pocket and go up onto the easy-angled ridge. (1973-1980)

2 Communist Crack 8m VS 5a   *
The fissure; mean and awkward. Off-width experts will find this a challenge. Young Turks may find laybacking more successful. (pre-1968)

Ten metres to the left, across a grassy slipway, a fine sharp arête springs up.

3 KGB 7m HVS 4c
Begin up the right side of the arête to finish airily on the left. (1977)

4 Finger of Fate 7m E1 6a   **
The left side of the arête. Friction offers more hope than fate! The horrendously thin wall to the left gives a 6c bouldering nightmare moving right to reach the arête 2m from its top. (1983)

5 Yankee Jam 8m VS 5a
The evil crack springing from the cave just to the left. (1973-1980)

6 Lenin 8m VD
Easier and more pleasant climbing up the crack just to the left. (pre-1968)

7 Legends of Lost Leaders 8m E2 5c   *
A stiff problem. Climb the centre of the wall to the left via an alarming mantelshelf and sprint layback finale. Finishing left from the mantelshelf is 5b. (1979)

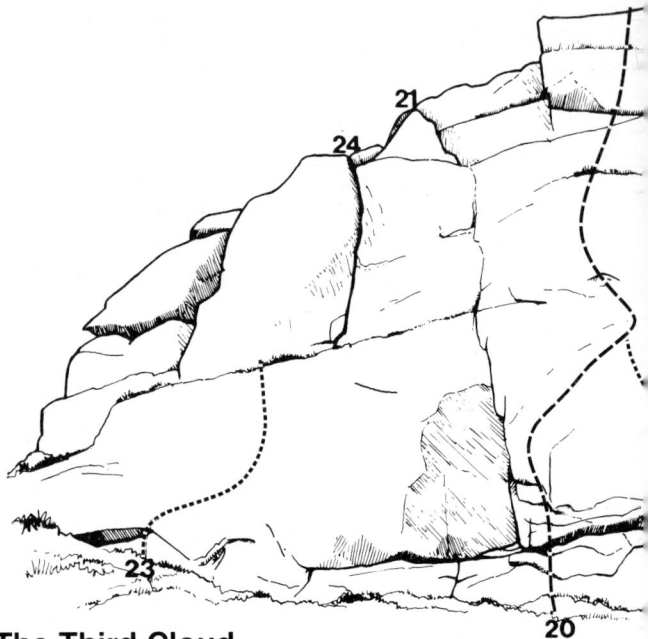

The Third Cloud

8 Stalin 8m VD
The crack to the left. Excellent stuff. (pre-1968)

9 Jimmy Carter 6m HVD
Amble up the wall to the left via flakes and ripples.

(1973-1980)

THE THIRD CLOUD

Altogether the Big Brother of The Clouds, the next hillock presents a sheer front face, a gully to its right and multiple features to the right again.

10 Pointless Arête 6m VS 4b
The arête at the right extremity of the wall. Possible escape gives the route its name. (1977)

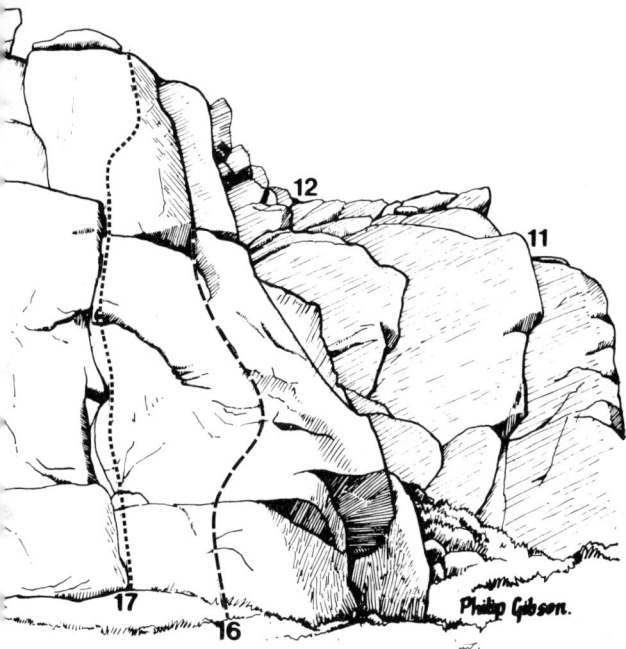

Philip Gibson.

11 The Big Flake 7m VD
The big flake gives an interesting exercise in chimneying.
(pre-1968)

12 The Little Flake 7m HVS 5a
The little flake is usually lustred in lichen. Slippery.
(pre-1968)

13 Tim Benzadrino 7m E3 5c
The vicious barrel-shaped wall just left. Pick your landing
before embarking on a solo ascent. (1979)

14 The Bender 7m VS 4b
Thin curving cracks, almost in the gully, left of the two
flakes. (1968-1973)

15 Icarus Allsorts 15m E4 6a *

The main rounded arête left of the gully provides the basis for this climb. From a block above the cave at the foot of the arête, teeter left onto a flake, then go up the slab to a ledge at the foot of a wide corner-crack. Step left onto the arête and leave the thin flake on badly-placed holds to gain the top; airborne retreat is not adviseable due to the brittle nature of the flake. Taking the right arête of the wide corner crack gives **Waxwing**, E1 5a. (1977/1979)

16 Flower Power Arête 15m E1 5c *

Climb the short rib forming the left side of the aforementioned cave to a scoop. Balance slightly right, then climb up onto a flake in a tight groove. Finish up the wide corner-crack from the ledge above. A long reach certainly helps. (1968)

17 Crabbie's Crack 15m HVS 4c ***

Gain the perfect hand-jam crack in the face to the left by direct ascent and climb it positively to gain easy ground. Make a rising traverse right to gain the arête and a fine finish in an exhilarating position. Magical. (1950s)

18 The Left-hand Variant 16m HVS 4c **

For the man who has done everything. From the foot of the crack move left and follow expanding flakes leftwards up the wall to easy ground above. (1968)

To the left, at the foot of the main wall, a small cave is usually full of charred remains.

19 Laguna Sunrise 15m E4 6c **

Ascend easily to stand in a break just right of the cave. Move up onto a flake, then shuffle frantically leftwards to join Appaloosa Sunset at the first jug. Technical wizardry. (1984)

20 Appaloosa Sunset 16m E3 5c ***

Quite superb. To the left is a scoop just off the ground. Climb the right arête of the scoop to a good hold and fix a runner in the crack above. Move up and rightwards on a line of holds and 'rockover' to gain a distant jug. 'Rockover' once more, then gallop on direct to the top passing a circular flake. Without a side-runner, the route is E4. A direct start is possible straight to the crux, **The Eclipsed Peach Start**, E1 6b. (1977/1983)

21 Rubberneck 15m HVS 5a   ***
THE classic route hereabouts. Bridge the open scoop with difficulty to gain the soaring crack. Rush up this and finish delicately up the slab above   (1967)

22 Cloudbusting 8m E4 6b   *
Climb the left side of the scoop of Rubberneck and fix a runner above. Stretch quickly up left for a distant edge and lunge frantically leftwards for victory.   (1986)

The smooth wall to the left is bounded by a 6a problem flake nick-named **Persistence**.

23 Who Needs Ready Brek? 7m E4 7a   *†
Wicked. From a few centimetres (!) up Persistence follow the non-break right to its end and somehow move up to the ledge above. Somehow is quite appropriate!   (1986)

24 Elastic Arm 5m HVS 5b
Above the ledge is a wide crack. Stretch, contort and squabble with this awful fissure. Knee-pads essential.
   (pre-1968)

25 Glass Back 5m VD
The easier and pleasanter crack left of Elastic Arm.
   (pre-1968)

26 Blue Bandanna 20m E1 5b   *
An excellent expedition. From the large block below Icarus Allsorts swing left above the lip of the cave then move across into Crabbie's Crack and out onto The Left-hand Variant. Move immediately left and cross Appaloosa Sunset via shaky flakes to reach Rubberneck. Finish up this or the slab to its left.   (1978)

THE FOURTH CLOUD

The next buttress is smaller but offers some fine problem-type routes. The face is bordered on the right by a rounded proboscis.

27 Roman Nose 7m E2 5b   *
Step left off a shelf and climb boldly up the small flakes in the face. There is no protection so do not fall.   (1977)

28 Chockstone Corner 6m D
The obvious corner.   (pre-1968)

29 Mantelshelf Route 8m D   *
A series of ledges, left of the corner.   (pre-1968)

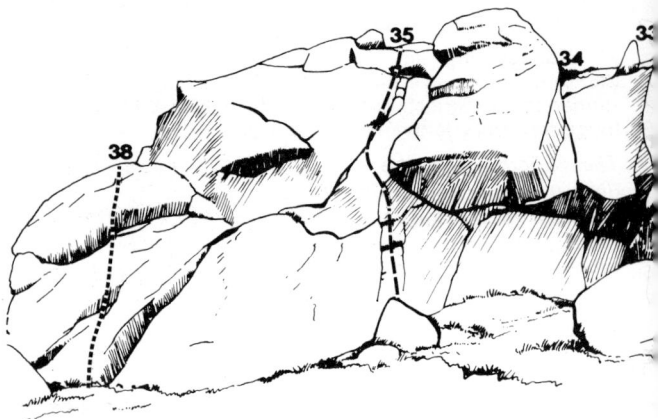

30 Mirror, Mirror 10m E4 6b ✳✳
A very technical problem. Follow small edges and a tiny
flake in the wall to the left to gain the break. Shuffle left,
then move up through an arch via a thin crack. Omitting the
thin crack by ascent to the right is 6a but nowhere near as
fine. (1979)

31 Boysen's Delight 9m HVS 5c ✳
The first obvious feature in the smooth wall to the left. A
difficult entry to the groove is fortunately afforded perfect
protection. (1968)

32 Private Display 9m E1 5b ✳
From a block just left, commit yourself to the faint rib and
thin crack. Tackle this direct by fine moves. (1970)

The slab round to the left can be ascended by using the left
edge at E1 5c; **Winter in Combat**.

In the recess to the left are:

33 Right-hand Block Crack 5m S (pre-1968)

34 Left-hand Block Crack 5m S (pre-1968)

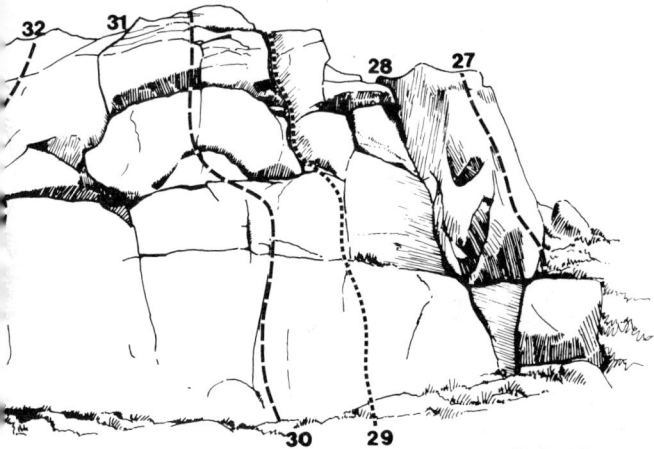

Philip Gibson.

The Fourth Cloud

The small block roof to the left is brushed but currently appears impossible.

35 Smun 9m VS 4c   *
From a crack below the block overhang, swing left and go
up via another crack.   (pre-1968)

36 Stranglehold 10m E1 5b
Gain the upper crack of Smun via an undercut and a
layback.   (1979)

37 Meander Variation 9m HVS 5b
The centre of the short steep wall round to the left is gained
via its easier counterpart: (1977)

38 Meander 8m VD   *
Climb the right-hand line up the slab to the left, then go
leftwards on the upper slab. Delightful.   (pre-1968)

39 Wander 5m VD
The crack to the left.   (pre-1968)

The left arête gives a 5b problem; **Static**.

A large block below and to the left gives fine bouldering. The right arête is 6b, the undercut slab is 6b and the left arête is 5c.

THE FIFTH CLOUD

The final buttress offers climbs on a large angular block with a smooth front face. A small overhang-capped buttress before this gives 6a smearing.

40 Fifth Cloud Eliminate 9m HVS 5a   *
From just left of the obvious arête, swing up right to a ledge. Move diagonally right to gain a shallow finishing groove. This can be gained direct, also at 5a.   (1969)

41 Cloud Nine 10m E2 5b   *
From the ledge at the foot of the arête move up and extend off a small edge for distant holds just right of the arête. Finishing is easier. A direct start gives a shin-scraping 6a.   (1977)

42 Foxy Lady 7m VS 5a   *
The crack in the steep left face of the buttress, exiting right onto the front face.   (1977)

FIVE CLOUDS LIST OF FIRST ASCENTS

Early-1950s	**Crabbie's Crack** Bob Downes, Miss Nea Morin
1967	**Rubberneck** Robin Barley, Tony Barley
1968 Spring	**Boysen's Delight** Martin Boysen First free ascent.
1968 Spring	**Flower Power Arête** Martin Boysen *Pre-placed protection was used. Named after the rather floral T-shirt worn by the first ascensionist.*
1968	**Flaky Wall** Colin Foord
1968	**Left-hand Variant** John Yates (solo)
Pre-1968	**Communist Crack** Hugh Banner
Pre-1968	**Lenin, Stalin, The Big Flake, The Little Flake, Elastic Arm, Glass Back, Chockstone Crack, Mantelshelf Route, Right Block Crack, Left Block Crack, Smun, Meander, Wander** *All of these routes appeared uncredited in the 1968 guidebook.*

1969	**Fifth Cloud Eliminate** John Yates (solo)
	Top-roped first.
1970	**Private Display** John Yates (solo)
	Named from the leader's split trouser seams.
1968-1973	**The Bender**
1977 April	**Foxy Lady** Dave Jones (solo)
1977 May	**Roman Nose** Dave Jones (solo)
1977 June 26	**Appaloosa Sunset** Dave Jones, Ian Johnson, John Gilbert
	A home-made protection device, for the hole at half-height, was measured for the ascent well in advance.
1977	**Icarus Allsorts** Al Simpson, Dave Jones
	The initial section had been climbed earlier in the year by Dave Jones and John Gilbert.
1977	**Cloud Nine** Jonny Woodward, Andrew Woodward
1977	**KGB, Pointless Arête** Ian Johnson (solo)
1977	**Meander Variation** Chris Hamper
1978	**Blue Bandanna** Dave Jones, Al Simpson
1979 June	**Stranglehold** Gary Gibson (solo)
1979	**Mirror, Mirror** Andrew Woodward (solo)
	An inaccurate description in the previous guidebook made this route somewhat easier. The actual line was clearly chalked for some time after the ascent.
1979	**Waxwing** John Codling, Dave Jones
1979	**Tim Benzadrino** Dave Jones, John Codling
1980 March 9	**Legends of Lost Leaders** Gary Gibson (solo)
1973-1980	**Marxist Undertones, Yankee Jam, Jimmy Carter**
1983 Nov. 15	**Finger of Fate** Simon Nadin (solo)
1983	**The Eclipsed Peach start** Allen Williams (solo)
1984 Aug. 21	**Laguna Sunrise** Simon Nadin (unseconded)
	Top-roped first. A spectacular fall was taken from just below the crux narrowly avoided the ground.
1985 Jan.	**Winter in Combat** Richard Davies (solo)
1986 April 2	**Cloudbusting** Simon Nadin (unseconded)
	The second ascent followed immediately.
1986 April 29	**Who Needs Ready Brek?** Simon Nadin (solo)

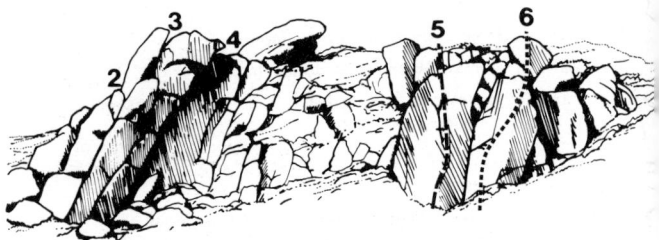

The Main Crag

THE Nth CLOUD/ROACH END

O.S. ref. SK 998635

by Gary Gibson

> *'Definitely terminally, terminal. John Allen only got the first ascent of The Pillar of Judgement by one week!'*

Jonny Woodward, 1979.

SITUATION and CHARACTER
This twin-faced outcrop lies below The Roaches escarpment and above the minor road, midway between the Five Clouds and Roach End.
The two main faces are separated by a grassy gully in which lies a smaller, boulder-type buttress. The excellent right-hand face affords a handful of immaculate face and crack climbs which become rather green in poor weather. The best routes lie in the higher grades.

APPROACHES and ACCESS
Approach proves quite problematic despite the proximity to the road. Either trudge across open moorland from The Five Clouds or descend from the ridge just north of the Hard Very Far Skyline Buttress on The Roaches escarpment following a track alongside a wall, then open ground, to the top of the right-hand face.

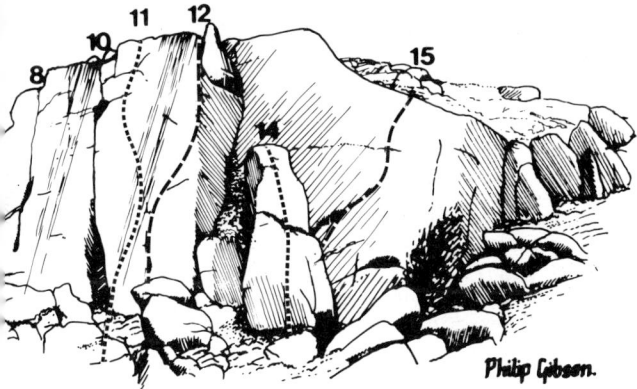

Philip Gibson.

Though access is not prevented, the farmer who owns the land below the crag is not too keen on access over it. The above mentioned approaches are best used to prevent any problems.

THE CLIMBS are described from LEFT to RIGHT.

1 Grenadier 12m HD
Attain a sentry-box on the front face of the left-hand buttress and exit via a crack. Finish up a short corner-crack.
(1960s)

2 Slanting Crack 12m HVD
The left-hand of two cracks in the side-wall of the buttress. From a ledge, finish up a depression. (1960s)

3 Mayhem 12m VS 5a
The right-hand crack. Move left into the left-hand crack at the overhang. An ugly battle. (1969)

4 Green Chimney 11m VD
The appropriately named chimney right again. Finish round the chockstone. (1960s)

The small, central, boulder-type buttress gives two problematical climbs:

5 Totally Unprecedented 7m HVS 5b
The left arête of the obvious corner. Start on the left and finish on the right. (1985)

The obvious corner is Very Difficult.

6 Crystal Voyager 6m E4 6c
A desperate trip up the smooth right wall of the corner via a
faint flake and poor pockets. Horrendous.   (1984)

Pride of place goes to the majority of climbs on the
right-hand buttress, all of which have an esoteric flavour.

7 Little Crack 6m VS 5a
The left-most crack gives exquisite moves which belie its
height.   (1969)

8 Rowan Tree Crack 9m S
Climb the next crack to the right. Treat the tree with care or
the route may have to be renamed.   (1969)

9 Ageing Adolescents 10m E4 6b
The smooth, featureless face just right again. Holds in the
adjacent cracks are strictly out of bounds, though protection
in Rowan Tree Crack has to be sought.   (1984)

10 Plumb-line 12m VS 4c   *
The third and right-most crack is often slippery.   (1969)

11 Judge Dread 15m E6 6b   **
An extremely bold and technical offering. Climb the blunt rib
right of Plumb-line to the half-height ledge on The Pillar of
Judgement. Step left to climb the awesome thin face above.
The route has yet to be led without the pre-placing of an
HB 1.   (1986)

12 The Pillar of Judgement 15m E4 5c   **
A classic frightener, rarely led on-sight. Climb the thin
pocketed crack in the face right of Plumb-line to the
half-height ledge. Step right and balance carefully up using
the arête to reach a short and awkward finishing crack. (1975)

Just right again a pillar leans against the face.

13 Barbeque Corners 18m HVD
Climb the corner formed by the right-hand side of the pillar
and finish up the corner just left of its summit.   (1960s)

14 The Pinnacle Start 15m HS 4a
A very pleasant start can be made by climbing the front face
of the pinnacle. Exit as for Barbecue Corners.   (1960s)

15 Metaphysical Scoop 9m E4 6a   *
From 4m up Barbecue Corners, step right and teeter up the
scoop, hands in your pockets, to gain holds! Finish directly.
(1987)

*For those with a penchant for bouldering, some good
problems can be found on the jumble of rocks 150m left of
the main outcrop.*

NTH CLOUD/ROACH END LIST OF FIRST ASCENTS

1960s	**Barbeque Corners, The Pinnacle Start, Grenadier, Green Chimney, Slanting Crack** North Staffordshire Mountaineering Club members
1968 Nov.	**Plumb-line, Little Crack, Rowan Tree Crack** John Yates, Colin Foord
1968 Nov.	**Mayhem** Colin Foord, John Yates
1975	**The Pillar of Judgement** John Allen, Mark Stokes *Previously named and top-roped by Colin Foord in November 1968.*
1984 March 23	**Crystal Voyager** Simon Nadin (solo)
1984 May 29	**Ageing Adolescents** Nick Dixon (unseconded) *With a deviation into Rowan Tree Crack.*
1984 June 30	**Ageing Adolescents** Simon Nadin (unseconded) *Without deviation but still with a side-runner.*
1985 April 23	**Totally Unprecedented** Gary Gibson (solo) *Certainly climbed before but never claimed.*
1986 April	**Judge Dread** Nick Dixon, Simon Whalley *Top-roped first.*
1987 Feb. 17	**Metaphysical Scoop** Andy Popp, Steve Lowe, Gwynn Hughes *Top-roped first.*

BACK FOREST and THE HANGING STONE

O.S. ref SJ 987653 to 974654

by Gary Gibson

---

*'The buttresses and gullies were labelled with
what were surely the most impressive names
ever applied to a crag of this size.'*

Colin Foord, 1973.

SITUATION and CHARACTER

These outcrops are close to the crest of the undulating
continuation of The Roaches escarpment. From Roach End,
the ridge runs north-west for just over 1km before curving
to the west for a further 2km and petering out near
Danebridge.

Not having the magnitude of the neighbouring crags, the
main attributes of these buttresses are their isolation,
pleasant aspect and fine views. The rock is usually fine and
clean though green in places but never crowded nor
imposing. The Main Crag is ideal for a quiet introduction to
the world of climbing whilst the occasional harder route
does exist for the expert searching for an evening's soloing.
The Hanging Stone is slightly more imposing and its routes
are both dramatic and interesting.

APPROACHES and ACCESS

For The Main Crag and Western Outcrop the best approach
is from Roach End, where ample parking is available. Cross
the wall to the north of the parking area by a small stile and
follow the path along the ridge; initially alongside a wall.
The path dips down to the left before meeting another wall
in a hollow where The Main Crag is situated. The Western
Outcrop lies farther along the ridge.

Whilst The Hanging Stone can also be approached along the
ridge, by far the best approach is from Danebridge (O.S. ref.
SJ 965652). From the bridge, follow a wide track upstream
on the Staffordshire side for 50m. Cross the fence on the
right via a stile and follow another path up through the
wooded valley, then cross the field to Hanging Stone Farm.
Pass between the farm buildings and continue on up the
hillside to reach the block.

No access problems have ever arisen.

THE CLIMBS are described from RIGHT to LEFT.

THE MAIN CRAG

Once over the wall, the initial section of crag is little more than 5m in height. Problems abound here. **Unseen Face**, 4b, lies above a stony recess, **Contract Worker**, 4a, is a thin crack topped by a bulge, and **Problem Arête**, 5c, is the arête to the left. **Dog-leg Corner**, VD, is the obvious wide corner, **Armstrain**, 5b, the undercut wall left of the corner, **Dog-leg Crack**, VD, the obvious crack, **Harrop's Pride**, 4b, an undercut and arête 2m left and **Simple View**, 5a, a thin crack and wall 2m left again.

The next feature, a chimney, is followed by **ROCKING STONE BUTTRESS** *which no longer has its stone.*

The right-hand edge of the buttress has a short Moderate problem up it.

1 Rocking Stone Ridge 7m VD
The left-hand edge after an undercut start. (pre-1931)

2 Grasper 7m VS 4b *
Tackle the centre of the wall to finish at thin cracks.
(pre-1973)

3 Requiem For Tired Fingers 6m HVS 5b
A tricky little problem up the green and often slimy crack in the left side of the wall. Finish slightly right. (1974)

The Hanging Slab Crack, M, lies in the corner which also bounds **BROKEN NOSE BUTTRESS**. **Thin Crack**, 4a, is the face 2m left again.

4 Not-so-central Route 6m S
Start at the foot of the buttress. Go up the ridge, then move right below the initial overhang and finish direct. (1973-1981)

5 Central Route 6m S
Follow the ridge to the second overhang and pass this to the right with a little discomfort. (pre-1931)

6 Green Shaker 8m VD
From the first ledge on Central Route, step left to a small flake, then move up rightwards to the top. (pre-1973)

The rounded face 10m to the left is **BASTION BUTTRESS**.

A smaller rounded buttress to the right has a poor Severe arête; **Filler In**.

7 Bastion Face 6m D
The right-hand side-wall via a break and a black flake.
(pre-1931)

8 Bastion Corner 7m VD
From the left-hand face, follow holds rightwards to finish
up the vague arête. (pre-1931)

To the left lies **BOLLARD BUTTRESS**. *A steep crack and
groove separate the two buttresses:*

9 Pseudo Crack 8m HVD   *
The groove and crack exiting right at the top, or finishing
left via an airy traverse and the arête. (pre-1931)

10 Toe Rail 8m HVS 5b   *
The right-hand face of Bollard Buttress passing a small
flake and bulge *en route*. (1979)

11 Bollard Edge 8m HS 4a   **
The best route in this area. Climb from the foot of the
buttress avoiding the overhang to the left via a crack to
reach the top of the bollard. Press on just left of the arête to
gain the top. (pre-1931)

12 Capstone Chimney 6m S
The obvious chimney is climbed by passing outside the
chockstone. (pre-1931)

13 Wrestle Crack 6m HS 4a
Attack the obvious undercut crack 1m left. (pre-1931)

Three metres left is a small slab below an overhang:

14 The Saucer Direct 6m S
Climb to the overhang and move right to pass it via a
wedged flake. A right-hand start is 4c. (1973-1981)

15 The Saucer 6m VD
Climb the slab and move left round the corner. Finish via a
crack. (pre-1931)

Left again is **KEEP BUTTRESS** *which is easily identifiable by
a gully to the right.*

16 Keep Face 6m S
Gain a ledge on the front face and use an L-shaped crack to
move up and left to a mantelshelf finish. (pre-1931)

17 Portcullis Crack 6m HVD ✦✦
Take the crack complete with chockstone on the left side of
the buttress. Pass the overhang and finish leftwards to the
arête. (pre-1973)

18 The Keeper 6m HVS 5a ✦
Gain the steep left-hand wall of the buttress by a quick pull,
then pass a ledge to finish up the right arête. (1979)

Across the sandy bank at a slightly higher level is **HOLLY
TREE BUTTRESS**.

Blow Hard, 4a, is a flaky crack right of the niche in the
buttress's right wall.

19 Holly Tree Niche Right Route 6m D
Attain the niche and finish up the corner. (pre-1931)

20 Holly Tree Niche Left Route 9m S ✦
The main arête of the buttress on its right-hand side. At the
first bulge move left and make awkward moves up the
left-hand side of the nose. (pre-1931)

21 Eye of Japetus 9m HVS 5a ✦✦
Climb a thin crack 2m left, gaining a second break above a
smooth section with interest. Finish via a faint flake. (1974)

22 Twin Thin 8m S
The twin, thin vertical cracks to the left. Finish to the left of
a vague groove. (1931-1973)

23 Green Crack 6m HVD
An appropriately named curving feature 1m left of Twin
Thin. (1931-1973)

On top of the edge, 100m to the left is **THE ROSTRUM**, *a
projecting platform of rock.*

Racer's Rock, 4c, lies at the right-hand edge of this group
of rocks.

24 John's Route 6m HVS 5a
The wall and bulges on the right-hand side of The Rostrum.
(1979)

25 The Rostrum 6m S ✦
Get onto the platform by an odd manoeuvre, then finish up
the left-hand edge of the bulges. (1931-1973)

Continue along the escarpment for a further 1km to reach:

THE WESTERN OUTCROP

Fifty metres before the obvious twin overhung buttress lies a small isolated crag.

26 Suspended Sentence 7m VS 5a
The crack through the overhang. (1974)

27 Double Overhang 11m E1 5b ✱✱
Outrageous climbing for the grade, through the main feature of the buttress. Pass the first overhang centrally via a long stretch for a super-jug on the lip. Use similar tactics to overcome the second overhang. (1971/1974)

28 Burnham Crack 9m VS 4c
The obvious and relatively steep corner left of Double Overhang. (1971)

29 The Gaping Void 11m D
Starting on the left side of the buttress, traverse right across Burnham Crack and go between the overhangs to finish on the right. (1971)

THE HANGING STONE O.S. ref. SJ 974654

THE CLIMBS are described from LEFT to RIGHT. Two plaques are secured to the rock; one commemorates the death of a dog and the other is a memorial to a notable member of the Brocklehurst family.

30 Left-hand Crack 8m VS 5a
The corner right of the steps leads to a break. Struggle with the crack through the overhang above to gain the top. (1931-1973)

31 The Bridge of Sighs 12m E3 5c ✱✱
An excellent and unusual pitch. Hard climbing just left of the leftmost plaque, gradually easing, leads to the break. Swing out left into the void and finish up the faint groove above the roof. (1977)

32 Hanging Stone Crack 11m HVS 5b ✱
Starting just right of the main arête, climb on small holds, one metal, to gain an upper crack which is followed by tricky jamming, or holds out to the right. (1931-1973)

33 Right Bow 8m E1 5b
Climb the bulging right wall of the buttress to gain a high
flake and finish up it strenuously.   (1977)

The buttress can be girdled from left to right at three points.
The Low Girdle is Severe, **The Drifter's Escape**, VS 4c, uses
the central break and **The High Girdle**, HS 4a, crawls along
the uppermost break.

BACK FOREST LIST OF FIRST ASCENTS

Pre-1931	**Rocking Stone Ridge, Central Route, Bastion Face, Bastion Corner, Pseudo Crack, Bollard Edge, Capstone Chimney, Wrestle Crack, The Saucer, Keep Face, Holly Tree Niche Right Route, Holly Tree Niche Left Route** *All appeared in the Rucksack Club Journal of 1931.*
1971	**Double Overhang** (1 pt.) Dave Salt, Colin Foord *The aid was a nut on the initial roof.* *Climbed free in 1974 by Jonny and Andrew Woodward.*
1971	**Burnham Crack, The Gaping Void** Dave Salt, Colin Foord *These routes may have been climbed before.*
1931-1973	**Grasper, The Green Shaker, Portcullis Crack, Twin Thin, Green Crack, The Rostrum, Left-hand Crack, Hanging Stone Crack** *All appeared for the first time in the 1973 Staffordshire Gritstone guidebook.*
1974 Aug.	**Eye of Japetus, Requiem for Tired Fingers, Suspended Sentence** Jonny Woodward, Andrew Woodward *Eye of Japetus appeared in the 1981 guidebook as Thin Wall by John Holt but had been done previously.*
1974 Aug.	**Double Overhang** Jonny Woodward, Andrew Woodward *First free ascent.*
1977	**Bridge of Sighs** Dave Jones, John Gilbert
1977	**Right Bow** Jonny Woodward
1979	**The Keeper, Toe Rail** John Holt (solo)
1979	**John's Route** Gary Gibson (solo)
1973-1981	**Not So Central Route, The Saucer Direct** *Appeared for the first time in the 1981 guidebook.*

HEN CLOUD

O.S. ref. SK 008616

by Gary Gibson

> *'Not everyone has been benighted on gritstone
> and one ought to be ashamed for want of
> prudence, the episode is delightful to me in
> retrospect; gritstone has its romance no less
> than granite.'*

John Laycock, 1909.

SITUATION and CHARACTER

The unmistakable fortress-like appearance of Hen Cloud
stands out proudly guarding the entrance to the Peak District
from the south-west, towering majestically over the A53
Leek-to-Buxton road 1km to its north. Set between the
spiky profile of Ramshaw Rocks and the long ominous
escarpment of The Roaches, The Cloud, as it is known to the
locals, provides one of the finest settings for an individual
gritstone outcrop in the area.

The character of Hen Cloud is unique and renowned for its
harshness and grandeur. Twin turret-like walls overlook a
central amphitheatre with tapering side-walls swinging
round and down to the saddles on either side of the
fortress. Majestic, strong and natural lines abound; sharply
defined cracks, often bottoming before the perfect hand-jam
is found, are punctuated by fine steep walls and striking
gargantuan arêtes. This is no place for the weak or faint of
heart. The climbing calls for a confident, insensitive
approach; the bold quick-thinking climber is well-rewarded
by a crag with tremendous charisma whilst the meek will
often retire battered and torn with the knowledge that they
have done battle with the elite of gritstone climbs. The
tapering side-walls offer a place for slight relief but their
routes should not be underestimated in terms of difficulty.
Make no mistake, some of the best routes on gritstone are
to be found on Hen Cloud.

The respect for The Cloud, coupled with its extremely open
aspect and lack of sunshine, often leaves many of the routes
more green and gruesome than they have been during more
popular days. It has its devotees but even their dedication
doesn't keep the lichen at bay and it returns after only a hint
of defeat from the climbing fraternity. A good brush (but not
wire) is a useful weapon for any little-frequented pitches

and every route is graded for a clean state. Add one or two grades if you feel the greenness to be of appreciable encumbrance.

APPROACHES and ACCESS

Approach as for The Roaches until the gateway through the barrier of trees (below the crag and skirting the road) is reached. Careful parking, without blocking the gate, is available but please be sensible so as not to cause any obstruction. The direct approach via the gateway, a dirt track and steep path, leads to Central Climb area from where all the climbs are easily reached.

The crag is Peak National Park property and though access is a formality, **please respect the crag and take your litter home!**

THE CLIMBS are described from LEFT to RIGHT starting with two routes on the attractive small pinnacle nestling just in front of the shoulder between Hen Cloud and The Roaches.

1 Starlight and Storm 7m E3 6b   *
The left arête of the pinnacle. A difficult problem start is followed by delightful moves past the break.   (1986)

2 The Aiguillette 6m S 4a
The easiest means to the top is up the right edge. Happily there is no telepherique so the route has to be reversed for escape.   (1913-1927)

The remainder of the routes are on the main escarpment starting with the short, square wall facing north-west.

3 Zoom Wall 6m VS
The obvious wall of the block. The left edge and centre are 4c; the right edge is 5a.   (1978)

Round to the right a long 7m-high wall extends to a curious pinnacle, the left-hand of three. The wall gives several routes and problems, none quite as fine as:

4 Nutted by Reality 7m E1 6a   *
Exquisite climbing up the centre of the smooth rippled wall 10m right of Zoom Wall. The wall to the right is also 6a.
                                                        (1978)

5 Slipstreams 7m HVS 5a
The twin 'empty' cracks 8m to the right lead to a finish up a short flake.   (1979)

6 Little Pinnacle Climb 7m VD
Climb a tiny corner just right into a second, larger, corner.
Move left then go up to and over a small pinnacle to reach
the top.   (1968-1973)

*To the right are three prominent pinnacles, the first of the
trio standing somewhat forward of the rest.*

7 November Cracks 12m S
Climb the awkward and insecure twin cracks on the front
face of the first pinnacle to a ledge. Finish up the corner
behind.   (1927)

8 Bulwark 12m E1 5b   *
Start at a higher level on the right wall of the first pinnacle.
Tiptoe daintily leftwards onto the crest of the pinnacle and
climb this on rounded breaks to an airy finish on more
positive flutings. Protection is poor and well-spaced.   (1957)

9 Slowhand 11m E1 5b   *
The right wall of the first pinnacle. Climb the crack right of
Bulwark until it begins to fade at a scoop. Negotiate this by
way of a rounded pocket and a twisted reach.   (1978)

Philip Gibson.

General View

10 Chockstone Chimney 9m M
The large chasm dividing the first pinnacle from the second.
(1947-1951)

11 Mindbridge 11m E7 6c †
Horrendous. Climb the right wall of the gully to some thin
flutings. Hard moves lead up, if you're lucky, to the top.
Bridging the chimney is illegal but obviously more
life-assuring? (1984)

12 Master of Reality 11m E6 6c ***
The stunning line via a prominent vein up the middle of the
second pinnacle. A formidable proposition. Climb the lower
wall on rugosities moving slightly left to gain the break by a
powerful move. Withering moves onto and up the vein lead
to a worrying finale. (1983)

13 The Notch 11m VS 4c
Gain the notch between the second and third pinnacles via a
thin crack or, harder (5b), by a scoop on the right. Finish up
the right wall of the notch via a flake. (1968-1973)

14 Chicken 12m E1 5a *
The thin crack cleaving the buttress right again. At its end,
swing up right (escape here reduces the grade to HVS), then
go back left to climb a slippery unnerving scoop. **Chicken**

Direct, E4 6b, follows the difficult prow just left of the top of the crack to gain the finishing scoop from the left. **Pullet**, pulls up the right arête at E1 5b. Both variations are as good as the original route. (1960s/1981/1978).

15 Piston Groove 11m VS 5a
The evil, tight groove right again. The curving crack in the right wall would have provided a good pitch had it not been for this route. (1957-1968)

16 The Mandrake 10m E5 6a   **
The only protection available is that in Victory (the obvious crack to the right) which proves less useful the higher one proceeds. Climb the wall 3m to the right of Piston Groove, then stretch reluctantly leftwards over the bulge to gain holds and a short crisp flake on the arête. Finish up this or the wall to the right. Typical gritstone boldness. (1980)

17 Victory 9m VS 4c
Confident thrutching up the obvious crack will yield success. (1957-1968)

18 Short 'n Sharp 8m E1 5c
Just before the corner. A balancy start is followed by a short flake and 'empty' crack. Use of the routes on either side is strictly taboo. (1978)

19 Green Corner 8m S
The slimy corner to the right. Easier if it ever dries out! (1957-1968)

The crag now stands forward offering a large, block-like, front face.

20 Blood Blisters 9m E4 6b   *
Boulder out the wall 2m right of the arête to reach a thin crack. Balance left to the arête and search frantically for adequate finishing holds amidst a sea of roundedness. (1981)

21 Electric Chair 9m E2 5c   *
Climb up just right again to a ledge, then traverse left to the short crack. Swing back up right to finish via the scoop and a delightful move. (1978)

22 Bad Joke 8m E4 5c   *
Take a direct line up the wall above the ledge on Electric Chair. Failure could be nasty but at least you may die laughing! (1979)

23 Gallows 8m E2 5b   *
Fine climbing up the arête to the right, started on the left
and finishing on the right. Direct on the right-hand side is
slightly easier, E1 5b.   (1978)

24 Recess Chimney 7m VD
There are two exits from the chimney to the right after a
common start.   (1957-1968)

25 Dog Eye Rib 8m E6 6b   *†
From the boulder in Recess Chimney, step right to climb the
rounded arête on its left-hand side by very rounded moves
on extremely rounded holds!   (1987)

26 The Sorcerer 8m E3 6a   *
Excellent. Starting just right of the right arête of the
chimney, boulder quickly up to the thin crack; protection
arrives too late for the hardest moves!   (1978)

27 High Tensile Crack 8m HVS 5a
The deceptive thin crack right again. A testing affair.   (1963)

28 Chockstone Crack 11m M
The obvious chimney almost in the corner and just before
the crag swings out onto the terrace beyond.   (1947-1951)

29 The Better End 11m E2 5c   **
Right again, a crack breaches the leaning wall. Climb the
crack to a ledge and a cramped rest. The remainder of the
crack gives an awesome struggle akin to laybacking up a
greasy pole.   (1963/1975)

30 The Raid 13m E4 6a
The second should take a belay! In the rounded arête to the
right is a broad scoop. Layback and smear energetically into
the scoop. A crack and easier ground appear before a move
left to a fine fluted headwall.   (1978)

*The cliff now swings round to present a superbly-featured
wall above a terrace.*

31 En Rappel 15m HVS 4c   *
On the front face of the buttress. Delightfully airy climbing
and a bold mantelshelf lead up the left edge of the wall until
moves rightwards gain a shallow chimney and a ledge.
Move rightwards to another chimney to finish. Moving left
and up before the final chimney provides a better but harder
(5a)alternative.   (1927/1961)

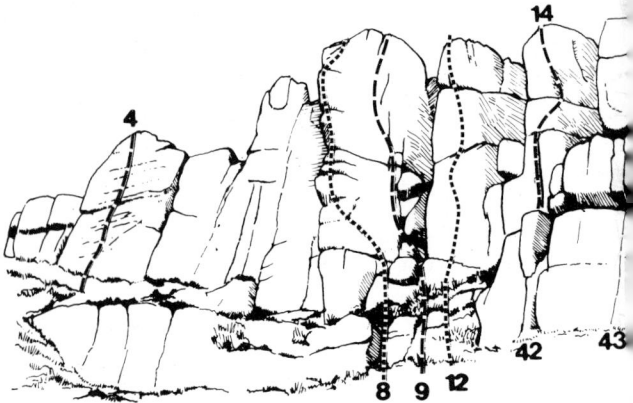

32 Caesarian 15m E4 6b ***
An outstanding test-piece accepting the central challenge of
the magnificent wall. Thin flakes lead slightly rightwards up
the centre of the wall to a break. Hard brisk pulls, easier for
the tall, lead up to a puzzling final crack. A cut above the rest.
(1978/1980)

33 Main Crack 15m VS 4b *
The wide crackline yields to a belly-roll and leg-kick
manoeuvre. More inhospitable for the larger climber.
(1951-1957)

34 Delstree 20m HVS 5a ***
A magnificent combination of delicate and strenuous
climbing, hence the name. Start at a lower level 8m right of
Main Crack. Move up a chimney and exit left onto a slab.
Cross this leftwards to the fine crack in the tower which

Philip Gibson.

Hen Cloud Left-hand End

provides a fitting conclusion. It is possible to gain the upper crack by a rightwards traverse from the foot of Main Crack.
(1957-1961)

35 Levitation 20m E3 6a   *
From the slab below Reunion Crack, and with protection above, move left to the arête and rise up, not right, to a flake finish. Quite good but only if the line is adhered to.
(1979)

36 Reunion Crack 20m VS 5a   **
Climb the chimney as for Delstree but exit direct up to the arching corner-crack. Layback quickly to better holds and the top.   (1957-1961)

To the right an easy line of ascent or descent, **Slab Way**, *Moderate, is obvious.*

37 The Pinch 20m E1 5c
The black tower to the right of Reunion Crack. From 6m up Slab Way, move left and climb up the right-hand side of the tower, threads, to the top break. Move left and make an alarming extension for the top. Completely impossible for the short, the grade is a compromise. (1978)

38 Fat Old Sun 50m E3 5c
A rather pointless traverse from the ledge on The Better End to the finish of The Pinch. Left, for the bent with a bent, to discover ad infinitum, ad libitum, ad nauseum! (1975/1978)

The next pair of routes lies on the terrace to the right of Slab Way *and can be used as top pitches to the routes below or as climbs in their own right. A large wall above a big ledge faces north-west.*

39 Quantas 8m E2 5c
The shallow groove and thin crack system in the left side of the wall. (1978)

40 Press on Regardless 10m E2 5b
From the break at 3m on Quantas, swing right to the arête. Climbed on its left side, this gives fine airy climbing; on its right it is escapable and perhaps not worthwhile. (1978)

At a lower level and directly below Electric Chair is a 10m-high, green wall often harbouring much seepage. When dry it gives:

41 Buster the Cat 8m HVS 5b
The innocuous green crack to the left of the main crack at the left-hand end of the buttress. This is not a good route. (1979)

42 Pug 8m VS 4c
The obvious main crack at the left end of the buttress finishing up a groove. (1968-1973)

43 The Stone Loach 10m E5 6b   **
Superb, when dry. Start below the roof-crack in the centre of the buttress. Boulder up then go right to reach a pod in a thin crack, good wire. Continue bouldering up the thin crack to the wide break. Either squirm right or struggle up the horrendous off-width. A must for the connoisseur of 10m-high, boulder problems! (1982)

Towards the right end of the wall is a box-shaped, shallow chimney.

44 Anthrax 13m E3 5c
Climb the green, thin crack in the left-hand arête of the
chimney with an awkward start to reach a ledge. Struggle
left along the break and finish via the awful roof-crack as
for The Stone Loach. (1975)

45 The Lum 10m HVS 4c
The box-shaped shallow chimney for the connoisseur of
'budge by an udge'. (1957-1968)

46 Bantam Crack 8m VS 4c
Pleasant jamming up the crack at the right-hand end of the
wall. Finish up a flake on the left. Walking off seems more
appropriate. (1957-1968)

*Returning to the area below and to the right of Delstree, an
extremely green, square wall is obvious to the right of Slab
Way.*

47 The Ape 11m E1 5b
The wide crack at the left side of the wall followed by a
'monkey' right via the flutings atop a large nestling block.
(1963)

48 The Monkey in Your Soul 15m E3 5c †
Mirrors The Ape. Climb the thin crack in the centre of the
green wall and traverse right along the break to finish up
the arête after a deviation to the right. (1978)

49 Broken Arrow 11m E1 5b
Start 6m right at the edge of the wall. A series of detached
(?) flakes lead to an impasse. Move right, then go back left
to climb the upper section of the arête. (1978)

50 Roof Climb 30m VS 4b,-
1. 20m. Climb a crack 5m to the right into a box-shaped
recess. Move right and go up via a groove, stepping back
left to continue up the wider groove to the terrace.
2. 10m. The straightforward block-filled chimney behind.
(1947-1951)

51 The Long and Short 25m E1 5b,5b
1. 15m. Starting from a grassy ledge 5m to the right and at
a slightly higher level, move into, and carefully go up, the
green groove above. Exit left and move up to the terrace.
2. 10m. Thrash frantically up the wide crack above, then exit
right and go up with relief. (early-1960s)

52 Anaconda 25m E4 6a,6a   *
This route snakes ungraciously up the green walls right of
The Long and Short. Better when clean.
1. 15m. Tackle the tight fingertip groove right of The Long
and Short to reach a small overhang. Pull left, then climb up
onto the green wall. Creep right to a flake, then go up it to
an unwelcoming exit.
2. 10m. Start at a thin crack and trend up leftwards towards
a black flake. Steep moves lead up to the finish of The Long
and Short.   (1976)

74

Philip Gibson.

60

59

58

Central Climb Area

53 Borstal Breakout 33m E4 4b,6a,6b   ***
Eminently more gracious than Anaconda, but unfortunately,
more often than not, no less lichenous. A tremendous and
audacious line. Start to the right of Anaconda and at a lower
level.
1. 8m. A crack leads to a belay ledge.
2. 15m. Climb the fine jamming crack until it ends at a
break. Move onto the wall above at the continuation crack
and where it fades make perplexing moves up to gain a
pocket. Move right, then go up to a sloping exit. Phew!
(1978)

3. 10m. A daunting problem. Starting as for Anaconda, continue straight up via a thin crack to a good ledge and an easier wall. (1980s)

54 Central Climb Direct 35m VS 4c,-,4a *
1. 15m. The awkward twisting crack to the right again. Continue up the next wide corner-crack to reach a ledge.
2. 10m. Climb the flake left of the corner to the top terrace.
3. 10m. Finish up the wide groove left of the top pitch of Central Climb. (1947-1951)

55 B4, XS 25m E7 6b **†
A major and substantial undertaking up the incredible arête forming the centrepiece of the main, front face. A thin, sustained and serious lead. From the first belay of Central Climb move out left, then go up onto the arête. Climb it moving onto its right side when necessary to gain obvious flutings and improving holds leading to the top. A Ferrari with the engine running (for the belayer) is essential, if parking space can be found! (1986)

To the right, a small cave lies at the foot of the crag. Right again, a large flake-crack provides the start to Central Climb, the classic route of the crag.

56 Standing Tall 33m E1 4c,4a,5a
1. 9m. Climb the rounded rib above the small cave. Belay on the first ledge.
2. 9m. Continue up the wall, using flakes, to the next ledge.
3. 15m. From 3m up the corner of Central Climb, move right to join Encouragement at the end of its difficulties. Climb the wall slightly to the left, first leftwards, then rightwards via a shallow groove. (1978)

57 Central Climb 36m HS 4a,-,-,- ***
A justifiably popular excursion up the front of the crag. Conquer the start and the remainder is sheer delight.
1. 9m. Climb the awkward and repellent flake-crack (hint: use holds inside) to reach sanctuary in the form of a belay ledge.
2. 8m. From the left end of the ledge, climb the corner to a second ledge.
3. 9m. Continue up another corner to the haven of the top terrace; a delightful place for lunch!
4. 10m. Finish by a saunter up the groove above exiting right to finish (or exit direct, slightly harder). (1909)

Directly below Central Climb lies a large boulder giving
excellent problems. The left arête and centre are 6a whilst
the right-hand side is 5c.

58 Encouragement 30m E1 5b,5b   ***
A fine groove is followed by a satisfying jamming crack; a
superbly balanced climb. Start below the hanging groove
just to the right of Central Climb.
1. 15m. Climb straight up the wall into the hanging groove.
Problematic bridging, followed by a positive pull, gains a
fine belay ledge.
2. 15m. Take the crack above with determination, then rush
for the final jugs. Finish easily up a shallow groove and a
ridge.   (early-1960s)

59 K2 30m S   *
1. 12m. Round to the right is a short steep corner which
leads up to a ledge.
2. 18m. The Y-shaped crack on the right is surprisingly
awkward and, not surprisingly, very polished. Climb this and
a groove above to gain the summit by an amble up the
obvious ridge.   (1927)

60 The Arête 30m VD   ***
Follow the excellent stepped ridge to the right. An awkward
move at half-height provides the crux and a
disproportionate amount of exposure for the grade.
       (pre-1913)

61 Arête Wall 18m HS 4a
The first crack encountered on the gully wall. From a block
move right and go up.   (1957-1968)

62 Easy Come 12m HS 4a
A thin crack 3m right again. Finish diagonally rightwards via
a slab onto The Arête.   (1978)

63 Easy Gully 35m M
The obvious broad boulder-strewn gully.   (1913-1927)

64 Songs of Praise 12m E1 5b   *
Wild. Undercut, then layback, the black flake on the right
wall of the upper reaches of the gully. Finish direct.   (1971)

65 Loose Fingers 9m E1 5c
An appalling pitch up the thin, dirty (understatement!), crack
3m right again.   (1980)

66 Prayers, Poems and Promises 11m E1 5b
Just to the right is an arête. Gain a ledge and continue to a large rounded hole. Exit awkwardly right and then up. Poorly-protected.   (1978)

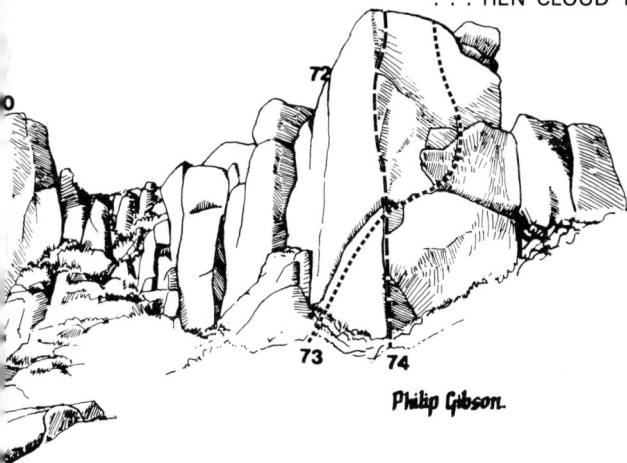

Philip Gibson.

The Amphitheatre

67 Modern 18m S   *
To the right again is a large flake. From a platform, follow
the flake and crack above to a ledge. Step right and climb an
awkward thin crack.   (1947-1951)

68 Flexure Line 18m HVS 6a
Start on a flat rock-ledge below a short smooth wall to the
right. Boulder out the wall and continue direct up the
rounded tower to gain the terrace. Finish up the right arête.
                                                       (1981)

69 Ancient 18m VD   *
Climb flakes almost in the gully to the right, again to the
terrace. Step left and finish up cracks.   (1947-1951)

70 Even Smaller Buttress 6m HVS 4c
The flakes on the left wall of the tower in the gully to the
right of Ancient. Pleasant.   (1985)

*To the right and up the hill, almost at the back of the
amphitheatre, is a large twin-faced block:* **BOW BUTTRESS**.

71 Small Buttress 6m HVS 5a
The even smaller buttress (!) in the gully just left of Bow
Buttress, taken on its front-face via the right arête.   (1979)

72 Bitching 7m E1 5b
The thin crack in the narrow left face of Bow Buttress. All
difficulties lie within the initial 3m. (1978)

73 Bow Buttress 8m VD
Spirals round the large twin-faced block. Starting on the left
wall, move right round the arête and go up by means of a
vandalised flake. (1924)

74 Solid Geometry 8m E1 5b *
Start below the arête. Gain the flake and continue up the
perfectly-formed arête by a series of fine postures to an
inelegant finish. (1980)

*The long tapering wall to the right offers probably the finest
collection of hard routes on the crag. The climber must have
a determined approach to be well-rewarded here.*

Problems on the shorter left-hand section of the wall are
plentiful. A ramp with a rightward exit gives a good 5a
problem whilst the small veins right again give a 5c
bouldering gem.

75 Stokesline 6m E2 6b
The first faint crackline towards the left-hand end of the
wall. A hideous start often made more difficult by the
greenness of the holds/non-holds. (1977)

76 This Poison 8m E3 6b *
Negotiate the bald wall 2m right by way of an appalling
rockover and a thin pebble pull. From the break finish
slightly leftwards. (1981)

77 Slimline 9m E1 5b
The next crackline is less subtle and provides balancy moves
with a gruelling finale. (1957-1961)

*The wall to the right sports a peculiar flake which is said to
resemble a hedgehog from various directions.*

78 Fast Piping 11m E4 6b **
Steep bouldering moves lead past a small undercut and faint
crack to the 'hedgehog' flake. Teeter carefully up to gain an
awkward prickly crack. (1981)

79 Hedgehog Crack 11m VS 4b **
The vertical widening crack just to the right gives a
non-prickly affair thanks to many years of wear.
(1947-1951)

*The wall now bows out once again. A crack splits its
left-hand side but fades out 5m above the ground.*

80 Comedian 12m E3 6a   **
Start below the obvious crack. Steep moves lead rightwards
to the obvious horizontal break, then an awkward
manoeuvre left gains the crack. Romp up this, then tackle
the bulge above to finish up an entertaining groove.   (1976)

81 Frayed Nerve 13m E5 6a   *
Two metres right again. Good holds in a shallow groove
enable the break to be gained, large nut runner. Sprint
quickly and positively up the wall above to a rounded little
groove. An enigmatic solution to a fine wall.   (1982)

82 Second's Retreat 15m HVS 4c
'Fine, if you like that sort of thing'. The green and gruesome
V-shaped groove to the right.   (1957)

83 Second's Advance 15m HVS 5a   *
The large bulge to the right of Second's Retreat is gained
direct and overcome by means of a crack and surprise jug.
    (1963)

84 Corinthian 17m E3 5c   **
Gain a faint bulging crack (complete with an old peg
runner!) just to the right and grapple with its roundedness
for success.   (1976)

85 Hen Cloud Eliminate 18m HVS 5b   **
Not an eliminate! A great pitch. Climb the awesome wide
fissure just right again to a renowned hazard; the
nose-grinding finish!   (1957-1961)

86 Cool Fool 20m E5 6b   **
Technical and superb. Start just left of the foot of the large
chimney. A faint groove leads to a boulder in the chimney.
Climb the arête on the left until holds allow protection to be
arranged in the crack on the right. Step back to the arête
and battle for every hold... and hopefully the top.   (1982)

87 Rib Chimney 20m HVD 4a   *
An awkward start gains the chimney. Bridge it gracefully or
struggle within its depths by a strenuous breast stroke.
    (pre-1913)

88 Rib Crack 20m VS 4c   *
The thin crack in the upper left wall of the chimney. An
elegant piece of esoteria.   (1963)

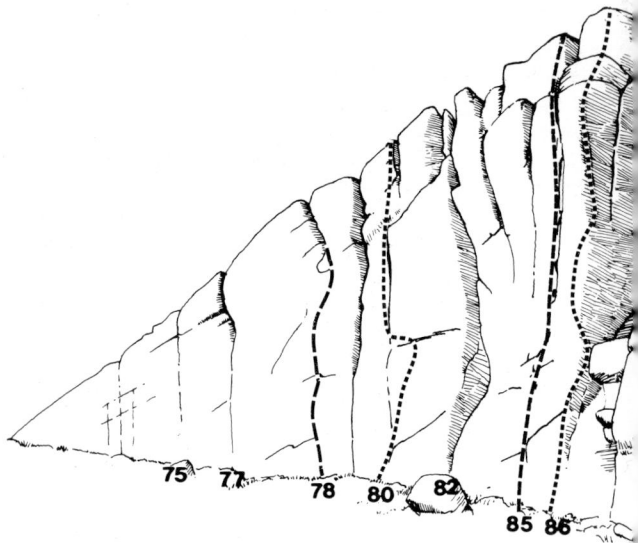

89 Caricature 22m E5 6a ***

Tortuous in line but absorbing throughout, this route tackles the headwall right of Rib Chimney. From 5m up the main chimney encroach delicately onto the wall via two small holes to a respite and a good flake runner. Use the flake to begin the wall above and progress direct with boldness and care, on rounded holds. (1976)

90 Chiaroscuro 27m E5 6a **†

An audacious eliminate 'twixt light and shade'. From the top of the thin bulging crack on Batchelor's Left-hand, step left and balance up the faint right arête of the gully to a junction with Caricature and easy ground. Move right, arrange a runner in the wide crack and climb the centre of the headwall moving left to a faint crack, then go up. Inspection advised. (1985)

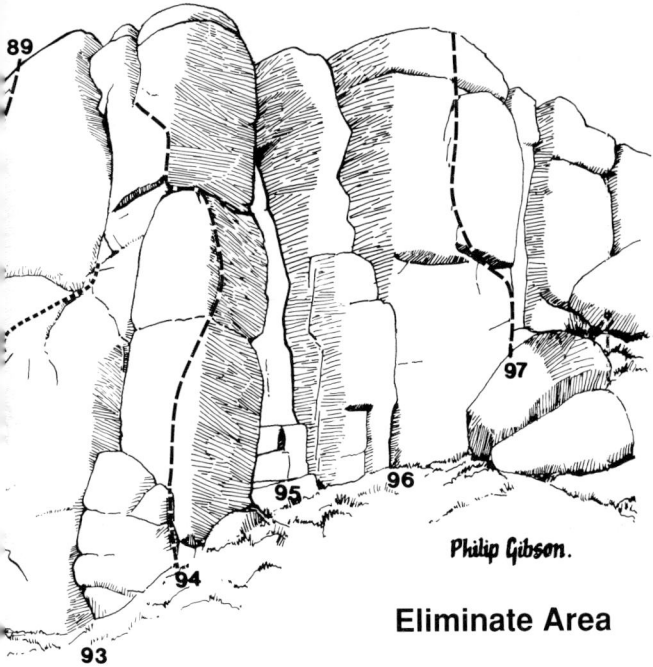

Philip Gibson.

Eliminate Area

91 Bachelor's Left-hand 25m HVS 5a   ***
A super-classic taking a beautifully varied line up the
highest part of the buttress. Gain the thin bulging crack 3m
right of Rib Chimney by a surprisingly awkward move and at
its end move right onto a flake. Reach a huge jug above via
a welcome pocket, then teeter right on a slab and move up
to finish via the wide cumbersome crack above. A legacy of
Whillans in brilliant form.   (1957-1961)

92 Parallel Lines 25m E6 6c   **†
A desperate encounter with the smooth wall to the right. A
side-runner in the initial crack of Batchelor's Left-hand is
of little assistance. Climb the initial thin crack and use two
poor layaways and an even poorer 'edge' to gain a slight
ramp and easier ground. Profoundly technical.   (1985)

93 Bachelor's Climb 27m VS 4b ✱✱
More classic stuff. Climb the fluted crack at the right-hand
end of the wall, past a ledge, to reach a fine pulpit stance.
Finish up Great Chimney round the corner or, better, step
back down and traverse left to the finishing crack of
Batchelor's Left-hand. (pre-1947)

94 Space Probe 20m E4 6a,5c ✱✱
Just round to the right is an immaculate arête bounding the
left-hand edge of a magnificent chimney.
1. 12m. Elegant climbing up the arête first on its left side to
the break, difficult protection, then on the arête proper leads
to the fine pulpit stance.
2. 8m. **The Helter Skelter** finish. Move up the left arête
above, then swing boldly out left (no mats!) to thankfully
reach easier climbing up a shallow groove. (1979/1977)

95 Great Chimney 18m S ✱✱✱
The magnificently formed chimney. Numerous variations
exist, including either corner direct or full bridging for its
entirety. The usual way is to climb the left corner to the
pulpit then to transfer to the right corner for the upper
section. Getting jammed in the wide corner-crack is not a
good idea! (1913)

96 Rainbow Crack 18m VS 5a ✱✱
The fine airy flake-corner in the right wall of Great
Chimney. Gain it via either of the cracks below. Take your
Friends! (1947-1951)

*The next route lies to the right and at a higher level, starting
below a similar, but smaller, chimney to that of Great
Chimney.*

97 Chameleon 12m E4 6a ✱✱
The varying opinions on the grade of this route adequately
match the changing colours of the lizard. Move up just left
of the left arête of the chimney, easier for the tall, and
undercut quickly left to a jug on the lip of the overhang.
Lurch frantically over, harder for the tall, then sprint more
easily, for all heights, up the disjointed flake. (1977)

98 Sauria 9m E3 5c †
The arête right of Chameleon. (1986)

99 Left Twin Crack 9m HS 4a
The left corner of the short, square chimney. Full-width bridging is impossible here and stilts are not for hire!
(1957-1968)

100 Right Twin Crack 9m VS 4b
The right corner of the chimney. Spectacular for the grade.
(1957-1968)

Continuing along the path below the crag for 30m brings one to a chimney.

101 Footpath Chimney 18m VD
1. 8m. The chimney with an awkward bulge.
2. 12m. Scramble over blocks and finish up an arête.
(pre-1913)

Still farther on, about 20m, lies **THOMPSON'S BUTTRESS**, *bounded to the right by a series of steps.*

102 Thompson's Buttress Route One 15m S   *
Climb the corner-crack in the centre of the buttress and finish up a crack.
(pre-1913)

103 Thompson's Buttress Route Two 15m VD
The obvious steps on the right-hand side of the buttress are followed by a wide crack above.
(pre-1913)

104 Tree Chimney 15m HVD
The chimney right again. An awkward section is passed to the right.
(pre-1913)

105 Tunnel Vision 12m HVS 5a
The face right of Tree Chimney. Climb it at its centre without escaping to the right.
(1979)

Right again, across a broad grassy gully, a large rounded buttress gives **THE INACCESSIBLE PINNACLE.**

106 Cold Sweat 8m E2 5b
The wall just left of the left arête of the buttress. Good climbing but escapable throughout.
(1979)

The front face of the pinnacle is composed of a smaller block leaning up against the main face.

107 Pinnacle Face 12m VS 4b   *
Climb the left side of the block to a small crack on the face behind. Move up this and the left-hand side of the face via small wrinkles, to finish up another short crack. (1947-1951)

108 Face Value 12m HVS 5a   *
Quite bold. Climb the front face of the subsidiary block via a
black flake to its top. Continue direct up the slabby wall
above by pleasant and delicate face-climbing.   (1978)

109 Pinnacle Rib 11m VS 5a
Awkward. Climb the crack on the right side of the block and
continue up the bulging arête.   (1957-1968)

110 Delusion 8m HS 4a
On the southern side of the pinnacle. Climb a groove and
skirt right, then go back left to the summit.   (1979)

111 Short Side 4m S
The back-side of the pinnacle. Surprisingly stiff. Descent is
by this route or a jump.   (1947-1951)

*Thirty metres to the right and slightly round the hillside, the
next buttress is divided by two gullies and presents three
rounded facets.*

112 Shoe Shine Shuffle 8m HVS 5b
The crack on the left side of the first facet. Step right and
belly-flop onto the top.   (1979)

113 Diagonal Route 12m VD   *
The pleasant slanting crack on the front face.   (1957-1968)

114 Triumph of the Good City 11m HVS 5b   *
Start round to the right at a small cave. Surmount the roof
of the cave and continue up the arête.   (1979)

115 Jellyfish 8m E4 5c
Wobble up the slippery slanting ramp on the left wall of the
first gully. Not for the timid.   (1979)

116 Pete's Back-side 7m VS 5a
The peculiar runnel on the front face of the next facet. Gain
it from the left.   (1979)

117 Central Tower 8m VD
Climb the narrow slabby face right again.   (1968-1973)

118 The Nutcracker 8m S 4a
The wide cumbersome crack just to the right. Large runners
should be carried well out of the way!   (pre-1913)

119 Heart of Gold 10m E2 5c   *
A gem of a pitch. Climb the clean arête of the final facet to
an unusual hole. Exit cautiously and reach the sloping top
with some relief.   (1976)

120 The Deceiver 7m VS 4b
The 'harder-than-it-looks' crack on the south face.
(pre-1913)

121 Touch 7m E4 6c   *
Hideously thin climbing on 'smears' up the micro-wall to
the right. Brilliant, but ferociously technical, bouldering. (1985)

*Fifty metres in front of Diagonal Route, and at a lower level,
is another lower tier.*

122 Hal's Ridge 11m VD
The broken ridge towards the left-hand side of the buttress.
(1962)

123 Short-man's Misery 9m HVS 5a
The prominent arête to the right is taken on its left-hand
side. A long reach will help. (1976)

124 Crispin's Crack 11m VS 4c
Climb a thin crack on the front face to a slab. Step right and
finish up the arête. (1962)

125 Duck Soup 9m E1 5a
The faint ramp right again. Finish as for Crispin's Crack.
(1978)

*The buttresses to the right provide several excellent
problems, often cloaked in pine needles. Needless to say,
these are best left to the connoisseur, though a sharp arête
and curving cracks give a good problem at 5b.*

*At a higher level again, but farther round the hillside, the
buttresses begin to reappear.*

126 Last View 6m VD
The small face to the left of the chimney, on the front face
of the first buttress encountered. (1978)

127 The Weirdy 11m VD
Start at the foot of the buttress right again. Move up past a
strange hole via a ramp to reach a ledge. Move left and
finish right of the chimney. (1968-1973)

*Fifty metres on again, the final buttress worthy of
description presents a large overhang above a block on the
ground.*

128 High Energy Plan 8m HVS 5a
Breach the roof direct and finish hastily on crisp rock. (1979)

129 Shortbread 10m HVS 5a
Start 3m right again. Move up to a groove, then traverse left
to black flakes and finish directly over a dirty bulge.   (1969)

130 Shortcake 8m E1 5b
Appalling finishing holds. From the groove on Shortbread,
finish slightly rightwards via a short diagonal crack. Don't
snatch for any straws.   (1976)

131 Gingerbread 6m HS 4a
Delicate climbing up the centre of the face to the right. (1976)

132 Ginger Biscuit 8m VS 4b
The obvious arête to the right gives pleasant climbing. (1976)

*It goes without saying that the buttresses farther right offer
innumerable boulder problems. However, due to the nature
of the lichen this wil probably remain a rarely used
bouldering ground. Then again.....*

HEN CLOUD LIST OF FIRST ASCENTS

1909	**Central Climb** John Laycock (unseconded) *A direct finish was added in 1927.*
1913	**Great Chimney** Siegfried Herford, Stanley Jeffcoat
Pre-1913	**The Arête, Rib Chimney, Footpath Chimney, Thompson's Buttress, Tree Chimney, The Nutcracker, The Deceiver** *The latter two routes were known as Hall Cracks 'A' and 'B' respectively. 'Exceedingly destructive to the climber's well-cut tweeds' – Rucksack Club Journal.*
1924	**Bow Buttress**
1913-1927	**The Aiguillette, Easy Gully**
1927	**November Cracks, K2, En Rappel** Arthur Burns *En Rappel was known as Blizzard Buttress until an ascent by Joe Brown.*
1947	**Bachelor's Climb**
1947-1951	**Hedgehog Crack, Rainbow Crack, Chockstone Crack, Chockstone Chimney, Roof Climb, Central Climb Direct, Modern, Ancient, Pinnacle Face, Short Side** *'Hedgehog Crack is beset with thorny problems, all of which can be solved if the hands can be persuaded to stay jammed' – 1951 guidebook.*
1951	*Climbs on Gritstone, Volume 3, published.*

1952 May	**Bachelor's Climb (left-hand finish), Second's Retreat** Joe Brown and party
1957-1961	**Main Crack, Delstree, Reunion Crack, Slimline, Hen Cloud Eliminate** Joe Brown
1957-1961	**Bachelor's Left-Hand** Don Whillans
Early-1960s	**Encouragement, The Long and Short, Chicken** Tony Nicholls
1962	**Second's Advance, Hal's Ridge, Crispin's Crack, Rib Crack** Bob Hassall
1962	**High Tensile Crack** Colin Foord
1962	**The Ape** Pete Ruddle
1962	**The Bitter End** (1 pt.) Dave Salt *Climbed free in 1975 by John Allen and Steve Bancroft.*
1957-1968	**Piston Groove, Victory, Green Corner, Lum, Bantam Crack, Arête Wall, Left Twin Crack, Right Twin Crack, Pinnacle Rib, Diagonal Route, Recess Chimney** *All of these routes appeared uncredited in the 1968 guidebook.*
1968	*Rock Climbs on The Roaches and Hen Cloud published.*
1969 May	**Shortbread** John Yates
1971 April	**Songs of Praise** John Yates
1968-1973	**Little Pinnacle Climb, The Notch, Pug, Central Tower**
1973	*Staffordshire Gritstone Area guide, Rock Climbs in the Peak, Volume 9, published.*
1974 Aug. 18	**Fat Old Sun** (1 pt.) John Allen, Steve Bancroft (AL) *Climbed free in 1978 by Steve Bancroft and Dave Humphries (AL).*
1975 Summer	**The Better End** John Allen, Steve Bancroft *First free ascent of The Bitter End, renamed from a spelling mistake in Crags magazine.*
1975 July 27	**Anthrax** Steve Bancroft, John Allen (AL)
1976 Feb. 26	**Comedian** Steve Bancroft, John Allen *Started on the right where Frayed Nerve now starts. The described start was climbed by Dave Jones in 1980.*
1976 June 20	**Heart of Gold** Nick Colton, Con Carey, Jim Campbell, John Tout
1976 June 20	**Short-man's Misery, Shortcake** Jim Campbell, Con Carey, John Tout, Nick Colton
1976 June 20	**Gingerbread, Ginger Biscuit** Con Carey, Nick Colton, John Tout, Jim Campbell

1976	**Corinthian** Steve Bancroft, John Allen
1976	**Caricature** John Allen, Steve Bancroft
1976	**Anaconda** John Gosling
1977 July 16	**Chameleon** Steve Bancroft, Nicky Stokes, Al Manson
1977	**Helter Skelter** Steve Bancroft, Al Manson
1977	**Stokesline** Mark Stokes *Named in absentia.*
1978 April 2	**Slowhand** Dave Jones, Roger Bennion, Gary Gibson
1978 April 2	**Electric Chair** Jim Moran, Simon Horrox, Geoff Milburn, Dave Jones, Roger Bennion
1978 April 2	**Nutted by Reality, Pullet** Simon Horrox (solo)
1978 April 2	**Gallows** Jim Moran, Geoff Milburn, Simon Horrox
1978 April 2	**Face Value** Gary Gibson (solo)
1978 April 5	**Short 'n Sharp** Dave Jones, Ian 'Hots' Johnson, Gary Gibson
1978 April 16	**Easy Come** Al Evans, Geoff Milburn
1978 April 17	**Borstal Breakout** Jim Moran, Al Evans, Simon Horrox *A day off work was needed as the route had been cleaned but not completed on the Sunday. Top-roped first by Simon Horrox on April 4. It was erroneously assumed for some time that Jim Moran et al had completed both pitches. The second pitch was actually climbed by Dave Jones with a nut for aid in 1978. The route in its described form remained unclimbed until after the production of the last guidebook which had described a free ascent! It had certainly been led clean by 1983 but who actually made the first complete free ascent will probably remain a bone of contention.*
1978 April	**The Monkey in Your Soul** Al Simpson, John Holt
1978 April	**Prayers, Poems and Promises** Al Simpson, Dave Jones
1978 April	**Duck Soup** Al Evans
1978 May 17	**Bitching** Gary Gibson, Kons Nowak
1978 May 17	**The Pinch** John Holt, Dave Jones
1978 May 17	**Broken Arrow** Dave Jones, John Holt
1978 May 20	**Fat Old Sun** Steve Bancroft, Dave Humphries (AL) *First free ascent.*
1978 May	**The Raid, The Sorcerer** Jim Moran, Al Evans
1978 May	**Quantas, Press on Regardless** Dave Jones, Al Simpson
1978 May	**Zoom Wall** Dave Jones (solo)

1978 June	**Caesarian** Martin Berzins, Bob Berzins *This was with a deviation to the left, avoiding the main difficulties. Climbed direct by Jonny Woodward in September 1980.*
1979 Feb. 25	**Space Probe** Jonny Woodward, Ian Maisey *Pre-placed runners were used in the break. These were eliminated in 1980 by Gary Gibson.*
1979 April 5	**Triumph of the Good City**, **Last View** Gary Gibson (solo)
1979 May 29	**The Mandrake** Jonny Woodward (unseconded) *'I placed runners in Victory, level with the overhang, but these are probably unnecessary since when a hold broke off from the flake I hit the deck despite the runners.'*
1979 June 7	**Cold Sweat** Gary Gibson (solo)
1979 June 10	**High Energy Plan** Gary Gibson, Phil Gibson
1979 June 10	**Shoe Shine Shuffle** Phil Gibson, Gary Gibson
1979 June 10	**Jellyfish** Gary Gibson, Phil Gibson *Top-roped first. On the second ascent Gary Gibson slipped from the crux, stripped a crucial wire and landed almost in Dave Jones' lap!*
1979 June 12	**Bad Joke** Gary Gibson, Ian Barker *Top-roped first. The ground was well-padded with clothing for the expected retreat.*
1979 July	**Levitation** Phil Burke (unseconded)
1979	**Slipstreams, Buster the Cat, Standing Tall, Tunnel Vision, Delusion** Dave Jones *All climbed during guidebook work.*
1980 Sept. 14	**Loose Fingers** Gary Gibson (solo)
1980 June	**Solid Geometry** Dave Jones (solo)
1981	*Staffordshire Area guidebook, Rock Climbs in the Peak Volume 6, published.*
1981 June 28	**Blood Blisters** Gary Gibsons (unseconded) *Top-roped first.*
1981 July 4	**Fast Piping** Gary Gibson, Jon Walker *The upper crack had been climbed previously as a variation to Hedgehog Crack.*
1981 July 5	**Flexure Line** Gary Gibson, Jon Walker
1981 July 7	**This Poison** Gary Gibson (solo) *Top-roped earlier. The route originally finished by a traverse off to the right. The direct finish was first climbed by Gary Gibson in 1983.*

1981 Aug. 10   **Chicken Direct** Gary Gibson, Rob Davies
Top-roped first.

1982 Aug. 2   **Cool Fool** Gary Gibson (unseconded)
Top-roped many times previously. The lower arête had been climbed as Charisma by Nick Postlethwaite in 1980.

1982 Aug. 12   **The Stone Loach** Gary Gibson (solo)
A long sling was clipped into a wire in the pod to protect the crux moves which had been practised extensively on an abseil rope.

1982 Aug. 17   **Frayed Nerve** Gary Gibson (unseconded)

1983 Sept. 22   **Master of Reality** Simon Nadin (unseconded)
The lower front face was climbed a few days later.

1984 Sept. 26   **Mindbridge** Simon Nadin (solo)
Top-roped first.

1985 April 18   **Chiaroscuro** Gary Gibson (unseconded)
Top-roped first.

1985 April 18   **Even Smaller Buttress** Gary Gibson (solo)

1985 July 31   **Touch** Simon Nadin (solo)

1985 Aug. 3   **Parallel Lines** Simon Nadin (unseconded)
Top-roped first.

1986 May 16   **Starlight and Storm** John Allen, Martin Veale

1986 June 6   **B4, XS** Simon Nadin (unseconded)

1986 Oct. 10   **Sauria** Martin Boysen (unseconded)

1987 May 6   **Dog Eye Rib** Andy Popp (solo)
Top-roped first.

RAMSHAW ROCKS

O.S. ref. SK 019622

by Richard Davies

> *'It is peculiar in that it really consists of three feet of 6b smearing in a very dangerous position.'*
>
> Nick Dixon, talking about Handrail Direct, 1986.

SITUATION and CHARACTER

The rocks run roughly north-east to south-west overlooking the A53, Leek-to-Buxton road, about 6km from Leek and 12km from Buxton. The escarpment forms an exposed and jagged ridge of rough natural gritstone which has been eroded by the elements over the years into a multitude of curious-looking buttresses and pinnacles.

The ridge catches even the slightest breeze which dries the rocks rapidly. Unfortunately, being shaded from the sun for the greater part of the day, there is a vigorous growth of lichen and unpopular routes rapidly return to their more natural-coloured state.

The short height of the climbs and inward dip of the strata favour climbers with powerful forearms, though the large profusion of overhangs and cracks infested with razor-sharp pebbles often cause unfavourable first impressions. For the persistent there are many pleasant surprises hidden along the edge, not least the numerous esoteric boulder problems. Although lacking the intense development and difficulty of The Roaches, the boulder problems have an isolated charm all of their own and it is rare to have to queue at the base of the crag for a route.

APPROACHES and ACCESS

The PMT X23 bus service between Hanley and Sheffield runs along the A53 approximately every two hours. The closest official stop is some distance from the edge at The Royal Cottage but on polite request the driver will usually make a special stop for passengers. The best car parking is on the grassy verge of the A53 directly beneath the rocks. Otherwise the short lane dividing the edge at its western end provides just enough room for a few vehicles. Be sensible not to block either the road or the entrance to farms farther up the lane.

The main crag is owned by Harper Crewe Estates and there are no access problems except for the 'Winking Eye' which

has been vandalised in the past. Climbers have been asked to **AVOID THE ROUTES ON THIS UNIQUE GRITSTONE FORMATION** to preserve it in its present state. The Lady Stone is on private land and climbers should seek permission to climb on it from the farm 150m to the north-east.

THE CLIMBS are described from LEFT to RIGHT.

One hundred and forty metres west of the lane dividing the edge is a curious pinnacle with three routes:

1 East Face 6m M
Climb the slab moving left to a notch and the top. (pre-1973)

2 After Eight 7m S
Climb directly up the wall to the nose on the south-east corner.   (1979)

3 Southern Crack 7m VD
A crack on the left is gained by rounded holds and leads to an awkward pull onto the fluted top.   (pre-1973)

Scoop, 3a, takes the shallow groove left of After Eight, **Playaway**, 5a, the layback crack to the left, **The Whale**, 6a, uses the mouth and eye to gain the brow 2m to the left and **Shallow Run**, 4a, takes a shallow runnel round the corner.

Philip Gibson.

11   13   15

Loaf and Cheese

The remaining climbs are all to the east of the lane. After 35m the edge begins with an unusual pinnacle known as **THE LOAF AND CHEESE**.

4 Assembled Techniques 8m E5 6a
Climb the front face of The Loaf and Cheese pinnacle with a difficult move to reach a flake. Finish using a hold on the left arête. A good sequence of moves.   (1986)

5 Loaf and Cheese 11m VS 4c
Near the right arête of the face is a slanting crack: this proves more than awkward and leads to a shelf. Scramble to the top of the pinnacle up either the front or the back face.
(pre-1973)

6 Dream Fighter 8m E3 6a
Across the gully. Climb the arête left of the green groove of Green Crack to the break; this point can also be by-passed to the right. Traverse left on the break until it is possible to pull onto the finishing slab.   (1984)

7 Green Crack 8m VS 5b
The green groove and wide thrutchy crack through the bulge. Precarious despite the chockstone.   (1972)

8 National Acrobat 9m E4 6c †
Climb the desperate blind crack/runnel through the bulge to the right. At the time of writing, still awaiting a second ascent. (1978)

9 Traveller in Time 11m E4 6a **
Just to the right is a hanging flake. Climb this and from its top swing left onto a jug. Mantelshelf onto this and scamper left across the scoop to an ungainly finish. (1977)

10 Body Pop 11m E4 6b *
From the top of the flake on Traveller in Time, move right to the arête and layback the rounded edge in a spectacular fashion. (1984)

11 Wall and Groove 9m VD
Go up under the prow left of the arête to the right, moving right to gain a ledge (or gain it direct; easier). Finish up the chimney which is harder than it looks. (pre-1973)

12 The Arête 9m S
Climb the overhang on large holds to reach the ledge. The rib above is hardest to start and succumbs to layaway or 'a cheval' technique. (pre-1973)

13 Louie Groove 8m E1 5b *
Climb the square-cut groove to the right. Over the years the holds have gradually eroded to make this an intimidating lead. (1968)

14 Leeds Slab 8m HS
Ascend the centre of the cutaway to finish up the notched rib. (1980)

15 Leeds Crack 6m D
The crack right of the slab provides introductory hand-jamming. (pre-1973)

16 Honest Jonny 6m D
The pleasant groove right again. (1976)

Fifteen metres right and higher up is a blunt-nosed pinnacle with a thin crooked crack on its front face.

17 The Undertaker 6m E2 6a
A grave problem up the finger-wrecking crack with a monster reach for the wider slot above. (1973/1976)

Pink Flake, 4c, is the flake in the wall to the right, gained from the right. **Pink Flake Direct**, 5a, gains the flake direct. **Mantel**, 4c, pulls onto the rounded shelf farther right and continues up the wall.

18 Overdrive 7m E3 5c
Up to the right is a small buttress with a triangular roof on the left. Climb the roof on its left-hand side. (1977)

19 Twin Cracks 6m D
The left-hand crack is slightly easier to a finish up the groove. (pre-1973)

20 Double Chin 6m S
Three metres right again, the rounded prow and friable nose above. (1973-1981)

21 Prowler 6m HVS 4c
Climb the roof to the right at its widest point and finish up the prow. (1973-1981)

Right again is a buttress with a prominent recessed crack to its left. Round the arête to its left are:

Equilibria, 4c, is a pad up the groove and **Steeper**, 4c, is the shorter, steeper groove just to the left.

22 The Great Zawn 8m HVS 5a   *
Climb the wide mean crack. For the tall a good hold at the top aids extraction. For the short a diabolical move still remains. (1950-1965)

23 Broken Groove 8m M
Start to the left of the crack on the buttress front. Gain the ledge and continue up the groove. (pre-1973)

24 Broken Groove Arête 8m D
The arête to the right. (pre-1973)

Ten metres right, beyond a double V-shaped gully, two prominent cracks breach a tiered overhang.

25 Gully Arête 6m E1 5c
Climb the steep arête in the gully on its right-hand side. The final upper arête is easier. Avoid all easier alternatives. (1986)

26 Wellingtons 8m VD
The wide left-hand crack is climbed direct or started up the slab on the left. 'Wellies' help overcome the crack but not the slab! (pre-1973)

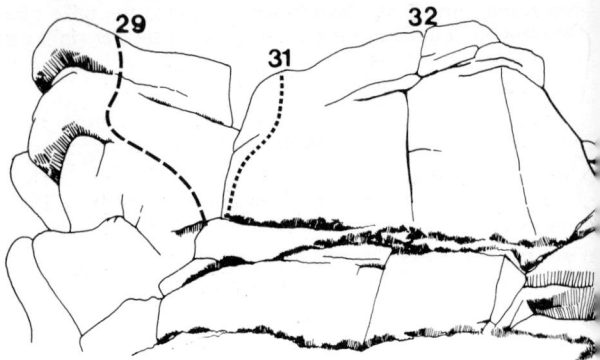

27 Masochism 9m HVS 5b
Traditionally 5a, the initial crack will halt almost everyone.
The upper crack is simply awkward and strenuous!

(1950-1965)

28 Trivial Traverse 6m HVS 5a
Traverse along the side-wall of the buttress using the
horizontal break to a foothold, then go up. Interesting. (1977)

29 T'rival Traverse 6m E2 6a   *†
Start from a ledge below the start of Trivial Traverse, runners
in the break above and right. Traverse delicately leftwards at
the limits of adhesion to gain a thin flake. Make an airy
mantelshelf to the left of this and finish direct.   (1987)

30 Rock Trivia 5m E2 6c   †
The right-hand side of the Trivial Traverse wall has a
desperate start but it is fortunately possible to place runners
above your head!   (1987)

To the right is a smooth wall above a grassy terrace.

31 Sneeze 6m E1 5b   *
Layback the left edge of the wall to reach the incipient crack
system above.   (1979)

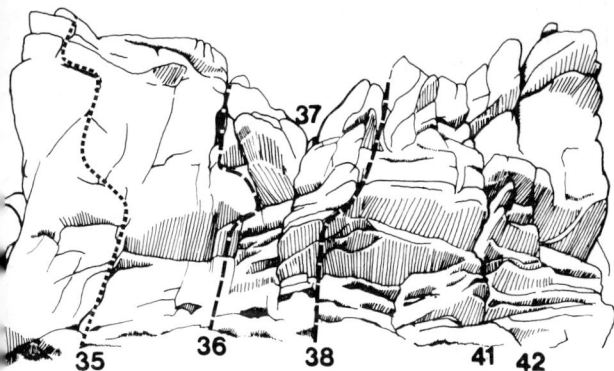

Philip Gibson.

South Buttress

32 The Crank 6m VS 5a   *
The short impressive crack in the right centre of the wall
gives perfect jamming to a struggle after its zigzag right. A
start up the shallow green groove in the lower wall is
available for the connoisseur.   (1950-1965)

The crag now reaches its full height at **SOUTH BUTTRESS**, *a
towering wall bounded on its left by a chimney.*

33 Chockstone Chimney 8m VD
The chimney eases after the battle with the chockstone.
                                              (pre-1973)

34 Maximum Hype 10m E3 5c   *
The prow above Chockstone Crack. Move out right to a
layaway flake and finish on the arête.   (1987)

35 Gumshoe 14m E2 5c   **
Ascend the shallow groove in the impending wall to the
right to reach a ledge. Move left and go up the wall
finishing leftwards with a long reach. Exhilarating climbing
with juggy surprises. A right-hand finish is also available
which moves right after the traditional crux, **Wine Gums**, E4
6a.   (1977/1985)

36 Tally Not 14m HVS 5c
The wall to the right has two hanging corners. Gain the lower corner from the left and with a quick 'udge' and a swing left reach the second, higher corner. This still requires care.   (1968/1972)

37 Battle of the Bulge 9m VS 4b   *
The prominent bulging crack right again. More elegant than a battle.   (pre-1973)

38 The Cannon 13m HS 4a   *
Some flakes 1m right again lead via a crack/groove to 'the cannon'. Finish direct.   (pre-1973)

39 Torture 12m E4 5c   *
The centre of the tiered overhang to the right on sandy holds. Fulfills its name only if you fall off!   (1981)

40 Whilly's Whopper 12m VS 4c
Just left of Phallic Crack is a slight hanging groove above the initial overhangs. Pull into this from the right, move left up the slab and pull round the 'Bobby's Helmet' to finish.
                                                                        (1979)

41 Phallic Crack 12m HVD   **
The steep chimney-crack, the line of the buttress, is climbed past a rock prow/phallus at 4m. A classic requiring numerous techniques to achieve success.   (pre-1973)

42 Alcatraz 12m E1 5b   *
Just right is a corner capped by an overhang. Follow this, pull round the overhang and then escape up the crack on its right-hand side. Sparse protection.   (1968)

Round to the right is an obvious corner, the left wall of which gives:

43 The Untouchable 11m E1 5b   **
Gain the crack from the right via a flexible flake; a long reach helps. Esoteric jamming eases towards the top. Much more pleasant since the invention of the camming device.
                                                                        (1968)

44 Corner Crack 8m S 4a
Traditionally harder than it looks.   (pre-1973)

45 The Rippler 8m VS 5a ✳

Use the veins on the small buttress to the right to reach a tiny ledge at mid-height. Move right to finish using carved holds. Careful use of the ripples will maintain the route's delightful nature. (pre-1973)

Rippler Direct, 6a, gains the ledge from just left of the left-hand arête.

46 Cold Wind 6m E2 5c

Climb the small arête to the right taking care not to use the boulder on the right. (1984)

Below and to the right is a smooth undercut face penetrable only at either end.

Midge, 6a, takes the bulge and twin cracks at the left-hand end and **Cleg**, 5a, the hanging groove at the right-hand end.

Farther right at a lower level, and much closer to the road, is **THE LOWER TIER.**

47 Crab Walk 15m S 4a

Start near the centre of the buttress and climb into a scoop. An ascending traverse leads leftwards to a crack leading past the left-hand end of the upper overhangs. (pre-1973)

48 Brown's Crack 14m E1 5b ✳✳

Master the roof-crack directly above the Crab Walk start. (1950-1965)

49 Prostration 14m HVS 5a ✳✳

This route takes the stunted crack 3m right of Brown's Crack. Climb straight up to the roof where a tricky move to gain an upright posture overcomes the short wall. (1950-1965)

50 Colly Wobble 11m E4 6b ✳✳†

Just to the right of Prostration is a square hanging wall, the site of four holes, the remnants of an old plaque. Climb the hanging wall with a very long reach. Protection is in the form of a half-sized tri-cam in one of the holes. (1987)

51 Don's Crack 11m HVS 5b ✳

Four metres right again, almost at the end of the buttress, a crack splits the overhang. Climb it on widely-spaced jams which require equally wide hands. (1950-1965)

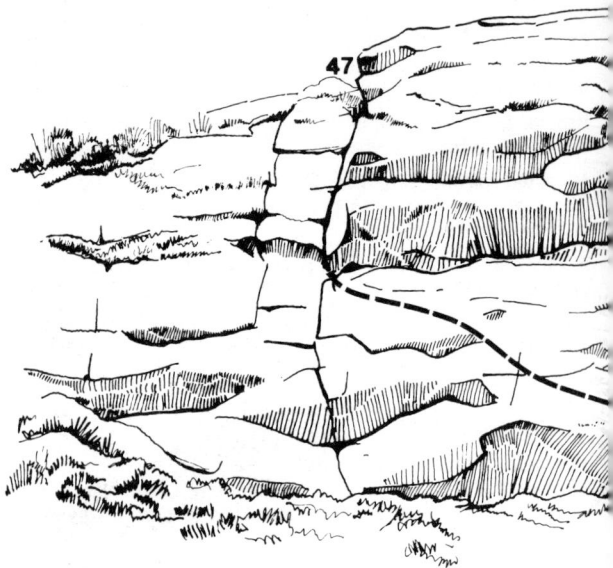

52 Tierdrop 8m E5 6b   ***
Cross the ceiling 2m right of Don's Crack via the obvious
pinch-grip to gain a runnel at the lip. A small finger-jug is
then within jumping distance, if you're lucky! The 'flat'
landing is acquiring a hollow. The best micro-route in the
Peak District.   (1980)

53 Tier's End 8m VS 5a
Pull gymnastically round the overhang to the right and finish
up a shallow groove.   (1979)

54 Abdomen 34m S
The upper girdle of the Lower Tier. Wriggle along the central
break.   (pre-1973)

A number of problems tackle the initial overhangs along the
base of The Lower Tier and can be used as rival crux moves
for the above routes.**Sensible Shoes** 5a, skirts the left end of
the Crab Walk overhang to a sloping ledge and shallow

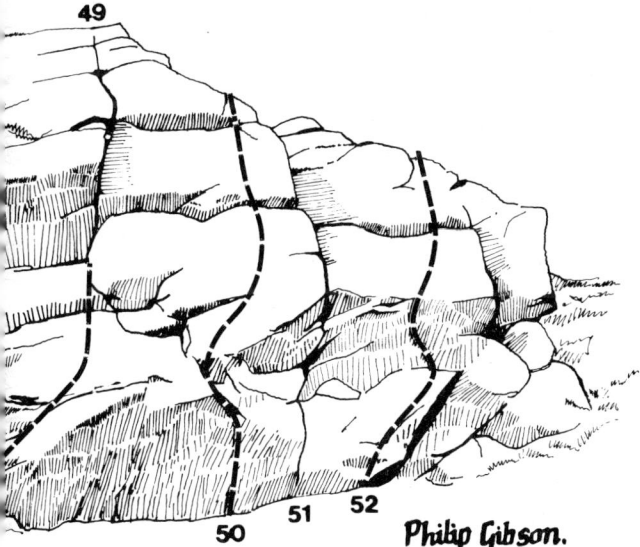

Philip Gibson.

Lower Tier

corner. **Crab Walk Direct** 5b, takes the vicious crack below the Crab Walk finish. **Overlap** 5b, surmounts the overhang right again and **Roll Off** 5c, rolls onto the shelf below the crack of Prostration.

55 Hem Line 35m 6a   *
A demanding traverse, never exceeding 4m above the ground. One usually starts left of Sensible Shoes, continues past Tierdrop, crux, and steps off at the right-hand end of the crag.   (1978)

At the same level, but 80m to the right, is a small undercut buttress giving three problems all at 4b, right, left and centre; **The Doleman**. Right of this wall, and at a slightly higher level, is an overhang giving a 5c problem when taken at its centre.

Returning to the path are two boulders.

Ossie's Bulge, 5a, climbs a flake and bulge on the right-hand boulder to a rounded finish. The runnel to its left is 5c.

The edge now recommences with two isolated buttresses.

56 The Comedian 9m VS 4b
Go directly up the front of the left-hand buttress until forced into a humourous (especially so for the large) stomach-traverse right. Exit precariously. Less-horizontal finishes exit left, 4a, or straight over the roof, 5a.   (pre-1973)

57 Camelian Crack 6m VD   *
The fine layback crack up the left side of the next buttress.
(pre-1973)

58 Dangerous Crocodile Snogging 9m E7 6c   ***†
Start below the prominent fin/arête and climb through the large overhang. Move round onto the left-hand side of the arête and launch up it moving left to gain a hold in the centre of the side-wall. Using pebbles, snap for a rounded finish. A dangerous sport!   (1986)

59 Elastic Limit 9m E2 5c   *
A crack on the lip of the overhang to the right can be reached by stretching from the back: certainly a knack, the key to which is a cunning toe-hook. Swing up and right to gain a ledge then finish direct. The ledge can be gained by traversing in from the left, VS 4c, or from the right, S 4a.
(1974/1977)

Below the right-hand start is a hard (6c) problem and on the edge behind is some good bouldering, the best being: The well-brushed wall, 6a, the left arête of the wall, 5c, the obvious hand-crack on the next boulder, 5a, or a mantelshelf onto the slab of the boulder at 5b.

The edge forms a more continuous stretch of rock 18m farther right. Two wide problem cracks face back down the edge.

60 Wriggler 6m HS 4a
The first (and appropriately named) crack on the front face.
(pre-1973)

61 Arête and Crack 13m VD
Take the blunt arête left of the cave then move left and ascend a crack to exit left.   (pre-1973)

62 Handrail 12m E2 5c
Near the top of Arête and Crack, a rising hand-traverse
leads right on dwindling holds to a short crack before the
prow. Strenuous. (1977)

63 Handrail Direct 9m E5 6b
Pad delicately up the scoop to join Handrail. Very serious
ground covered in a few very short metres. (1984)

64 Assegai 11m VS 4c
The corner-crack right of the cave is hardest at the bulge.
(pre-1973)

65 Bowrosin 12m VS 4c
Climb the slab right of the cave, then the awkward bulging
crack above. (1969)

66 English Towns 12m E3 5c *
A bold proposition. Follow good holds up the wall to a
junction with Bowrosin which is avoided by mantelshelving
out onto a hold on the right. Continue steadily up
easier-angled rock above. Protection in Bowrosin reduces
the E factor but increases peace of mind! (1979)

67 Boomerang 12m VD **
The immaculate diagonal flake 12m right again. A route to
return to. (pre-1973)

68 Wick Slip 12m E5 6b **
The obvious blunt arête emerging from the foot of
Boomerang gives superb delicate climbing. Runners up and
left can be placed in Boomerang. (1987)

69 The Watercourse 15m HS 4a
The wide groove/scoop farther right is often sandy. Scramble
up the second groove and traverse left to finish up a cracked
nose. (1969)

Arthur Scargill's Hairpiece is Missing, 5b, follows the
right-hand side of the small prow to the right.

70 Dan's Dare 9m VS 4c
At a higher level. Climb an awkward flaky groove just right
of a short chimney. Continue up the arête on the right. (1969)

71 Gully Wall 10m HVS 5a
The left wall of the next gully, starting 2m from the arête. A
thin move near the top adds zest to an interesting route.
(pre-1973)

72 Little Nasty 13m E1 4c,5b
1. 5m. The vile undercut crack just right of the gully soon capitulates.
2. 8m. Stroll back to climb the side-wall at a shallow crack.
(1968)

73 Electric Savage 15m E3 5b,5c   *
1. 7m. An impressive route. Having started Little Nasty, finger-traverse right to a flake, then go up to a large shelf.
2. 8m. Swing onto the large hanging flake on the left-hand side of the large overhang and balance up to a shocking finish.   (1978/1979)

74 Ramshaw Crack 6m E4 6a   ***
The gently widening crack splitting the centre of the massive overhang above the shelf. This hides delights rarely encountered elsewhere.   (1964/1976)

Philip Gibson.

Ramshaw Crack Area

75 Four Purists 7m VS 4c
The old start to Ramshaw Crack provides a route in its own
right. Climb the crack on the right of the buttress to reach
the shelf below the overhang. Escape off leftwards.

(pre-1973)

76 Never, Never Land 12m E6 6b   ****†**
The very impressive side-wall of the buttress. Place a large
runner at the top of the crack of Four Purists and fly right to
reach a flake. Using this, slap for a good hold, crux, then
continue carefully via the upper wall. (1986)

77 Green Corner 6m S
Climb the steep crack in the corner; much better than it
looks. (pre-1973)

78 Zigzag Route 10m VD
Begin up the first undercut crack right of the short gully,
then take the wide crack on the right, moving right again to
finish. Harder starts exist up twin cracks to the right, 4c, or a
slanting crack farther right again. (pre-1973)

79 Imposition 7m HVS 5a   *
The steep undercut crack beyond an impressive leaning wall
9m from Zigzag Route. A good test of off-width technique.
(pre-1973)

80 Iron Horse Crack 6m D
The much friendlier crack 3m right.   (pre-1973)

81 Scooped Surprise 6m E3 6a
From the short blind crack just right of Iron Horse Crack, use
pebbles to pull into the scoop, then finish direct.   (1984)

82 Tricouni Crack 6m HS 4a
The thin slanting crack on the right yields to good fat
finger-jams.   (pre-1973)

83 Rubber Crack 6m VS 4c
The incipient flaky crack and groove 2m right, gained via a
stretch.   (1973)

84 Darkness 9m S
Begin up the slab below Rubber Crack. Bridge the steep
corner-crack curving right, crux, and finish up the first crack
on the left.   (pre-1973)

85 Army Route 12m D
Start on the lower section. Traverse left below a small prow
to a cracked rib and grassy ledge. Finish up the broken
chimney.   (pre-1973)

86 Scout In Situ 8m HVS 5a
The wall just right of the prow on Army Route.   (1987)

87 Dusk 12m D
Go up the boulder-topped gully right of the prow to a
ledge. There are various exits up the chimney and crack
system above.   (pre-1973)

To the right rises the pinnacle of **FLAKY BUTTRESS**.

88 Flaky Gully 6m M
The gully to the left of the wall.   (pre-1973)

89 Flaky Wall Direct 14m VS 4b   *
Climb steeply up the right-hand side of the wall on good
holds to reach a ledge. Move leftwards past a
wicked-looking spike guarding entry to the exhilarating
groove above.   (pre-1973)

90 Flaky Wall Indirect 16m VS 4c   *
From the ledge of Flaky Wall Direct, go rightwards up some
flakes and move round the corner. Finish up the front face,
crux, on small holds.   (pre-1973)

91 Cracked Gully 12m D
The shallow groove on the front face of the pinnacle.
            (pre-1973)

92 Cracked Arête 12m VD
The arête immediately to the right is taken direct.   (pre-1973)

93 Arête Wall 9m D
The V-shaped groove. The groove and rib on its left side
give another start.   (pre-1973)

A gully separates Flaky Buttress from, **MAGIC
ROUNDABOUT**, *the slabby buttress right again.*

94 Crystal Tipps 7m E1 5c   *
Step delicately right from the gully onto the slab and aim for
the layback flake almost on the left arête of the buttress.
            (1976)

95 The Ultra Direct 7m E2 6b   **
Pull desperately round the lower bulge 2m right and climb
the slab to finish over a prow.   (1984)

96 Magic Roundabout Super-direct 7m E1 5c   *
Ascend the layaway flake in the bulge to the right and climb
the slab above to finish between the normal route and The
Delectable Deviation.   (1975)

97 Magic Roundabout Direct HVS 4c
Climb the shallow groove right again, then step right on the
break and finish up the green strip above a niche. (pre-1973)

98 Magic Roundabout 9m S   *
From the niche, tiptoe along the lowest rising break across
the slab to finish up a black flake on the crest.   (pre-1973)

99 The Delectable Deviation 9m VS 4c
Start 2m up and right of the niche. Tread delicately along
the upper crease to the black flake.   (pre-1973)

100 Perched Flake 9m D
Climb left, right or centre up a flake to the right. Go up a
blunt arête to finish.   (pre-1973)

*The next two routes take the slab on the back of this
buttress.*

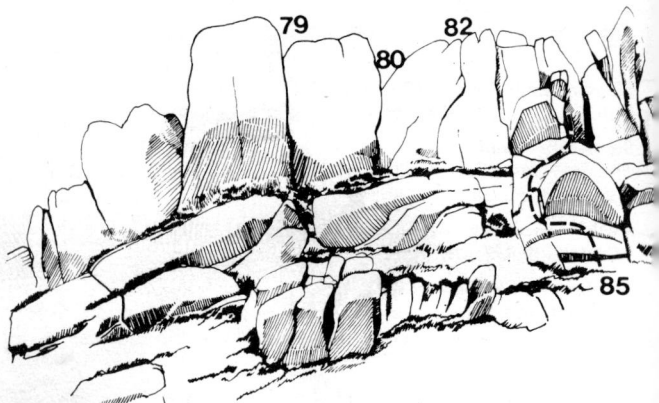

101 Force Nine 9m E4 6c   *
Ascend pebbles direct to a good (?) hold and finish direct.
Easier variations exist out to the left.   (1985)

102 Be Calmed 6m E2 6c
The scoop left of Force Nine gives food for thought.   (1986)

Magic Arête, 5c, follows the arête to the left on its
right-hand side, whilst **The Finger**, 4a, is any means of
ascent onto the solitary 'finger' of rock just right.

*Farther right are three square blocks containing a multitude
of problems:*

The left-most chimney is 4c, the left arête of the next
chimney is 6a, the chimney itself is 4b and the flake on the
right-most arête is 5a.

*Below Magic Roundabout is a small buttress with a trio of
cracks.*

103 Port Crack 8m S
Start by bridging from below or from the slab on the left.
                               (pre-1973)

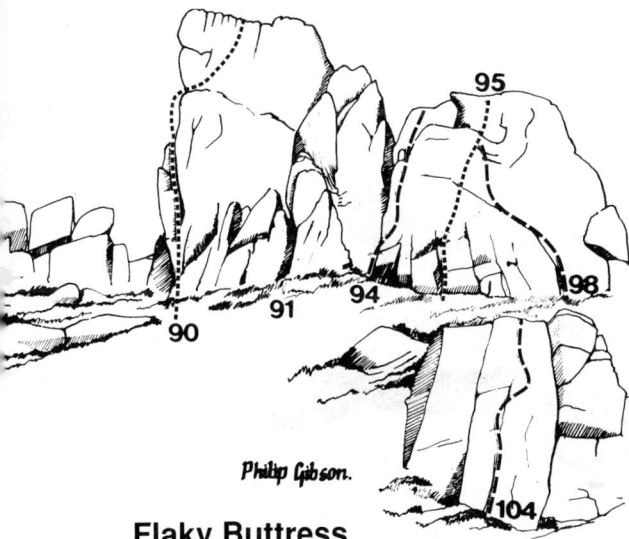

Philip Gibson.

Flaky Buttress

104 Time Out 9m E2 5c   *
The central crack. Moving right to a subsidiary upper crack
provides the crux.   (1979)

105 Starboard Crack 9m E1 5b
Contort up the right-hand, pebble-infested crack. Most
painful at the outset.   (pre-1973)

At the same level and farther right is the famous **WINKING
EYE BUTTRESS**. Due to serious damage caused to this
unique feature, **PLEASE AVOID THIS BUTTRESS**. Routes 106
to 112 are included purely for completeness.

106 Owl'ole 6m D
Climb past an eroded hole, just right of the pinnacle.
      (pre-1973)

107 Middle Route 6m S
The crack through the bulges to the right.   (pre-1973)

108 The Shoulder 6m HVD
The corner left of the face. Go straight up or move left at
half-height onto a protruding flake, then go over a bulge.
      (pre-1973)

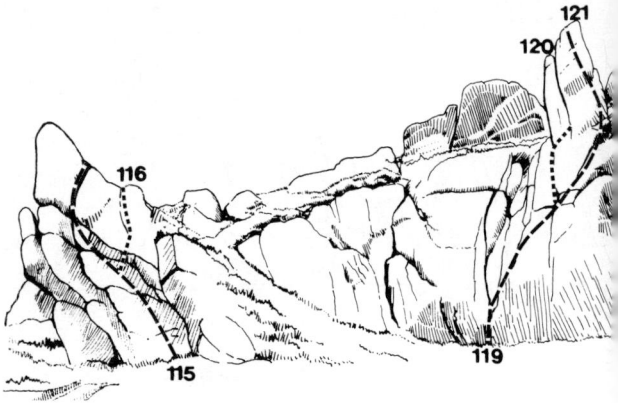

109 South Cheek 6m HS
Traverse right from the corner and go awkwardly up to the
eye. Step on the nose and mantelshelf onto the forehead.
(pre-1973)

110 North Cheek 8m VD
Climb the slab and corner on the right until a traverse left
leads to the 'eye' and the manoeuvres of South Cheek.
(pre-1973)

111 Collar Bone 8m D
The pock-marked slab to the right of the corner.   (pre-1973)

112 The Veil 20m S
Traverse the buttress at half-height via the eye from either
direction.   (pre-1973)

END OF FORBIDDEN SECTION
*Returning back to the ridge, some 70m right of Magic
Roundabout is* **ROMAN NOSE BUTTRESS**.

113 Big Richard 10m S
Climb direct, or from the right, to gain a spike at 10m.
Squirm through the chimney above to a ledge and finish up
the reachy wall on the right.   (pre-1973)

114 The Proboscid 10m E1 5b
From the ledge on Big Richard, layback the exposed and
serious nose.   (1980)

Philip Gibson.

124 125

The Pinnacle

115 The Crippler 10m HVS 5a ✳✳
A Ramshaw classic. Start 4m right of the spike. Trend leftwards under and round the main overlap to climb the flaky groove. A direct start to the spike is of a similar standard. (1969)

116 Escape 8m HVS 5b
Climb the wall to the left of the man-eating chimney. Difficult to avoid capture at the top. (1977)

117 Mantrap 8m HVD
Don't get caught in the chimney! (pre-1973)

Across the wide gully is **THE PINNACLE** *which has a sharply undercut groove to its left.*

118 Great Scene Baby 10m S
Gain the crack by traversing from the left and climb it and the neb above. (pre-1973)

Direct Start, 5b: a finger-wrecking problem can be connected to a somewhat artificial variation up the slab to the right.

119 Groovy Baby 10m HS 4b
The start is 'uncool', the remainder disappointing. (pre-1973)

120 Pile Driver 17m VS 4c   *
After the start of Groovy Baby, move right to gain a
corner-crack and climb to its top. Step right and go up a
worrying crack in the exposed nose. **Direct Start**, 6b, gains
the groove dynamically.   (pre-1973)

121 The Press 15m E1 5b   **
Follow Pile Driver to a swing right at 5m onto the leaning
wall. Squeeze into the hand-crack above and finish right of
the arête.   (1971)

122 Night of Lust 14m E4 6b   *
Starting below the right-hand side of the undercut prow,
pull desperately through the bulge to attain easier ground.
Finish up the right-hand side of the prow to finish.   (1984)

123 Curfew 12m HVS 5b   *
The severely undercut crack just right yields to a layback
with an unusual 'no hands rest' in the lower section.
                                                          (pre-1973)

124 Foord's Folly 10m E1 6a   ***
The overhanging single crack system to the right provides
an exasperating and strenuous test-piece. Unique.
                                                    (1968-73/1973)

125 The Swinger 13m HVS 5a   *
From the right end of the wall, ape up left using two
slanting ramps to reach a ledge. Continue up the exposed
arête behind.   (1972)

126 Screwy Driver 30m VS 4c   *
A rather contrived girdle crossing the prow at two-thirds
height. Start at the gully left of Great Scene Baby and finish
up a crack right of The Swinger.   (1968-73)

*Thirty-five metres to the right is an undercut nose with a
short wall above and to the left:*

127 Slow Hand Clap 8m E2 5c
Climb the wall just right of centre starting easily directly
below. A mega-reach at the top.   (1979)

128 Modesty Crack 8m D
Go up the crack on the left-hand side of the nose and finish
over blocks on the right.   (pre-1973)

129 The Brag 9m VS 5a   *
Climb the easy-looking slab just right of Modesty Crack
with difficulty. Move up left via cracks to an easier finish.
      (pre-1973)

130 Shark's Fin 5m 5a   ***
The obvious roof on the edge above. Climb the flake. A
traverse of the lip also proves amusing. Beware of the huge
frog.   (pre-1973)

*The next buttress, 20m to the right, has a blocky groove on
its left side.*

131 Early Retirement 6m D
Climb the groove to the slot on the right and shuffle
backwards to the top.   (pre-1973)

132 Rash Challenge 8m E1 5a
Tackle the frontal overhang. Climb the right-hand edge to
gain a slab below the main roof. Surmount it from the left,
swinging rightwards to a flake.   (1976)

133 Honking Bank Worker 8m E2 5c
Climb the short arête just right and continue up the wall
above on untrustworthy holds.   (1984)

134 Extended Credit 9m HVS 4c   *
The interesting right wall of the buttress leads to a shallow
finishing groove. Treat the holds with respect.   (1973)

*Twenty-five metres right is a buttress with a
leftward-slanting crack:*

135 Caramta 12m S
Jam the crack then pull directly over the twin noses.
      (pre-1973)

136 The Prism 9m VD
Bridge up the undercut corner on the right and then climb
either the cracks on the left or the groove on the right.
      (pre-1973)

137 Approaching Dark 9m E1 6a
Struggle round the centre of the overhang to the right. (1984)

138 Lechery 9m HS 4a
Take the overhanging arête to the right on spaced jugs.
Continue delicately to the top block for a gymnastic finish.
      (pre-1973)

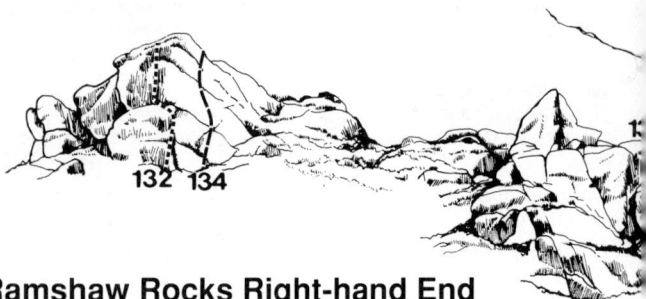

Ramshaw Rocks Right-hand End

Twenty-five metres right are two outcrops, one above the other. The upper one gives:

139 Ceiling Zero 6m HVS 4c
Gain huge jugs on the lip starting through a smaller overlap
below. (1980)

140 Pocket Wall 6m HS 4a
Climb the hanging bulging wall on sufficient holds, just right
of a large block. (pre-1973)

Farther right are two problems; **Problem Crack** *and* **Slab**
both 4a.

141 Curver 9m HVD
On the lower outcrop. Cross the slab under the prow, from
left to right, to finish up a flake. (pre-1973)

142 Old Fogey 12m E3 5c   **
From 4m up the gully to the right, traverse right along a
small ramp to reach the arête. Climb this on its far side via
a fine flake. (1977)

143 Old Fogey Direct 15m E4 6b   ***
The lower pebble-dashed wall is crossed diagonally
leftwards to a junction with the original route at the fine
flake. A brilliant combination. (1980)

144 King Harold 9m S
Climb the chimney to the right. (pre-1973)

Philip Gibson.

145 Little Giraffe Man 12m HS 4a
An amusing excursion. Climb the arête to the right of King
Harold, cross the chimney and continue left and up the thin
crack in the roof above. (1968-73)

Two hundred and thirty metres along the ridge is **THE LADY
STONE**. *Permission should be sought from the farm 200m to
the north-east. A short 4a slab is on the left side of the
stone.*

146 Lady Stone Chimney 6m D
The chimney right of the slab. (pre-1973)

147 Farmhouse Arête 9m HS
From the chimney, move right on parallel cracks to the
finishing arête. (pre-1973)

148 Childhood's End 9m HVS 5a *
From 3m right again, start with a fingery move, then go
rightwards through the overhangs to a final slab. (1978)

149 Ladies' Route 10m S
The diagonal crack to the right has an undignified start. Exit
right. (pre-1973)

150 Evil Crack 8m HVS 5a
Approach the roof-crack farther right via a pocket. Climb it
by standing on the nose to the left. Strenuous. (1973)

*In the centre of the field is a buttress giving several
problems.*

RAMSHAW ROCKS LIST OF FIRST ASCENTS

1950-1965	**Brown's Crack**, **Don's Crack**, **Prostration**, **The Great Zawn**, **The Crank** Joe Brown, Don Whillans
1964 Sept.	**Ramshaw Crack** (some aid used) Joe Brown *Climbed free by Gabe Regan in 1976.*
1968 Oct. 9	**Louie Groove** John Yates, Colin Foord
1968 Oct. 9	**The Untouchable** Colin Foord, John Yates
1968 Oct. 16	**Alcatraz** Dave Salt
1969 Jan. 15	**The Watercourse**, **Dan's Dare** Pete Ruddle
1969 Jan. 16	**Bowrosin** Barry Marsden
1969 Feb. 5	**The Crippler** John Yates
1971 Oct.	**The Press** Bob Hassall
1972 Aug.	**Tally Not** (1 pt.) Bob Hassall, Norman Hoskins *Climbed free by Martin Boysen in 1972.*
1972 Oct. 9	**Green Crack** Pete Harrop
1968-73	**Screwy Driver** Bob Hassall
1968-73	**Foord's Folly** (2 pts.) Colin Foord *Climbed on a wet day to keep the lads amused. First free ascent by John Allen in 1973.*
1968-73	**Little Nasty** Dave Salt *Only the finish was climbed. The first crack had obviously been done before, probably by Joe Brown.*
1968-73	**Abdomen**, **Little Giraffe Man** North Staffordshire Mountaineering Club members
1972	**The Swinger** Martin Boysen
1972	**Tally Not** Martin Boysen *First free ascent.*
1973 July 7	**The Undertaker** (1 pt.) Dave Salt, Barry Marsden *Climbed free by Jonny Wooward in 1976.*
1973 July 7	**Pink Flake Direct** Barry Marsden, Dave Salt
1973 July 8	**Rubber Crack** Steve Dale, Dave Salt
1973 July 8	**Evil Crack**, **Extended Credit** Dave Salt, Steve Dale

Pre-1973	**East Face, Southern Crack, Loaf and Cheese, Wall and Groove, The Arête, Leeds Crack, Twin Cracks, Broken Groove, Broken Groove Arête, Wellingtons, Battle of the Bulge, The Cannon, Phallic Crack, Corner Crack, The Rippler, Crab Walk, The Comedian, Camelian Crack, Wriggler, Arête and Crack, Assegai, Boomerang, Gully Wall, Four Purists, Green Corner, Zigzag Route, Imposition, Iron Horse Crack, Tricouni Crack, Darkness, Army Route, Dusk, Flake Gully, Flaky Wall Direct, Flaky Wall Indirect, Cracked Gully, Cracked Arête, Arête Wall, Magic Roundabout Direct, Magic Roundabout, Delectable Deviation, Perched Flake, Port Crack, Starboard Crack, Owl'ole, Middle Route, The Shoulder, South Cheek, North Cheek, Collar Bone, The Veil, Big Richard, Mantrap, Great Scene Baby, Groovy Baby, Pile Driver, Curfew, Modesty Crack, The Brag, Shark's Fin, Early Retirement, Caramta, The Prism, Lechery, Pocket Wall, Curver, King Harold, Lady Stone Chimney, Farmhouse Arête, Ladies' Route** *These routes marked the publication of the 1973 guidebook which was the first to attempt to describe all of the routes on Ramshaw Rocks. Many of these had almost certainly been climbed before in the dim and distant past, yet all were named, and some were climbed for the first time, by the North Staffs. M.C. who did as many routes as possible in one frantic weekend.*
1973	*Staffordshire Gritstone Area guidebook, Rock Climbs in the Peak, Volume 9, published.*
1973	**Foord's Folly** John Allen (solo) *First free ascent.*
1974 Autumn	**Elastic Limit** Andrew Woodward (solo) *Gained from the right.*
1975 Oct.	**Magic Roundabout Super-direct** Jonny Woodward (solo)
1976 Spring	**Honest Jonny** Jonny Woodward (solo)
1976 April 10	**Crystal Tipps** Andrew Woodward (solo)
1976 Aug.	**Rash Challenge** Jonny Woodward (solo) *Top-roped first. Counterclaimed as Overdraught by Martin Boysen in August 1977.*
1976 Aug.	**The Undertaker** Jonny Woodward (solo) *First free ascent.*
1976	**Ramshaw Crack** Gabe Regan *First free ascent.*
1977 March 27	**Elastic Limit Direct Start** Nick Longland (solo)

1977 April **Gumshoe** Martin Boysen

1977 June 2 **Traveller in Time** Andrew Woodward, Jonny Woodward
Counter-claimed by Martin Boysen as Jumbo in July 1977.

1977 July **Trivial Traverse, Overdrive, Midge, Handrail, Escape, The Press Direct Start** Martin Boysen
'Arrive there on a warm summer evening , fighting fit and determined – preferably with a few preliminary bouts under your belt – crash the jams in, move quickly and the climbs submit. Arrive on a bad day, and it is a different story; the rock will maul you and you will retire bloodied to lick your wounds' – Martin Boysen, Crags 19.

1977 Aug. **Old Fogey** Martin Boysen

1978 March 26 **Childhood's End** Jonny Woodward

1978 April 7 **National Acrobat, Electric Savage** Jonny Woodward (unseconded)
Only the top pitch of Electric Savage was climbed and after top-rope inspection.

1978 April **Hem Line** Nick Longland (solo)
As described in the current text.

1979 April 27 **After Eight** Nick Longland (solo)

1979 June 3 **English Towns, Time Out** Gary Gibson, Ian Barker

1979 June 13 **Electric Savage** Nick Longland (solo)
Only the first pitch was climbed. The second pitch had previously been climbed by Jonny Wooward in 1978.

1979 June 28 **The Sneeze** Nick Longland, Dave Jones

1979 Aug. 8 **Tier's End** Nick Longland (solo)

1979 Aug. **Slow Hand Clap** Gary Gibson (solo)

1979 Aug. **Whilly's Whopper** Dave Jones, Gary Gibson, Nick Longland

1979 **Cleg** Nick Longland (solo)

1980 April 10 **Ceiling Zero** Gary Gibson, Derek Beetlestone

1980 April 13 **The Whale** Nick Longland (solo)

1980 May 6 **Thinner Mantel** Nick Longland (solo)

1980 May 9 **Old Fogey Direct Start** Jonny Woodward (solo)
Top-roped first. A significant addition. 'Three snatches for crystals'. Some of these have now gone.

1980 May 15   **Tierdrop** Nick Longland (solo)
Success after months of attempts, many bad landings and the incentive of Jonny Woodward coming very close to success.

1980 May 19   **The Proboscid** Nick Longland (solo)

1980 May   **Leeds Slab** Nick Longland (solo)

1980   **Sensible Shoes** Dave Jones (solo)

1973-1981   **Double Chin, Prowler**

1981   *Staffordshire Area guidebook, Rock Climbs in the Peak Volume 6, published.*

1981 Aug. 10   **Torture** Gary Gibson (solo)

1984 March 21   **Handrail Direct Start** Simon Nadin (solo, with a hanging rope)
Soloed without the hanging rope and on-sight by Andy Popp in 1985.

1984 March 21   **Scooped Surprise** Simon Nadin (solo)

1984 May   **The Honking Bank Worker, Arthur Scargill's Hairpiece is Missing** Allen Williams (solo)

1984 Sept. 4   **Approaching Dark** Richard Davies (solo)
Many visits were required before the lichen was dry enough to allow an ascent.

1984 Sept. 14   **Dream Fighter** Richard Davies (solo)

1984   **Body Pop, Night of Lust** John Allen, Mark Stokes.

1984   **The Ultra Direct** John Allen (solo)
The first ascent is something of a bone of contention. Certainly it may have been climbed before by either Allen Williams or Richard Davies. The route name would seem to be a sensible compromise.

1984   **Cold Wind** Richard Davies (solo)

1985 April 27   **Force Nine** Simon Nadin (solo)

1986 May 4   **Be Calmed** Graham Hoey (solo)

1986 May 7   **Dangerous Crocodile Snogging** Simon Nadin (solo)
Top-roped first.

1986 May 26   **Never, Never Land** Simon Nadin, Richard Davies
Top-roped first.

1986 July 2   **Assembled Techniques** Richard Davies (solo)
An obvious line hinted at in the 1973 guidebook.

1986   **Gully Arête** Richard Davies (solo)

1987 April 16   **T'rival Traverse** Graham Hoey, John Allen, Martin Veale

1987 April 16   **Rock Trivia** John Allen (unseconded)

1987 April 16   **Maximum Hype** John Allen, Graham Hoey, Martin Veale
Martin was surprised to find Graham's car keys en route. Graham was even more surprised as he didn't realise that he had lost them. It might have been a long walk back!

1987 July 16   **Scout In Situ** Pete Oxley (solo)
Almost certainly done before.

1987 Aug. 6   **Wick Slip** Nick Dixon, Andy Popp

1987 Sept. 28   **Colly Wobble** Simon Nadin, John Perry
The four drilled holes were not the work of the first ascensionists. They were created well before the advent of bolt protection!

NEWSTONES AND BALDSTONES
by Gary Gibson

> '*Under the American system Ray graded this route 5.11c in comparison with Ramshaw Crack which he only gave 5.10d!*'

Crags, referring to Ray Jardine's ascent of Ray's Roof 1977.

SITUATION and CHARACTER
These rocks lie on a small north-to-south ridge roughly 2km north of Ramshaw Rocks. They can be seen clearly from the A53 Leek-to-Buxton road just west of Morridge Top.

Whilst many of the climbs here are short, the buttresses offer ample entertainment in quiet surroundings. The rock can be green though the popular routes are free from this hazard. It is worth noting that the crags face east and receive only morning sunshine.

APPROACHES and ACCESS
The normal approach is from the A53. The minor road dividing the southern end of Ramshaw leads, after 2km, to a small grassy triangle in the road. Limited parking is available here. This point can also be gained by the small road leading northwards from the crossroads just west of The Winking Man Inn. From the small triangle, a rough track leads behind the obvious small cottage to the first rocks. Ownership is not known and no access problems have arisen.

THE CLIMBS are described from LEFT to RIGHT starting with the obvious overhanging buttress beyond the fence on the left of, and 100m up, the deeply-rutted track.

NEWSTONES
O.S. ref. SK 019638

1 Leather Joy Boys 6m E3 6c
On the left wall of the buttress. Gain the obvious break by hard moves on sloping holds and traverse hastily right to exit above the nose. (1984)

2 Charlie's Overhang 6m E2 5c   *
The main overhang direct. Gaining the lip is a formality, establishing oneself above it is not! (1970s)

Newstones Left-hand End

3 Newstones Chimney 6m D
Either of two short cracks leads to the upper chimney.

(1951-1973)

4 Moonshine 6m HVS 5a
The bulging wall to the right is very green. Take it at its
centre.   (1973-1981)

5 Praying Mantel 6m VS 4c
Grovel onto the prow to the right and slither up the shallow
depression.   (1973-1981)

Traversing the buttress from either direction gives
unbalanced 5a climbing.

Also behind the fence, a small 'snout' to the right gives a
fine 5a problem whilst a slab just right of the end of the
fence gives tricky 5b starts.

The next buttress is bounded by a rippled side-wall and a
rounded undercut nose.

The rising vein on the side-wall gives complex finger
changes; **Ripple** 6a. A lower traverse on a rounded break
offers delicate footwork; **Martin's Traverse** 5b. The rounded,
undercut nose gives a strenuous problem; **Direct Start** 6a.
The rugosity-covered, undercut wall just left of the obvious
chimney is hardest at the start; **Short Wall** 5a. **Short
Chimney** is Very Difficult.

The front face of the buttress gives lengthier problems.

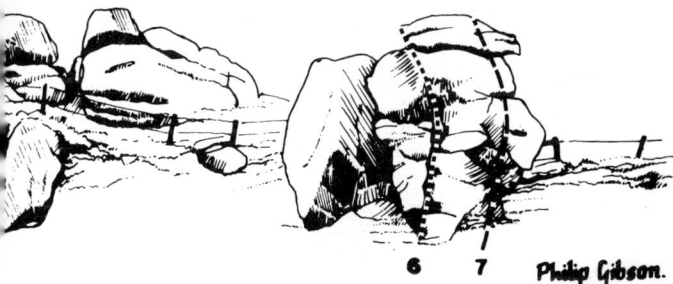

6   7   Philip Gibson.

6 Hazel Brow Crack 6m HVD
The obvious crack. Lurch left over the bulge at the top using
a long reach.   (1951-1973)

7 Hazel Barn 8m VD   *
Delicately tackle the faint groove just to the right. The
ripples just right again are Severe. Both variations take the
block direct to finish.   (1951-1973)

8 Nutmeg 8m HS 4b
The right side of the wall. Finish via the right side of the
block. A 5c 'blinkers' problem is just to the left; do not use
the ripples.   (1973-1981)

*Fifty metres farther on, the next buttress has a bay in its
centre:*

Scratched, 5b, tackles a bulge just left of a jamming crack
on the first rocks. The crack is **Scratch Crack**, 4b. The left
wall of the bay can be tackled direct at 6a, or more usually
from the right at 5b, **Itchy Fingers**. **Bridget**, 4b, is the
micro-slab at the back of the bay whilst **Peel's Problem**, 5c,
gains the rugosity-crack on the right wall directly.

The right arête of the bay forms an obvious crack:

9 Rhynose 8m VS 4b   *
Climb the crack and bridge out above the void to exit.
                                                          (1951-1973)

10 Hippo 8m VD
A shallow groove and a chimney just right lead out onto the
upper face which is itself taken direct.   (1951-1973)

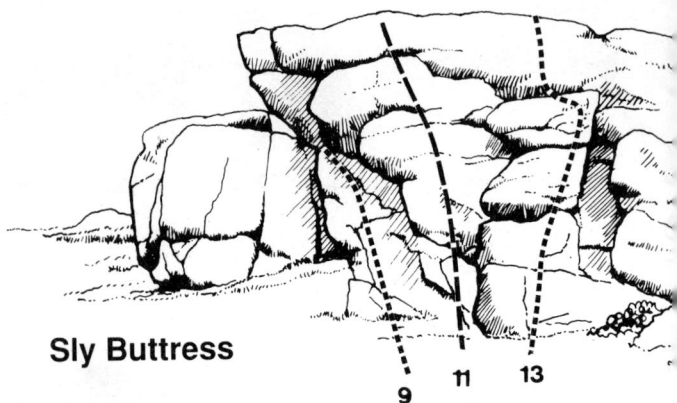

Sly Buttress

9   11   13

11 Rosehip 8m S
Ascend the bulge and the wall above, just left of some
'piled-up' boulders.   (1973-1981)

12 The Witch 8m D
Climb the left side of the 'piled-up' boulders to a tunnel.
Step left and go up to finish.   (1951-1973)

13 Candy Man 6m S
Trend rightwards up the front face of the boulders via twin
bulges.   (1951-1973)

*The final buttress is certainly the largest at Newstones, lying
10m to the right again:* **SLY BUTTRESS**.

14 Trepidation 8m E2 5b
From the gully on the left side of the butress move right
along a sloping crack, then storm up the headwall to a bold
and balding finish.   (1975)

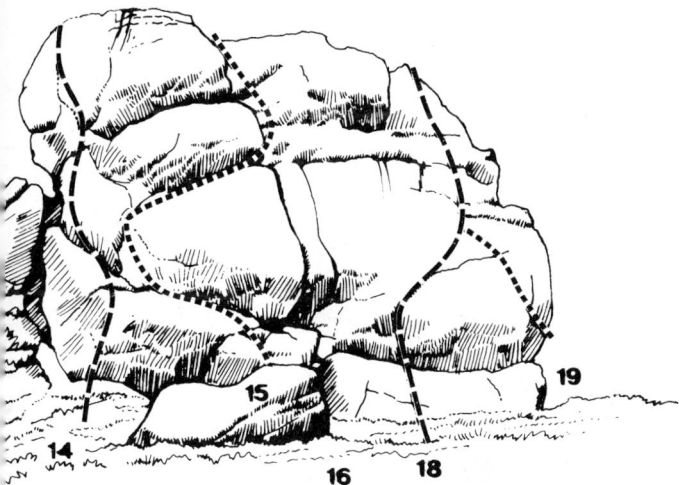

Philip Gibson.

The remainder of the routes lie on the front face which has prominent twin cracks in its centre and a long curving vein on the face to their right.

15 The Snake 12m S
Swing up left onto the thin catwalk left of the left-hand twin crack; most appropriate for the short. Move left along it, go up and then move back right by a degrading thrutch and chimney finish. (1951-1973)

16 The Fox 9m HVS 5b
A wily beast requiring resourcefulness and off-width technique. Do battle with the wide left-hand crack. Even more punishment is dealt out to those who cannot reach the chockstone! (1951-1973)

17 The Vixen 9m VS 4b
The right-hand crack is, as the name might suggest, a much friendlier affair. (1951-1973)

The long curving vein provides the substance of some excellent problems.

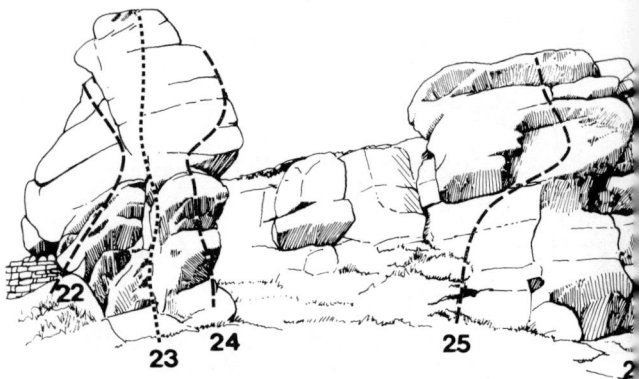

The Main Crag

18 The Sly Mantelshelf 9m HVS 5a   *
Swing up from the left end of the vein and mantelshelf at its centre. Finish direct. **Sly Super-direct** 5b, gains the centre of the vein directly and finishes in similar fashion.   (1951-1973)

19 Sly Corner 9m VS 4c   **
Start round the arête to the right. Move up onto the right end of the vein and make delightful balance manoeuvres along it to gain its centre. Finish direct again. **Sly Direct** 4c, hauls straight onto the vein just left of the arête. (1951-1973)

Numerous other problems exist round to the right, but none are of the quality of those already described.

BALDSTONES   O.S. ref. SK 019644

Continue in the direction of the ridge and after 450m, just beyond the brow lies a large 'thumb' of rock with a flat front face is the location of the best routes hereabouts.

20 Perambulator Parade 11m D   *
Start on the left side of the pinnacle at a ruined stone shelter. Follow a slanting groove and amble up the slab at the back of the pinnacle to the top, passing a bulge to the left. Descent is by the same line.   (pre-1951)

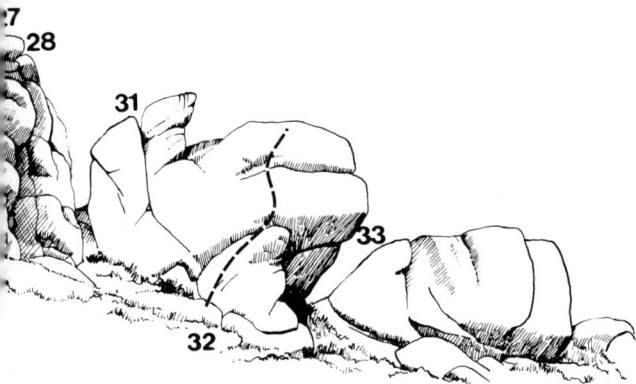

Philip Gibson.

21 Incognito 9m HVS 4c
Climb direct up the centre of the hanging slab just to the
right of the ruin to a scary exit. (1973-1981)

22 Baldstones Face 11m VS 4b ******
Move right along the break below the slab of Incognito onto
the left arête of the front face. Delightful climbing up this
leads to the summit. (1951-1973)

23 Original Route 9m E2 5b ******
Start in the centre of the front face. A difficult start up the
obvious central groove is followed by bold climbing up a
depression in the middle of the face. (1960s)

24 Baldstones Arête 11m HVS 4c *******
A superb route combining fine climbing with airy positions.
Start just right again. Haul over the bulge on good flakes
and step up before moving right to gain the arête above the
overhang. Saunter up this to the top. (1951-1973)

*Eight metres to the right, and across the obvious gap, is a
long buttress bounded on the left by a square, hanging
scoop.*

25 Gold Rush 10m E4 5c
Enter the scoop easily from the left, then shuffle right above
the void and pull over the bulge with difficulty to gain a
short finishing crack. Unprotected and, at the time of writing,
filthy.   (1976)

26 Goldsitch Crack 12m VS 4c
In the centre of the face is a short wide crack above a
half-height break. Gain the crack via an undercut start 2m
to the right and thrutch and curse up the crack to the top.
                                                         (1951-1973)

At the right-hand end of the wall lies an obvious chimney.

27 Blackbank Crack 12m VD
The crack just left of the chimney leads to a wider crack
farther left. A direct start via a short layback crack is 4b and
an indirect start 2m left again gives a 5c lunge.   (1951-1973)

28 Forking Chimney 9m D
The obvious chimney.   (pre-1951)

29 Bareleg Wall 9m VS 4b
Move up a groove 3m right again and shuffle rightwards
along a break before finishing up a curving crack.   (1970s)

30 Morridge Top 9m VS 4c
Take the green wall to the right again at its centre.   (1970s)

*The face almost at rightangles to the right again yields two
climbs.*

31 Minipin Crack 6m VD
The dog-legged crack just left of a curious pinnacle.
                                                         (1951-1973)

32 All-stars' Wall 6m HVS 5a
At the right end of the wall. Climb direct from a 'beak' of
rock via a pocket and a break. Harder for shorties.   (1970s)

33 Ray's Roof 8m E6 6b   ***
The delightful, off-width roof-crack skulking round the
corner to the right. Mean to all-comers and appears to be
standing the test of time.   (1977)

*The last-but-one buttress provides climbs of a bouldering
nature.*

Ganderhole Crack, 4a, lurks behind an obvious boulder.
Fielder's Indirect, 5a, moves right around the rib on the right
to climb the wall on pockets. **Fielder's Corner**, 6a, takes the
short hanging corner direct by means of a wicked pull on a
one-finger pocket. **Elephant's Ear**, 4c, climbs the delightful
flake round to the right and **Elephant's Eye**, 5c, breaks out
left to climb the wall on pockets; easier for the tall.

*The final buttress lies 20m farther on and is bounded by an
easy chimney.*

34 Pyeclough 6m VS 4b
Climb the awkward crack through the obvious nose.
(1951-1973)

35 Heathylee 6m D
The rightward-slanting rake, right again. Alternative finishes
direct or left provide harder alternatives. (1951-1973)

A boulder 40m right again gives only one route:

36 End Game 8m HS 4a
The wall and prow at the highest point of the buttress. Other
problems exist hereabouts. (1973-1981)

Across the Black Brook and through an area of fir trees lies
GIB TORR *but first you will have to read:*

NEWSTONES/BALDSTONES LIST OF FIRST ASCENTS

Pre-1951	**Perambulator Parade, Forking Chimney** *The latter route was originally known as Y-chimney.*
1960s	**Original Route** Martin Boysen
1951-1973	**Baldstones Arête** North Staffordshire Mountaineering Club members
1951-1973	**Newstones Chimney, Hazel Barn Crack, Hazel Barn, Rhynose, Hippo, The Witch, Candy Man, The Snake, The Fox, The Vixen, The Sly Mantelshelf, Sly Corner, Baldstones Face, Goldsitch Crack, Blackbank Crack, Minipin Crack, Pyeclough, Heathylea** *Described, but uncredited, in the 1973 guidebook, the first to describe routes on these two crags in detail.*
1973	*Staffordshire Gritstone Area guide, Rock Climb in the Peak, Volume 9, published.*
1970s	**Charlie's Overhang** Tony Barley *Also known as Barleyman.*

1970s	**All-stars' Wall** Martin Boysen (solo)
1975 Nov. 2	**Trepidation** Jim Campbell, Con Carey
1976 June 19	**Gold Rush** Jim Campbell, Nick Colton
1977 July	**Ray's Roof** Ray Jardine, Clive Jones
1977	**Morridge Top, Bareleg Wall** Jonny Woodward (solo)
1973-1981	**Moonshine, Praying Mantel, Nutmeg, Rosehip, Incognito, End Game** *A number of problems lay unrecorded but had obviously been climbed, thus posing a problem for the editor of the new volume. They were described and hurriedly named.*
1981	*Staffordshire Area guidebook, Rock Climbs in the Peak, Volume 6, published.*
1984	**Leather Joy Boys** Mark Stokes (solo)

GIB TORR

O.S. ref. SK 018648

by Gary Gibson

SITUATION and CHARACTER
This small outcrop is situated on the same north-to-south ridge as Newstones and Baldstones, 500m north of the latter and across Black Brook.
This crag is similar in many ways to Newstones and Baldstones as well as other esoteric Staffordshire crags. It can be green during long spells of wet weather and receives only the early morning sunshine on its faces.

APPROACHES and ACCESS
The best approach is from the A53 Leek-to-Buxton road. Turn off at Morridge Top and follow the minor road to within 50m of the crag.
Access has never been a problem here although the owner is not known.

THE CLIMBS are described from RIGHT to LEFT, beginning on **THE LOWER TIER**.

At the right-hand end, a jumble of walls provides minor problems including a 5c layaway move. The first obvious feature is a green slab:

Right: Among the superb routes on the Third Cloud, **Appoloosa Sunset** (p108) takes centre stage – here Marcus Payne gives a matinee performance. Photo: Simpon Nadin

eft: **Delstree**
130) one of Hen
loud's finest,
rrows down a
ugh challenge in
e HVS grade.
hoto: Ian Smith

ght: **K2** (p137)
ves a fabulous
evere climb up the
entre of Hen
loud's biggest
ce. Photo: Ken
ilson

verleaf: Graham
bey makes the
al moves of
aesarian (p130)
E4,6b 'a cut
ove the rest
hoto: Keith
arples

Above: John Goding powers up **Charlie's Overhang** (p183), one of the best of the big boulder problems of Newstones. Photo: Chris Wright

Previous Page: Jonny Woodward leads one of Hen Cloud's most challenging routes – the exposed and frugally protected **Caricature** (p142). Photo: Ian Smith

Right: Woodward in action on Joe Brown's **Ramshaw Crack** (p166). Photo: Ian Smith

1 Gibble Gabble Slab 8m D
Climb the slab moving right to reach the arête, then go up
on the edge of a wide crack. (pre-1973)

2 The Gibe 11m VS 4b *
Start just left of a block on the ground, 3m to the left. Go up
a flake and move right to gain a small ledge. Continue right
via a ramp beneath the roof to escape on the edge
overlooking Gibble Gabble Slab. The crack above the ramp
is reputed to have also been climbed. (1970s)

3 Montezuma's Revenge 9m E3 5c *
From the ledge on The Gibe, move up left on poor holds,
then go through the bulge using a blind crack and 'ear'.
(1979)

4 Porridge at Morridge Top 9m E5 6b **
Climb easily up the thin flake in the wall to the left to reach
a bulge. Pull over using poor holds and finish via a
depression. Superb technical moves. (1984)

5 Gibber Crack 6m S
The twisting crack at the left end of the wall leads to an
ungainly exit. (pre-1973)

6 Gibbering 6m HVS 6b
Climb the undercut wall to the left, finishing up the slab.
(1986)

7 Gib Sail 12m M
Climb the easy-angled slab round to the left. (pre-1973)

8 Gibbon Take 15m VS 4b *
A traverse of the buttress starting up Gibber Crack and
exiting as for The Gibe. (1977)

*At the very left-hand end of the lower tier is a large 'chin'
of rock.*

Right Fin 5c, tackles the right wall of the 'chin' on rounded
nubbins, **The Fin** 6b, takes the front of the 'chin', head on
and **Left Fin** 4c, takes the filthy crack on the left wall.

Above lies **THE UPPER TIER** *which is composed of two
buttresses, the right-hand giving the first routes:*

9 Giblet Crack 6m VD
Grovel up the chimney at the right-hand end of the buttress
and finish up the flake to its left. (pre-1973)

Left: Dean Hammond on the hard move on Baldstone's classic 4c boulder test
Elephants Ear (p191). Photo: Gene Hammond

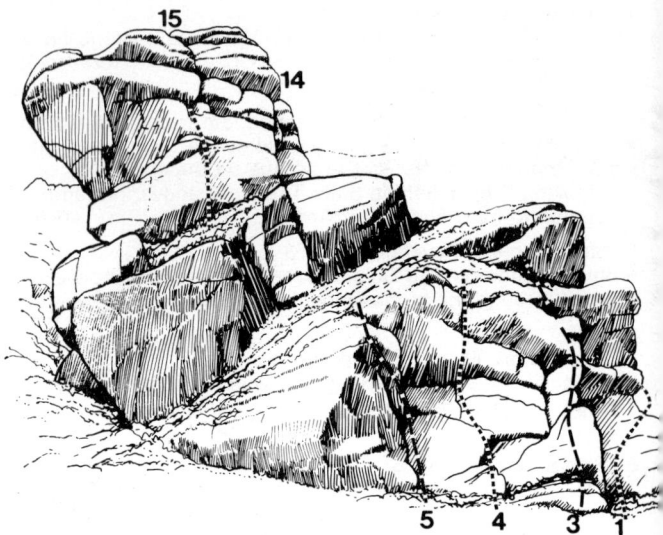

10 The Gibbet 11m HVS 5a *
From 2m up Giblet Crack, traverse diagonally up leftwards to
exit at the arête. (pre-1973)

The hanging arête to the left sports a large flake.

11 Gib 9m E2 5c **
Hard starting moves from either the left or the right gain the
flake. This soon leads to a crack and easy ground. (1970s)

12 The Ensign 9m HVS 5a
The finger-crack in the bulging corner to the left. (pre-1973)

13 Gibraltar 8m S
The next crack to the left. (pre-1973)

The left-hand buttress lies 5m to the left.

14 Gibling Corner 8m S
The vague corner on the right-hand side of the buttress.
Move onto the slab on the right to finish. Alternatively finish
direct at 4a. (pre-1973)

15 Gibbon Wall 8m VS 4c
From a ledge at 3m, gain the obvious short crack in the wall
to the left. Take the finishing bulge direct. (pre-1973)

Philip Gibson.

The Main Crag

The huge roof on the left provides an incredible 7a top-rope test-piece.

16 Gibeonite Girdle 14m HVS 5b
Traverse at two-thirds height from right to left until forced above the overhang to finish. (pre-1973)

GIB TORR LIST OF FIRST ASCENTS

Pre-1973	**The Ensign, The Gibbet** North Staffordshire Mountaineering Club members *Climbed during guidebook work.*
Pre-1973	**Gibble Gabble Slab, Gibber Crack, Gib Sail, Giblet Crack, Gibraltar, Gibling Corner, Gibbon Wall, Gibeonite Girdle** *Described, but uncredited, in the 1973 guidebook, the first to describe routes on this crag.*
1973	*Staffordshire Gritstone Area guidebook, Rock Climbs in the Peak, Volume 9, published.*
1970s	**The Gibe, Gib** Martin Boysen (solo)

1977	**Gibbon Take** Jonny Woodward (solo)
1979	**Montezuma's Revenge** Nick Longland
1981	*Staffordshire Area guidebook, Rock Climbs in the Peak Volume 6, published.*
1984	**The Fin** John Allen (solo)
1984	**Porridge at Morridge Top** Paul Mitchell (unseconded) *The most major line on the crag, bar one!*
1986	**Gibbering** Tom Leppert (solo) *Named in absentia.*

GRADBACH HILL

O.S. ref. SK 001653

by Ian Dunn

> *'It should only be E2 5b really, but don't quote me on it!'*
>
> Claudie Dunn, referring to The Phantom, 1987.

SITUATION and CHARACTER

These outcrops lie near the crest of the ridge called Gradbach Hill about 1.5km east of the Back Forest Crags and 1km roughly north-east of Roach End; the crags face south-west. There is an atmosphere of quiet isolation about these rocks which, though only having a small number of climbs, are situated in a most pleasant and pleasing environment. The most conspicuous features are a large pinnacle (The Phantom), easily visible from The Roaches/Back Forest ridge (and almost anywhere else in the surrounding area), and 150m farther south a substantial block on top of the edge is known as The Yawning Stone. The rock here is sound natural gritstone.

APPROACHES and ACCESS

From the A53 Buxton-to-Leek road, follow either of the minor roads past Newstones (forking right at the grassy triangle) or Gib Torr (the road just after the four houses on Morridge Top). These two lanes merge after a further 1.5km and cars can be parked a further 130m on at a sharp right-hand bend (O.S. ref. SK 008651). From the west, turn off the Congleton-to-Buxton road at Allgreave towards Quarnford beside the Rose and Crown public house. Go over Burntcliff Top and cross the River Dane. After 250m, turn right and continue for another 1.5km before parking besides the sharp bend previously mentioned. From the parking area follow a track due west until it begins to descend and then bear rightwards along the top of the escarpment to the rocks; approximately 10 minutes walk.

Ownership is unknown though no access problems have so far arisen.

THE CLIMBS are described from RIGHT to LEFT, the normal way when approaching the crag from the parking area.

The first features of any note are two slabs 100m south of the large block on top of the crag: **THE YAWNING STONE**.

1 Feed the Enemy 8m HS 4b
The blunt arête of the right-hand slab. (1978)

Two metres left, the slab gives a 5a problem. On the left-hand slab the right edge and left side are 4a and 4c respectively.

The Yawning Stone itself can be climbed by numerous problems. The biggest face is 4b and an intricate girdle can be made at 5a.

Directly below The Yawning Stone is a small cliff with a prominent crack through an overhang towards its right-hand side:

2 Sense of Doubt 8m E1 5b   *
Start through an undercut 2m right of the crack. Follow the blunt arête closely with a hard move above the horizontal crack. The wall to its right awaits someone with sufficient finger power to climb it. (1980)

3 The Gape 8m VS 4c
From the horizontal crack on Sense of Doubt, step left and go delicately up the front face past a short ramp. Pleasant.
(1980)

4 Chockstone Crack 8m S   *
The prominent crack. A big jug eases the passage of the overhang. (1969)

5 Anniversaire 8m E2 5c
Climb directly through the overhang immediately left of Chockstone Crack. Technical. (1985)

6 Marsden's Crack 7m VS 4c
The thinner crack through the overhang. (1969)

7 Barbiturate 7m S
Left again is a large corner. Ascend the slab to its right and
finish up the corner-crack. (1969)

8 Sleepwalker 9m HS 4b
Climb the crack on the left wall of the corner to a double
overhang. Traverse strenuously left, then trend rightwards up
the delicate slab. (1969)

9 John's Arête 9m HVS 5a *
Climb the arête right of the oak tree, then go directly up the
slab. Pleasant climbing. (1980)

10 French Connection 9m E1 5c
Climb the slab left of John's Arête, then go over the bulge
and up the slab. (1985)

11 Oak Tree Crack 6m VD
The crack behind the oak tree leads to an easier finish.
(pre-1973)

*Between leaving this outcrop and before The Pinnacle, there
are some small buttresses with various problems. Three of
these are worthy of note:*

12 Little Arête 6m VD
The arête. Skirt the overhang to the left. (1980)

13 The Overhang 6m HVS 5a
Fondle the big jugs on the obvious overhang. (1986)

14 Thin Crack 5m HVS 6a
The thin crack topped by a small roof, 20m before The
Pinnacle. (1986)

*One hundred and twenty metres along the ridge from The
Yawning Stone is* **THE PINNACLE**. *The short side is Difficult
and the side just to the left is Severe. A dry-stone wall runs
up to its front face.*

15 The Phantom 15m E3 5b **†
From the wall, go up a crack for a few metres. Step left onto
a small ledge and gain the break, large thread runner. Climb
onto the ledge above the break and move up past a ghost of
a bolt to a big ledge 3m below the top. Move 3m left, then
go over the top bulge by a thin crack, or climb direct to the
summit from the ledge. Peg and Friend belay. A superb but
scary route. (1971/1977/1986)

16 Green Crack 12m HS 4b
Climb the obvious green crack 3m left of the dry-stone wall
to a junction with: (1980)

17 The Cleft Route 12m VD
Four metres past the stone wall. Climb first right and then
left into the cleft. Follow this past a chockstone and move
round to finish up the easy back route.   (pre-1973)

*Twenty metres left is a buttress with a ledge at two-thirds
height.*

18 The Cue 6m VD
The crack on the right side of the buttress passing the right
edge of the ledge. Thrutchy.   (pre-1973)

19 The Chalk 8m HVS 5a
Climb the wall just to the left to the ledge. Finish up the top
wall. Pleasant.   (1980)

20 The Billiard Table 9m S   *
From the lowest point of the buttress, climb a crack to a
bulge. Go over this awkwardly to the ledge and exit up the
corner-crack.   (pre-1973)

21 Pot Black 9m E2 6a
Climb the wall immediately left of the previous route to a
ledge round the arête. From the ledge on the previous three
routes, climb the left arête passing an obvious snapped flake
by some technical moves. Don't fall off rightwards!   (1986)

One hundred metres left of The Pinnacle is **CYNIC'S
BUTTRESS**

22 Old Son 8m VD
Climb the corner-crack and arête above, right of the central
crack.   (1980)

23 For Tim 9m D
The wide central crack.   (1980)

24 Fat Old Nick 9m VD
Climb a crack on the left of an overhang, then move right
and go up the front slab. **Al's Abdominal Start,** takes the
overhang direct on large rounded holds at 5a.   (1980)

GRADBACH HILL LIST OF FIRST ASCENTS

1969	**Marsden's Crack, Chockstone Crack, Barbiturate, Sleep Walker** Barry Marsden
1971	**The Phantom** (2 pts.) Colin Foord *The bolt appeared in mysterious circumstances when, it was claimed, a Boy Scout placed it on abseil but was then unable to use it for aid due to its being out of reach.*
1971	**The Phantom** (1 pt.) John Yates *Climbed free by Jonny Woodward in 1977 with the bolt for protection and without by Ian Dunn and Claudie Dunn in 1986.*
Pre-1973	**Oak Tree Crack, The Cleft Route, The Cue**
1973	*Staffordshire Gritstone Area guidebook, Rock Climbs in the Peak, Volume 9, published.*
1977	**The Phantom** Jonny Woodward (unseconded) *First free ascent. The bolt was used for protection.*
1978 May	**Feed the Enemy** Gary Gibson (solo)
1980	**The Gape, Sense of Doubt, John's Arête, Little Arête, The Chalk, Old Son, For Tim, Fat Old Nick** Nick Longland, John Holt
1981	*Staffordshire Area guidebook, Rock Climbs in the Peak, Volume 6, published.*
1985 March 30	**French Connection** Ian Dunn, Claudie Dunn
1985 April 2	**Anniversaire** Ian Dunn (unseconded)
1986 Aug. 31	**Pot Black** Ian Dunn (solo)
1986 Sept. 20	**The Phantom** Ian Dunn, Claudie Dunn *The bolt was finally chopped and this rather unoffensive crag relieved of a very contentious issue. The main issue that remains is the grade of the route which may well be undergraded at E3!*
1986	**The Overhang, Thin Crack, Green Crack** Ian Dunn (solo) *Climbed during guidebook work, they may have been climbed before.*

OUTLYING CRAGS IN THE GRADBACH AREA

LUDCHURCH   O.S. ref. SJ 987656

This remarkable ravine, steeped in history (and vegetation), is on the north-eastern slopes of Back Forest Ridge. Receiving practically no sunshine, its side-walls are cloaked in vegetation and most of the rock remains wet and greasy except after a drought. Ludchurch thus affords a rare environment for thirsty plants suffering photophobia and as such is thought to be of greater significance to the botanist and ecologist than to the climber.

Although a few routes have been unearthed on the north wall in the past, such as **Subterranean Sidewalk** and **Dead Man's Creek**, they should remain as historical epitaphs to the climbers who no longer come here. **CLIMBERS ARE REQUESTED NOT TO CLIMB HERE.**

CASTLE CLIFF ROCKS   O.S. ref. SJ 985658

There is a group of shattered pinnacles near Ludchurch which offers a few minor problems unworthy of climbers' attention.

GIBBONS CLIFF   O.S. ref. SJ 971664

One kilometre downstream from Allgreave Bridge, Clough Brook winds through a short length of wooded valley with very steep sides. There are a number of outcrops here which are in the main overwhelmed by vegetation. The two cleanest buttresses are situated on the west bank directly above the ruins of an old mill. The old mill provides marginally more attractive problems than these rocks.

THE BALLSTONE   O.S. ref. SK 013658

This is a gigantic perched boulder in the grounds of Green Gutter Stake Farm. Whilst it offers excellent bouldering the farmer is understandably unwilling to allow climbing since it lies in his back yard!

FLASH BOTTOM ROCKS   O.S. ref. SK 018657

An excellent but small crag consisting of two buttresses 8m in height. Some fine little routes, mainly in the easier grades, can be found here as well as some tough problems. Just about worth the trek.

THE UPPER CHURNET

'**Esoteria** – meant for the initiated; private, confidential.'

The Pocket Oxford Dictionary.

SHARPCLIFFE ROCKS
by Gary Gibson

O.S. ref. SK 015520

SITUATION and CHARACTER
The rocks lie on the crest of a ridge in the grounds of
Sharpcliffe Hall, 2km from Ipstones.
Perhaps the most unusual of The Upper Churnet crags,
Sharpcliffe Rocks is abundant in numerous excellent boulder
problems along with some bigger, more serious routes on
the main crag. The rock, Triassic Conglomerate, gives the
crag its appeal. Numerous bands of pebbles, some Bunters,
give it a pebble-dashed appearance which is quite
off-putting on first acquaintance. Die-hards will find true
reward from the solitude of the climbing hereabouts.

APPROACHES and ACCESS
From Ipstones, take the B5053 northwards for 1km to a
crossroads on the crest of the ridge. Turn left and follow the
road for a further 1km to limited parking space at a sharp
right-hand bend and a small cottage, Sharpcliffe Lodge.
Continue on foot down the unmade road straight ahead for
400m, then break out right over the fence to the beginning
of the rocks and a series of boulders in the field.
The rocks lie in the grounds of Sharpcliffe Hall and though
access is technically forbidden, if carried out discreetly,
climbing does not appear to be prevented.

HISTORY
Obviously climbed upon in early years by hostellers at the
nearby hall, the 'discovery' of these rocks was the result of a
recce by John Yates, the Dale twins (Brian and Steve) and
Barry Marsden. Their visit resulted in most of the easier
routes along with Yates soloing some good problems:
Puffed Wheat, Blu-tac, Stickfast as well as the superb
Kaleidoscope and *Special K:* both are now Upper Churnet
Valley classics. The cliffs were left in that state and a script

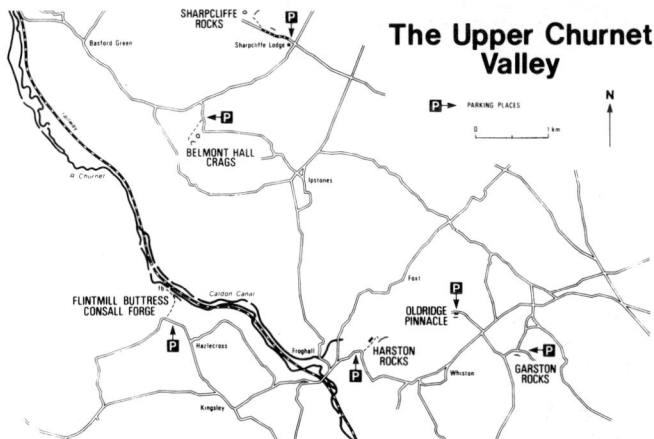

The Upper Churnet Valley

was prepared.

Quite separately, on a tip from John Perry, Gary Gibson and friends paid a visit in 1978 and tackled the main rock with a repeat of *Kaleidoscope*, thought at the time to be a first ascent, *Killjoy* and *Kudos* and left impressed. The potential was obvious, the big lines crying out for leads. Painstaking effort resulted in a number of visits and hours whiled away creating *Pebblesville* whilst Ian Johnson soloed *Johnson'sville*. With Kons Nowak, Gibson led *Kobold* and *Krakatoa*, and eventually, the evil *Knossos* after numerous abortive attempts. He returned a year later for the last two routes on the main crag with *Krushna* and *Kenyatta*, whilst rare visits from marauding locals since the 1980 guidebook have accounted for the odd crumb; Jonny Woodward's *Bond It* and Ian Dunn's *Cannabis Arm*.

THE CLIMBS are described from LEFT to RIGHT. Only technical grades are used for the smaller, problem-type, routes as a solo ascent will be normal.

The first group of boulders encountered is **STRAW BOULDERS** *which offer numerous problems. A large arched block gives:*

1 Peep Show 5m 4a
The left-hand flake on the front face. (1973)

2 Cabana 5m 4b *
The right-hand flake is blacker and meaner, though only
slightly more so. (1973)

*Continue on through the minefield of boulders to reach a
more continuous stretch of rock. Stop briefly at* **BLURRED
BUTTRESS** *for the gem problems of:*

3 Pebblesville 5m 5b
The left-hand side of the face, left of the first crack. (1979)

4 Hush Puppy 5m VD
The first crack proves to be wide and cumbersome. (1973)

5 Hot Dog 6m 4b
The slanting groove right again. (1973)

6 Johnson'sville 7m 5b
Small 'dinks' and holes up the wall to the right. The pebbles
seem to be shedding fast. (1979)

7 Bowcock's Chimney 7m VD
Tackle the cracked chimney to the right. (1973)

8 Cannabis Arm 6m 6a
The arête to the right. Precarious. (1984)

9 Puffed Wheat 6m 5b *
The centre of the final wall. Neat moves, perhaps too
short-lived. (1973)

Saunter on for a further 50m to meet **GROGAN BUTTRESS**,
characterised by a fine steep wall dashed with rugosities.

10 Gorgonzola 6m 5a
Ascend the left-hand side of the wall. Well-wired! (1973)

11 Mr Grogan 8m 5b *
Take the wall at its centre. Pockets, pebbles and rugosities
provide excellent entertainment. (1973)

12 Charlie Farley 8m 4c *
Even better entertainment up the shallow groove in the
right-hand side of the wall. Pockets, pebbles, then buckets!
(1973)

13 Rusks and Rye 6m 5b
The evil bulging crack on the front face. More brutal than
Ramshaw Crack! (1979)

14 Comeback S
Scramble over large blocks right again. (1973)

15 Clinic Kid D
The nice boulder and slab above. (1973)

Turn the corner for **TROUBLE AND STRIFE BUTTRESS**.

16 Vice 8m S
A wide crack complete with chockstone. (1973)

17 Veroa 7m 4c
The thin crack and easier ground right again. (1973)

The final wall yields:

18 Genetix 5m 5b
A crack in the side-wall. (1979)

19 Bond It 6m 5c
The arête. Better than it looks? (1981)

20 Blu-tac 6m 5c *
A good problem up the left-hand side of the front face.
Careful with the landing. (1973)

21 Stickfast 6m 5b
Tackle the centre of the wall. (1973)

22 Raven 6m 4a
Just right, ascend the wall before the arête. (1973)

23 Spirella 11m 4a
Waltz along the obvious break for a traverse. (1973)

24 Meninges 6m D
A slab on the right. (1973)

A further 100m brings **SHARPCLIFFE ROCK** *to hand. Grab
your rope, some runners and a tube of glue!*

25 Underhung Chimney 11m S 4a
The first shallow chimney on the approach from the
previous routes. (1973)

26 Konsolation Prize 12m HS 4a *
The pleasant arête to the right, just before the main rock.
(1980)

27 Marsden's Eliminate 12m M
The large chimney bounding the left side of the rock. (1973)

28 Knossos 18m E5 5c **†
An uncompromising proposition, the result of much hard
work and eventual stupidity! The crumbling front face of the
buttress. Climb up to a break and swing left along it, then
go up to a wide crack; large runners and a crow's nest! Exit

frantically right and upwards. A more difficult left-hand start, 6a, leads to the wide crack. A prior inspection is strongly advised. (1979)

29 Krushna 16m E4 6a *†
Tackle the pink-flecked wall right of Knossos to gain a break and struggle strenuously from the right to your prize — a mean, hand-crushing, final jam crack. (1980)

30 Kenyatta 15m E3 5c *
Less-friable and more amenable than Krushna, though of slightly less quality. Climb the wall 2m right again, passing the break and awkward bulge, to reach flutings leading to the top. (1980)

31 Kaleidoscope 16m E1 5a ***
Classic esoteria, Staffordshire style. From behind the large boulder at the foot of the slab, climb up left via a break to a bulge. Pull over this using a spike to gain a small groove and short finishing wall. (1973)

32 Killjoy 14m E2 5b **
To the right is a diagonal crack. The wall to the left of the diagonal crack leads to the break. Continue up and slightly leftwards, via a scoop. (1979)

33 Kobold 14m E3 5c *
The diagonal crack. From the break, press on direct to the top via small pockets and boldness. (1979)

34 Krakatoa 9m E4 5c
To the right is a grassy platform at a higher level. From its left-hand side climb direct up the thin slab, keeping left of easy ground. (1979)

35 Kudos 8m VS 5a *
The 'easy ground' right of Krakatoa. Any of a number of lines are possible via an initial bulge and shallow depression. (1979)

36 Special K 18m HVS 4c **
Technically the easiest of the routes on the main crag. From the platform, step down left to gain the break and follow it left to reach flutings and an airy finish. (1973)

The main rock is bounded to the right by a final undercut wall.

37 Golden Sovereign 5m 4a
The pleasant wall left of the obvious undercut arête. (1973)

38 Doubloon 6m 5a *

The undercut arête itself. Nowhere hard but enjoyable
throughout. (1973)

39 Pieces of Eight 8m 4a

Wander anywhere on the slab right of the arête. (1973)

Boulder problems abound in this area offering some thrilling
ways of whiling away the hours, unless you meet the nearby
owner!

BELMONT HALL CRAGS   O.S. ref. SK 007504

by Nick Dixon

SITUATION and CHARACTER

The two buttresses lie in a small dale overlooking a stream
2km west of Ipstones village.

An unusual crag, hidden and often green after prolonged
bad weather. In dry conditions the crag gives good climbing
without the attendant popularity found on other cliffs. The
rock is excellent sound gritstone.

APPROACHES and ACCESS

It is possible to approach from either end of the dale,
though it is easier from the north. Take the Basford road out
of Ipstones down past The Marquis of Granby, through
Stocks Green and Above Church. Follow the road down
through a sharp bend and steep hill to park at the bottom.
Halfway down the hill, a path leads off on the left to reach
the crag. From the southern end of the dale, at Belmont
Pools, follow a path on the right to the right-hand buttress.
There appears to be no access problems as the land is quite
public. No difficulties have ever arisen.

HISTORY

The first mention of any activity on these crags was in 1962
when, in the Midlands Association of Mountaineers Journal,
routes such as *Cave Crack, Cave Rib, The Flake Traverse,
Deadwood Crack* and *Vertigo* were described as having been
climbed by the club's members. Later in the same year a
visit from Bob Hassall and Dave Sales resulted in one route
each; *Kneewrecker Chimney* and *Sales' Bulge*. Returning
again, this time in the company of Graham Martin and John
Wilding, *Deadwood Crack, Hassall's Crack, Twisting Crack*
and *Wigglette* were accounted for. The crag lay quiet for

nine years until Norman Hoskins visited it in 1971 and added *The Clown* and *The Joker*, each route requiring an aid point. Following the 1973 guidebook, the Woodward brothers, Jonny and Andrew, visited briefly to eliminate these aid points. Gary Gibson then stamped his name on the cliff with *The Jester* and *Life in the Wrong Lane* whilst preparing a script for a new guidebook, then once again the crag was left alone. The remaining gaps were inevitably filled; Paul Pepperday created *Crimes of Passion* whilst Ian Dunn and Nick Dixon stepped in to climb *Life in the Left Lane* and *Face* respectively, the latter route being the cliff's hardest route to date. It will probably remain that way!

THE CLIMBS are described from LEFT to RIGHT as the normal approach is from the north.

LEFT-HAND BUTTRESS

The northern-most outcrop is the stage for the crag's best routes.

1 Vertigo 14m VD
At the extreme left-hand side of the cliff are two cracks facing north. Climb these. (1962)

2 Life in the Wrong Lane 14m E1 5b
Three metres right of Vertigo is a blunt rib with an overhung start. Climb over the first two bulges, then step right to climb the left-most of three grooves (somewhat artificial). Finish leftwards. (1979)

3 Life in the Left Lane 14m E3 5c   *
Follow Life in the Wrong Lane past the first two bulges, then follow the rib over the next and largest bulge with disheartening protection on a ledge. (1986)

4 The Clown 15m E2 5c   **
Three metres right of the blunt rib is a fingerhold just over the overhang. Gain this and struggle into a standing position above the roof. Using one-finger pockets gain the central small groove, peg runner, and finish directly. Technical moves on clean rock with adequate protection.
(1971/1974)

5 The Jester 15m E4 6a   **

A hard route with a good line and varied climbing, however the usually-present green carpet renders it rarely climbed. Climb the roof just left of Kneewrecker Chimney and take a direct line to gain the steep crack in the upper face. Follow this with increasing fatigue.   (1979)

6 Kneewrecker Chimney 15m HVS 4c   **

The obvious central cleft is magnificent. Climb the narrowing chimney between the buttocks of the crag.   (1962)

7 Face 15m E5 6b   ***

The obvious clean wall right of Kneewrecker Chimney is climbed to a cheeky peg runner. Crux moves past this gain a good flake and an intimidating finish. Low in the grade.

(1986)

8 The Joker 15m E3 6a   *

From 6m up the obvious slanting groove to the right, swing left to the base of a steep groove. Climb this, good wire protection, to some loose blocks and an exposed finish.

(1971/1974)

9 Deadwood Groove 11m HVS 4c

The obvious slanting groove is surprisingly tricky at its finale.   (1962)

10 Allen's Fingers 6m E1 6a

A problem up the wall between Deadwood Groove and Deadwood Crack.   (1984)

11 Deadwood Crack 11m VS 4c

The crack 5m right of Deadwood Groove past a rotting tree to an equally rotten finish.   (1962)

12 Crimes of Passion 11m E4 6a   **

Technical excellence is the key to the incipient ramp right of Deadwood Crack. From the obvious hole finish directly up the slab.   (1982)

RIGHT-HAND BUTRESS

Situated 100m downstream, and clearly identified by its central cave, this green crag has a haunting atmosphere.

13 Sales' Bulge 6m VD

At the left extremity of the crag, climb the crack and bulge above the shallow cave.   (1962)

14 Twisting Crack 8m D

The crack on the right.   (1962)

15 Hassall's Crack 9m VD
The crack just left of the left-hand rib of the front face.

(1962)

16 Cave Rib 12m HS 4a
The obvious rib. Finish right round the overhang.   (1962)

17 Cave Crack 11m HS   **

Start at the large central cave. Bridge out of the cave to the
obvious crack which is followed with difficulty to a hard exit
onto a ledge with a tree. Back-and-foot the tree to finish.
The crack can be climbed direct from the back of the cave at
5c.   (1962)

18 Flake Traverse 15m S
Climb the obvious flake 5m right of Cave Crack to a good
ledge at 9m. Traverse left to finish up Cave Crack.   (1962)

19 Wigglette 6m VS 4c
The face to the right.   (1962)

HARSTON ROCKS   O.S. ref. SK 032477

by Nick Dixon and Gary Gibson

SITUATION and CHARACTER
A small north-facing crag lying on the side of a heavily
wooded valley just to the north-west of Froghall Village.
With the exception of the main Harston Rock, the small
buttresses do not get much sunshine and are therefore often
green and uninpsiring but nevertheless provide some good
bouldering when conditions are perfect. The Rock itself is
probably the Upper Churnet's *'piece de resistance'* and offers
excellent routes on good rock which is perhaps a little sandy
but much less green than the surrounding bluffs. It is well
worth a visit.

APPROACHES and ACCESS
Follow the A52 Stoke-to-Ashbourne road out of Froghall
and go up the steep hill to its top and limited parking on the
left just before the village of Whiston. Walk back down the
hill and after 100m turn right through a gap in the wall and
go up a farm track to the farm; parking is not permitted
here. The start of the cliffs are 25m up the hill to the right
and gained via a well-formed path in the woods.
Access is not a problem since the owner lives at the nearby

farm and is usually notified by the very problematic dog. A polite request here usually bears fruit and helps good relations.

HISTORY

The rocks were first stumbled upon by Oread Mountaineering Club members who set to work with spades and shovels to create many of the easier routes. The driving force was David Penlington who accounted for *The Helix* (the classic of the pinnacle), *Fandango* and *Titian's Wall* as well as other less-important routes. Ernie Marshall climbed *Glyph* whilst Martin Ridges grabbed *Via Trita*. In 1957 the overhanging wall of the pinnacle was ascended on aid but was later ascended free by John Yates and named *The Impending Doom*; quite appropriate since the protection was then (and is now) only meagre. Little was then done until 1970 when Austin Plant, on a 'recce' for a new guidebook, discovered *The Cheek, The Nose* and *Ostentation*. Martin Boysen was also on the scene in the 1970s and came well-versed in jungle warfare for *Black Widow* and *Palsy Wall*. Then, in 1977, Steve Bancroft appeared to capture one of the pinnacle's fine arêtes; *DNA* was to bring Harston Rocks well up to date with modern climbing standards. These standards were continued as Jonny Woodward tackled *Much Ado About Nothing* and whilst preparing another guidebook John Codling did such gems as *Melancholy Man* and *Taming of the Shrew*. This new guidebook spoke of one final challenge, the pinnacle's remaining unclimbed arête. A gauntlet was laid down and a fair competition requested. This challenge was met one spring evening in 1984 when Nick Dixon, a lad from the North-East, well-versed in sandstone horrors, got to work and produced the awesome *One Chromosome's Missing* a route well ahead of any nearby competition, and showing the direction of evolution.

THE CLIMBS are described from RIGHT to LEFT as the normal approach is from the farm. The first crag is:

DEVIL'S ROCK

A bulging nose on the front face is bounded by a tapering wall to the left.

1 Introduction 8m VD

Saunter up green slabs right of the bulging nose.   (1952)

2 The Nose 8m HVS 5b
Usually started direct, the bulging nose gives an awkward
finish. The groove on the left can also be used as an
approach. (1970)

3 The Cheek 8m VS 4c
From 3m up The Nose, traverse left round onto the face,
then go up to finish. It is possible to start direct at 5a. (1970)

4 Devil's Crack 6m S
Quite an awkward little crack in the tapering wall. (1952)

5 Rugosity 6m S 4a
Pleasant. Just to the left of Devil's Crack. (1952)

6 Footpath 6m VD
A line of chippings left again. Naughty! (but nice?). (1952)

7 Alternative Ulster 5m 4b
The final wall and crack. Microscopic. (1978)

8 Saunter 9m S
Traverse across the wall at any applicable height. (1952)

Twenty-five metres onwards brings **GIB BUTTRESS**. *A shelf
on the left is an obvious feature.*

9 Wave 11m D
The right wall and bulge above a ledge. (1952)

10 Ripple 12m VD
Just right of the corner, finishing up a slight groove. (1952)

11 Crest 12m VD
Gain the shelf via a crack and finish direct up the slab.

(1952)

12 Break 14m HVD
Go up the corner just left of Crest. Traverse left and climb a
crack and a wall.

(1952)

13 Backwash 12m VD
The corner, crack and wall. (1952)

The buttress below and to the left is **BISCAY BUTTRESS**. *A
bay is formed by two walls and a prow on the left
dominates.*

14 As You Like It 6m M
A simple groove on the right wall. (1952)

15 Emerald Groove 6m VD
The groove just to the left is predictably green to a finish
either side of the overhang. (1952)

16 Flake Wall 9m HS 4a
The brittle flake to the left has a tricky start. Finish above the
ledge via cracks. (1952)

17 Original Route 11m VS 4c *
The main angle. The finish is awkward and often slimy. A
good line. (1952)

18 The Web 15m HS 4a
The wall left of the corner. Move left below the prow to
finish up its left face. (1952)

19 Black Widow 12m E3 5c
The prow. From the break move awkwardly up its
right-hand side, then swing left and go up its left wall.
(1970s)

20 Emerald Wall 11m VD
Climb the lowest face by its front wall, then the corner on
the right to finish up the left wall of the prow. (1952)

21 Corner Traverse 21m HD
Crosses the bay at half-height via a break and a ledge,
gained from a birch tree on the left of the buttress. (1952)

The next buttress is bottle-shaped and named **PINNACLE
BUTTRESS**.

22 Moore's Crack 11m D
At the top of the gully. A wide crack and slabs. (1952)

23 The Sting 9m E1 5a
The shallow groove, left of the crack. (1970s)

24 Titian's Wall 15m E2 5a
The front headwall gained from pockets on the right and
finished via a crack. Terrifying! (1952)
Direct Start, 5b † (1988). Climb the lower front wall of the
buttress over the undercut at the bottom, using a poor crack
to the left.

25 Ostentation 15m E2 5a
Even more terrifying. The wall to the left gained from the
chimney on the left. Pass the overhang with trepidation.
(1970)

26 Fandango 15m HS 4a
Traverse left from the chimney of Ostentation below an
overhang to a pocketed finishing wall. (1952)

27 Magenta Corner 14m HS 4a
The corner 4m left, then slabs and a pinnacle above. (1952)

28 Glyph 12m S
Use a vague crack to gain the pinnacle of Magenta Corner.
(1952)

29 Rotondas 9m S
Climb to a sloping shelf 2m left, then move left and go up
on pockets. (1952)

*There are three isolated buttresses to the left each one
giving a single route.*

30 Oak Spur 12m D
The first, right-hand, buttress. (1952)

31 Moss Rose 12m VD
The narrow central buttress. (1952)

32 Frequency 11m S
The third buttress. A difficult wall and 'fine' crack. (1952)

CAVE BUTTRESS *comes next. The reason for the name lies
at its foot in the centre.*

33 Vereker's Venture 9m VS 5a
The wall's right edge. A l– o– ng stretch to start. (1952)

34 Taming of the Shrew 9m HVS 5c
Step left from Vereker's Venture to climb the bulge and wall.
(1978)

35 Much Ado About Nothing 9m E3 6a *
The fine thin crack just right of the cave. Excellent with a
well-protected, single hard manoeuvre. (1975)

36 The Cave Crack 9m S
A painful affair with the obvious fissure. (1952)

37 Palsy Wall 9m E2 5c
The scooped wall to the left finishing on pockets.
Worthwhile. (1970s)

38 Palpitation 9m HVD
A corner on the front face to a finish off right. (1952)

39 Shelf Route 8m HVD
Climb direct up the left extremity of the buttress. (1952)

TECHNICIAN'S WALL *lies 100m left again and is usually cloaked in greenery.*

40 The Technician 6m 5a
Filthy. Climb the right-hand wall or, better still, don't bother! (1978)

41 Tiptoe 6m HVD
Just right of the central chimney. (1952)

42 Diagonal Crack 6m D
The chimney. (1952)

43 The Clam 6m 5b
The rounded left arête. (1952)

44 Limpet 6m 4a
The left-hand face is taken direct. (1952)

45 Megalomania 9m 5b
Traverse from left to right. Interesting moves. (1978)

HARSTON ROCK

One hundred metres left (north) of Technician's Wall is the bastion of Upper Churnet climbing, a 20m high tower of the best gritstone, set on an idyllic bracken-clad hillside.

46 Via Trita 14m HVS 5a *
An enlightening route offering highly technical moves for the grade but with only lean protection. Climb the crack in the right-hand (south-facing) face of the pinnacle. Arrange protection before a tricky mantelshelf leads to the delightfully rippled finishing wall. (1952)

47 The Helix 22m HVS 5a **
An expedition of uncompromising length and character for gritstone. Start as for Via Trita but after 3m break out left to an overlap. Traverse left to a small ledge, then go up a slab to gain a horizontal break. Follow the break leftwards across the exposed front face to finish up a goove above the far arête. (1952)

48 Melancholy Man 14m E2 5c *
An eliminate line based on the lower part of The Helix leads to a crux finishing wall. Start just left of Via Trita and traverse left along the small slab. Pull onto the hanging slab above which leads to a break. Step right and climb the steep wall. (1978)

49 DNA 18m E3 6a   **

A superb and classic product of the Seventies centred on the
right arête of the front face. Gain the undercut scoop in the
prow by some committing moves. Leave it on the left using
a horizontal break, then make technical moves up the rib to
the next horizontal break. Finish up the steep wall as for
Melancholy Man.   (1977)

50 One Chromosome's Missing 18m E7 6b   ***†

The right-hand side of the isolated arête left of DNA has no
worthwhile protection, save a very poor hand-placed peg in
the upper break. A gritstone gem to rival any in the Peak
District.   (1984)

51 The Impending Doom 18m E3 5c   **

Grand climbing up the steep flakes in the wall left of One
Chromosome's Missing leads to a difficult, rounded finish.
Poor, corroding pegs protect this route less securely each
year.   (1970)

52 Hatschek's Groove 14m HVS 5a   *

Ascend the broken crack to the large ledge. The shallow
groove above is both perplexing and dangerous. A good
route.   (1952)

The overlaps at the back of the pinnacle lead to the summit.
This also provides the easiest means of descent.

HARSTON QUARRY *exists down and to the left of Harston
Rock. It is not worth the effort to get to it.*

OLDRIDGE PINNACLE   O.S. ref. SK 043480

by Nick Dixon

SITUATION and CHARACTER
An obscure but pleasant gritstone pinnacle, this obelisk
stands amidst lush, open pasture in fields 1km east of
Harston Rock. Whilst there are no easy routes here it gives
pleasant esoteric climbing *'a la norm'* for The Upper
Churnet.

APPROACHES and ACCESS
Approach from Harston Rock is possible via an old and
increasingly overgrown railway track. However it is best to
approach from the A52 Stoke-to-Ashbourne road by taking

a left turn 1km outside Whiston (opposite Blakeley Road which leads to Garston Rocks). This track leads to a farm; ask the farmer for permission to climb as it is usually granted but do not block his access when parking.

HISTORY

The Pinnacle was initially discovered in 1952 by David Penlington who ascended the easiest three routes; *South-east Crack, South-west Crack* and *North Face*. In 1978 *Tour de Force*, an established top-rope route, received its first lead from John Codling. The 1973 guidebook had referred to an unclimbable south face to this pinnacle. Five years later Codling dispensed with this accolade by climbing the fine *Gateless Gate* and *Qui Vive*. The two remaining lines were duly picked off by Nick Dixon; *Boats for Hire* and *The Fatalist's Canoe* are the latest offerings on this strange outpost.

THE CLIMBS are described in a CLOCKWISE direction starting at the extreme right-hand side of the south face.

1 South-east Crack 9m VS 4a   *
The obvious wide corner-crack facing uphill, south-east. The easiest route to The Pinnacle's summit is by no means a pushover. (1952)

2 Qui Vive 9m E3 6a   **
The right arête of the overhanging south face leads, via 'rockovers', to a thread runner and a rounded finish; crux. (1978)

3 The Gateless Gate 9m E3 6a   **
The sometimes dirty central line up the overhanging south face starting via a crack and hole, is both strenuous and frustrating. Good wires protect the finish. (1978)

4 The Fatalist's Canoe 9m E4 6a   **†
Climb the obvious small flake to the left of The Gateless Gate to reach a hole. A rounded finish lies above. (1987)

5 Boats for Hire 9m E3 6a   **
The left arête of the overhanging south face gives a route with a split personality. Climb the horrendously steep crack, then traverse left above the dry-stone wall to finish delicately up the bulging slab. (1984)

6 The South-west Crack 8m VS 4b
The awkward fissure just left of the dry-stone wall on the west face. (1952)

7 Battle Royal 12m E3 5c
To the left is an arête which faces the farm. Climb this, the
crux being to leave the small groove. A good route which is
unfortunately often dirty. (1978)

8 Tour de Force 13m E1 5b
The very green north face just left of Battle Royal. Move up,
then right to a hidden hole near the arête. Use this to gain
the shelf, then finish up the wall above. (1978)

9 The North Face 16m VS 4b
Gain the top of the boulder in the centre of the north face,
then climb the thin crack up the face proper. Usually very
green. (1952)

10 Nom de Guerre 9m E1 5b
The thin crack just right of the arête. (1978)

11 Ivanhoe 9m VS 4c
Climb the square-cut arête directly below the shelf. (1978)

GARSTON ROCKS   O.S. ref. SK 051476

by Gary Gibson

SITUATION and CHARACTER
The rocks lie to the east of the A52 Stoke-to-Ashbourne
road and are easily seen from the road appearing as two
buttresses.
It is a pleasant crag composed of good sandstone with
weathered features and holds. Although there is some
friable rock, the easy-angled nature renders this an
insignificant problem.

APPROACHES and ACCESS
One kilometre out of the village of Whiston turn right along
Blakeley Lane (the first right on the long straight), then turn
left after 500m to below the crag. Limited parking below.
**Access is at present strictly prohibited. Those hoping to
climb should first ask permission from the nearby farm. It is
unlikely to be granted. Please respect this refusal.**

HISTORY
Climbing development here took place in two main phases.
Initially discovered in 1952 by Alan Simpson and Martin
Ridges, the easier and most obvious lines were then
ascended. Development then halted, though regular parties

visited for the existing routes. John Codling and Gary Gibson had other intentions in 1978. Codling plugged most of the gaps, notably *Don Quixote,* just beating Gibson to the majority (not all!)of the lines. Ewan Murray probably accounted for the first ascent of *Tequila Sunrise* named in absentia, whilst Mike Hernon toppled down, (before up!) the aptly named *Runaway*. Nothing remains.

THE CLIMBS are described from RIGHT to LEFT.

1 Tequila Sunrise 8m HVS 5a   *
A sharp arête, beginning precariously on the right.   (1978)

2 Runaway 8m E2 5c
The difficult bulging left-hand wall of the gully.   (1978)

3 Feet of Strength 6m HS 4a
Climb/struggle up the first wide crack left of the gully. (1952)

4 The Arête 12m S   **
A very pleasant affair with good climbing and surprising features. Start left or right, pass through a scoop but not through the thread. Mantelshelf to finish.   (1952)

5 Technocrat 11m HVS 5a
Avoiding the routes either side enables the wall and scoop just left to be climbed.   (1978)

6 Hole and Corner Crack 9m S   *
The crack to the left halts briefly for a small cave.   (1952)

7 Don Quixote 11m E3 6a   **
A bouldering gem. A peculiar porthole to the left enables a scoop to be gained, followed all too briefly by a wall. (1978)

8 Skull Crack 11m S   **
Cross your bones to climb the awkward wide crack.   (1952)

9 Tricky Woo 9m HVS 5a
Move right from the corner to the left and pass a break to gain the top via a small vague rib.   (1978)

10 The Chute 8m VD
The corner is open and pleasing.   (1952)

11 Pillow of Winds 8m VS 4b
The left arête of the corner. The name seems rather over-the-top.   (1978)

12 One Knight Stand 6m HVS 5b
Climb direct up the centre of the well-formed wall. Delicate at first only.   (1978)

13 The Bishop's Move 9m VS 4a   *
Move up just left again to reach the slanting crack. Follow it
to finish just left of the corner. Excellent.   (1952)

14 All the King's Horses 18m HS 4a   *
A girdle! From the arête of The Bishop's Move continue into
Tricky Woo and on into Hole and Corner Crack. Description
seems superfluous.   (1978)

*Problems abound at the back of the bay. The following
routes are on the left-hand buttress, starting on its
right-hand side.*

15 Larva Wall 8m VD
A slab and overhang on the buttress's right extremity.   (1952)

16 The Stadium 8m HVS 5b
Thin moves over the bulge to the left lead to a short slab.
                                                                (1978)

17 Left Arête 8m S
Quite an awkward start is followed by pleasant climbing.
                                                                (1952)

18 Cave Wall 8m VD   *
Climb to the obvious cave, exit onto the wall and climb via
cracks to a finishing bulge.   (1952)

19 Rainbow Recess 8m VD

                                                                    *
Gain a ledge 2m left, then step right and go up.   (1952)

20 Triack 6m HS 4a
A series of cracks on the left extremity of the buttress. (1952)

*The track (not Triack!)running eastwards leads past the farm
to a field containing a number of boulders. The largest of
these, much like a small pinnacle, offers* **The Last Post**, *E1
5b, up its arête.*

CONSALLFORGE, FLINTMILL BUTTRESS

by Gary Gibson   OS. ref SK 004484

SITUATION and CHARACTER
This cliff lies on the southern bank of the River Churnet 2km
south of Consall Station and 1km north-west of Froghall.
A large crag bristling with bulges and overhangs, the

buttress is much steeper than it looks. It is also often damp and the routes described were the result of painstaking gardening. They will probably require re-gardening before further ascents can be attempted. It is doubtful whether a visit has been made since the previous guide.

APPROACHES and ACCESS
The best approach is from the A52 Stoke-to-Ashbourne road. A small lane runs between Kingsley and Kingsley Moor, through the villages of Hollins, Hazles and Hazles Cross. Between the latter two a public footpath runs down to Consallforge and is well-marked. From the footbridge over the River Churnet, immediately below and right of the crag, strike up through the undergrowth to reach the cliff. The cliff appears to be quite public and no access problems have arisen.

HISTORY
The crag was discovered in 1970 by Austin Plant and Bob Hassall when in June of that year Norman Hoskins led *Constant Rumble*. In 1971 Hassall returned with Ralph Fawcett and bagged *Manifesto* and Hassall did *The Missus*. Suitably aware of the potential Fawcett returned with Barry Marsden, Pete Harrop and Jeff Wincott to clean and ascend *Nosey Parker* whilst Hassall with Dave Salt bagged *Full Frontal*. 1974 saw Marsden pegging up *Death Wish* and in 1977 Steve and Brian Dale found *Indecent Exposure* and *Grumbling Wall* to their liking along with *Peeping Tom* and a finish to The Missus in 1978. That's how things look like staying.
THE CLIMBS are described from LEFT to RIGHT.

Towards the left extremity, a disjointed groove merges to an overhanging chimney. Left again is:

1 Grumbling Wall 18m VS 4b   †
Climb up onto the wall via a rib, then traverse right and cross the smooth slab above the overhang.   (1977)

2 The Constant Rumble 15m HVS 5a   †
The obvious line has an awkward exit.   (1970)

A thin crack through the overhang to the right gives **Miller's Melody** VS A2 *whilst the big roof right again gives the* **Death Wish** A3.

Nine metres right again are twin grooves.

3 Full Frontal 20m HVS 5b (1 pt. aid)   †
Climb the right-hand groove, then swing right and go up
via a slab, moving left below the bulges for 3m. Use a peg
for aid, gained by a long reach, then climb the crack above
passing a small ledge to finish up the overhanging groove
with two further peg runners.   (1971)

4 Indecent Exposure 20m HVS 5b (2 pts. aid)   †
At the point where Full Frontal meets the overhangs, go
over with a peg for aid and use another peg to gain a
difficult corner.   (1977)

Three metres to the right a tree 'erupts' from the cliff.

5 Manifesto 20m HVS 5a   †
Climb past the tree and at the roof (peg runner)up left, pull
up to the next. Pull over again and finish up the crack. (1970)

6 Peeping Tom 20m HVS 5a   †
Starting just right, climb a crack and slab, then traverse right
below the roof to a groove. Move steeply up this to reach
good holds and then a large ledge. Continue up the wall to
gain the top.   (1978)

7 Nosey Parker 20m E1 5b u[pts. aid)   †
The indefinite crack 5m right leads to a steep groove. Use
two pegs for aid to start, then continue direct.   (1971)

8 The Missus 25m VS 4b   †
Start 5m right. Climb the slab then step awkwardly right to a
ledge. Step up left and climb the steep cracked chimney to a
slab on the left. Traverse left to finish up Nosey Parker.
     (1971/1978)

9 The Spearhead 11m VS 4c   †
The centre of the buttress to the right of the gully.

PRICE'S CAVE CRAG   O.S. ref. SK 002493

A small cliff overlooking the Black Lion Inn at Consallforge.
Scrambling is available on poor-quality rock.

WETLEY ROCKS   O.S. ref. SK 967495

These lie on the northern side of the Stone-to-Leek road.
Whilst they have been climbed on for years, they offer little
for the accomplished climber. A good ridge is available at
Difficult standard and is situated to the left of the service
station.

THE UPPER CHURNET LIST OF FIRST ASCENTS

1951 Spring	**Original Route** David Penlington, Michael Harby
1951 Aug.	**Cave Crack, Magenta Corner, Flake Wall, Devil's Crack** David Penlington, P Gardener, M Moore
1952 Spring	**The Helix, Titian's Wall, The Web, Fandango** David Penlington Titian's Wall, direct start S Alsop, solo, 18th September 1988
1952 Spring	**Hatschek's Groove** John Fisher
1952 Spring	**Glyph** Ernie Marshall
1952 Spring	**Via Trita** Martin Ridges
1952 Spring	**Introduction, Devil's Crack, Rugosity, Footpath, Saunter, Wave, Ripple, Crest, Backwash, As You Like It, Emerald Groove, Flake Wall, Emerald Wall, Corner Traverse, Moore's Crack, Magenta Corner, Rotandas, Oak Spur, Moss Rose, Frequency, Vereker's Venture, The Cave Crack, Palpitation, Shelf Route, Tiptoe, Diagonal Crack, The Clam, Limpet** Oread Mountaineering Club members
1952 June	**The Arête, Hole and Corner Crack, Skull Crack, The Shute, The Bishop's Move, Larva Wall, Left Arête, Cave Wall, Rainbow Recess, Triack** Alan Simpson, Martin Ridges
1952	**The South-east Crack, The South-west Crack, The North Face** David Penlington
1957	*Climbs on Gritstone Volume 4, Further Developments in the Peak District, published.*
1962 June	**Vertigo, Deadwood Crack, Cave Rib, Cave Crack, The Flake Traverse** Midland Association of Mountaineers members
1962 Autumn	**Kneewrecker Chimney** Bob Hassall, Dave Sales
1962 Autumn	**Sales' Bulge** Dave Sales, Bob Hassall
1962 Autumn	**Deadwood Crack, Twisting Crack, Hassall's Crack, Wigglette** Combinations of Bob Hassall, Dave Sales, Graham Martin, John Wilding
1970 Spring	**The Nose, The Cheek, Ostentation** Austin Plant
1970 Spring	**The Impending Doom** (2 pts.) Austin Plant *Climbed free in 1970 by John Yates.*
1970 June	**The Constant Rumble** Norman Hoskins
1970 June	**Manifesto** Bob Hassall, Ralph Fawcett

1970 July	**The Impending Doom** John Yates *First free ascent.*
1971 May 16	**The Clown** (1 pt.) Norman Hoskins *Climbed free by Jonny Woodward in 1975.*
1971 May 20	**The Joker** (1 pt.) Norman Hoskins *Climbed free by Jonny and Andrew Woodward in 1975.*
1971	**The Missus** Bob Hassall
1971	**Nosey Parker** Ralph Fawcett, Barry Marsden, Pete Harrop, Jeff Wincott
1971	**Full Frontal** Bob Hassall, Dave Salt
1970s	**Black Widow, Palsy Wall, The Sting** Martin Boysen
1973	*Staffordshire Gritstone Area guidebook, Rock Climbs in the Peak, Volume 9, published.*
1973	**Puffed Wheat, Blu-Tac, Stickfast, Special K, Kaleidoscope** John Yates (solo)
1973	**Peep Show, Cabana, Hush Puppy, Hot Dog, Bowcock's Chimney, Charlie Farley, Comeback, Clinic Kid, Vice, Veroa, Raven, Spirella, Meninges, Marsden's Eliminate, Golden Sovereign, Pieces of Eight** combinations of Steve Dale, Brian Dale, John Yates, Barry Marsden
1974	**Death Wish** Barry Marsden
1975 June	**Much Ado About Nothing** Jonny Woodward
1975 July	**The Clown** Jonny Woodward (solo) *First free ascent.*
1975 July	**The Joker** Jonny Woodward, Andrew Woodward *First free ascent. Top-roped first.*
1977	**Grumbling Wall, Indecent Exposure** Steve Dale, Brian Dale
1977 Aug.	**DNA** Steve Bancroft, Nicky Stokes
1978	**Peeping Tom, The Missus, new finish** Steve Dale, Brian Dale, Barry Marsden
1978	**Tequila Sunrise** Ewan Murray
1978	**Runaway** Mike Hernon
1978	**Technocrat, Don Quixote, Tricky Woo, The Gateless Gate, Ivanhoe, Taming of the Shrew** John Codling (solo)
1978	**Pillow of Winds, One Knight Stand, All the King's Horses, The Stadium, The Last Post, Megalomania, Alternative Ulster** Gary Gibson (solo)

1978	**Tour de Force** John Codling (roped solo) *Named from a previous top-rope ascent.*
1978	**Qui Vive, Nom de Guerre, Battle Royal, Melancholy Man** John Codling
1979 May	**Killjoy** Gary Gibson, John Perry
1979 May	**Kudos** Gary Gibson (solo)
1979 July	**Knossos** Gary Gibson (unseconded) *Top-roped many times first.*
1979 July	**Kobold, Krakatoa** Gary Gibson, Kons Nowak
1979 Aug.	**The Jester** Gary Gibson, Mark Hewitt *Top-roped first.*
1979 Aug.	**Life in the Wrong Lane** Gary Gibson, Mark Hewitt
1979 Aug.	**Pebblesville, Genetix, Rusks and Rye** Gary Gibson (solo)
1979 Aug.	**Johnson'sville** Ian Johnson (solo)
1980 May	**Konsolation Prize** Gary Gibson (solo)
1980 May	**Krushna, Kenyatta** Gary Gibson, Dave Williams
1981	*Staffordshire Area guidebook, Rock Climbs in the Peak, Volume 6, published.*
1981	**Bond It** Jonny Woodward (solo)
1982	**Crimes of Passion** Paul Pepperday (unseconded)
1984 May 16	**Boats for Hire** Nick Dixon, Steve Lowe
1984 May 22	**One Chromosome's Missing** Nick Dixon, Andy Popp *A major addition. Whilst at first 'only' graded E6, it has become clear that this route is much harder. Possibly the first gritstone E7 in the country.*
1984 May	**Allen's Fingers** Allen Williams (solo)
1986 May	**Cannabis Arm** Ian Dunn (solo)
1986 May	**Face** Nick Dixon (unseconded)
1986 May	**Life in the Wrong Lane** Ian Dunn (unseconded)
1987 Sept.	**The Fatalist's Canoe** Nick Dixon (solo) *On-sight, after many attempts in the rain.*

THE LOWER CHURNET

by Steve Dale

'All hope abandon, ye who enter here'.

Dante.

SITUATION and CHARACTER

All the crags are within 5km of the village of Alton, 8km from Cheadle and 14km from Ashbourne.

The best access to most of the crags in the district is from the narrow road between Oakamoor and Alton, known locally as The Red Road.

The scenery here is most spectacular. Castles and towers stand out on either bank of the river suggesting picturesque Rhineland rather than rural Staffordshire.

On the south bank is a great 'castle', in reality a nineteenth century Roman Catholic Church and Convent, now a preparatory school. On the opposite side is Alton Towers – famous now as Europe's largest leisure-park attracting millions of visitors during the summer months and offering an excellent alternative to anyone disillusioned with the climbing hereabouts.

Steepness and vegetation are very evident and the rock itself varies from being fairly sound to very pebbly, and rotten to even something resembling solidified mud! Despite superficial shortcomings some of the rock is solid enough and one soon learns to judge the likelihood of any particular hold (or pebble) staying in place (or not!). Much nervous tension is built up when negotiating this type of terrain but overcoming it safely is a very satisfying experience, a sterner joy than that obtained from solving practical problems of balance or strength without any decision having to be taken on the nature of the support. Some (not many) may enjoy this sort of thing better than purely physical pleasures of muscle co-ordination demanded by climbs with no such insecurity. Few new climbs have been reported since the last guidebook: lots of untouched rock exists, just no enthusiasm!

HISTORY

Some of these crags were visited by David Penlington and members of the Oread Mountaineering Club in the Spring of 1951 but they left no records of any routes. *Ina's Chimney*

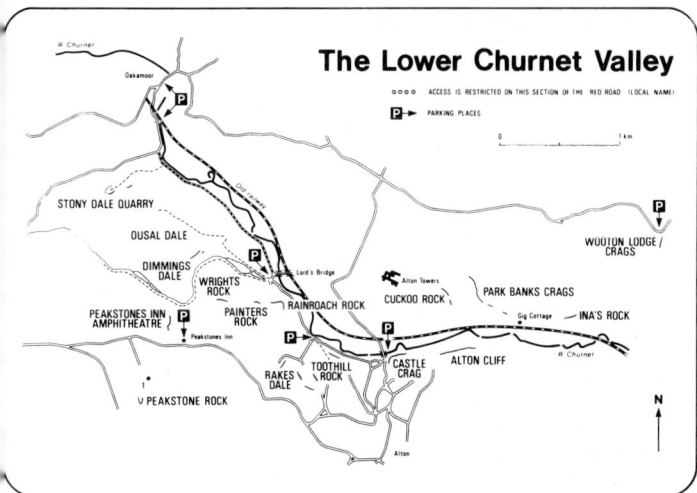

The Lower Churnet Valley

○○○○ ACCESS IS RESTRICTED ON THIS SECTION OF THE RED ROAD (LOCAL NAME)

🅿➤ PARKING PLACES

R. Churnet

Oakamoor

STONY DALE QUARRY

OUSAL DALE

DIMMINGS DALE

WRIGHTS ROCK

PEAKSTONES INN AMPHITHEATRE

Peakstones Inn

PAINTERS ROCK

RAINROACH ROCK

Lord's Bridge

Alton Towers

CUCKOO ROCK

PARK BANKS CRAGS

WOOTON LODGE / CRAGS

Gig Cottage

INA'S ROCK

V PEAKSTONE ROCK

RAKES DALE

TOOTHILL ROCK

CASTLE CRAG

ALTON CLIFF

R. Churnet

Alton

N

and *Brad's Chimney* on Park Banks crag had most certainly been climbed prior to Penlington's visit. Between 1959 and 1963 David Hudson and members of Denstone College Climbing Club did the majority of the routes on the right-hand side of Park Banks Crag including *Hollybush Hell, Defiance, Chilton's Superdirect* and *Left* and *Right Twin Cracks* and the three easier routes to the left. During the same period they visited Wright's Rock and climbed *Central Crack* and *Tunnel Chimney*. In early-1969, Austin Plant and John Stubbs of the North Staffordshire Mountaineeering Club climbed *Spreadeagle* on Rainroach. Plant returned later that year with Bob Hassall and climbed *The Taxman, The Unveiling* and *The Fly*, the latter with some aid.

Castle Crag was attacked in January 1971; Hassall, John Yates and Norman Hoskins climbed *The Gallows* and finished up the Castle wall. Yates led the direct start to *Pasiphae*, Plant and Hassall did *Minotaur* and the excellent *Labyrinth*; Hoskins produced *Daedalus* and the exit to *Theseus*. The same group turned to the impressive Ina's Rock. Hoskins led *Initiation Groove, Ground Support, Rawhide* and *Bloody Crack*. Hassall led *Tactical Weapon* and Plant climbed *Gladiator*. They also attacked *Atlas* which was climbed with a large wooden wedge for aid in the final overhang. Hoskins then climbed *The Renaissance* on Park

Banks Crag. The end of Spring found them on Wootton Lodge Crags where Hassall found *The Long Traverse* and *Central Route*. Hoskins led *Ungodly Groove* and the party went on to trundle and dig elsewhere.

The Winter of 1970/71 was a mild one and, in January, Yates visited Wright's Rock and led *Sauron*, *The Hob* and the variant finish on *Tiger's Wall*. On the same day he led *The Highwayman* and *Hot Pants* on Toothill Rock. Hoskins was back amongst the rhododendrons in February when he led *Mark* and *Stephen* on Park Banks Crag. Dave Salt took a rest from writing up other people's routes and led *The Prodigal* and *Per Rectum*. Yates produced *Extractum* and *Honest John* on Park Banks and Barry Marsden found *Tre Cime*.

Yates now moved his attention to Peakstone Rock in April, when he led *Peakstone Crack*, *Stumblehead*, *Plebble* and *Marajuander*. Marsden was responsible for *Afrodizzy Crack*. These two spent some time in the undergrowth behind Peakstone Inn producing *Scoop Wall*, *Right Wall*, *Scout Wall* and *B.J.M.* Hassall put up two new routes on Ina's Rock in April: *Donor* and *Amazing Grace*.

Hoskins, Salt and Hassall climbed *Icarus* on Castle Crag. The following week the trio returned and Hoskins led the first pitch of *Theseus* in a thunderstorm. He then turned on *Zeus* (perhaps in retaliation) and in almost total darkness forced his way over the overhang using a sling on a large nut in the crack.

Yates, Marsden, Pete Ruddle and Chris Cartlidge visited Wootton Lodge where Yates led the first complete ascent of *Ungodly Groove*, the very thin *Pull John*, *Quasimodo*, *Cripple's Corner* and *Wootton Wanderer*. Marsden and Ruddle tried alternately to lead *Hanging Crack* until Ruddle used a big nut for aid and powered himself over.

Hoskins paid a visit to Alton Cliff and climbed *The Brothers*. Later with Salt and Ruddle he returned to show his find and Ruddle led *Rig a Dig Dig* somewhat artificially.

In March 1972, Hassall visited Lion Rock and climbed most of the routes. For two years following the publication of the 1973 guidebook little or nothing was climbed in the valley.

In February 1975 Jonny Woodward and his brother Andrew attacked Wootton Lodge Crags, removed the aid from *Quasimodo* and *Hanging Crack* and added *A Phoenix Too Frequent*. Later that year the same pair dispensed with the aid on *Zeus* on Castle Crag, *The Fly* on Rainroach and

Tactical Weapon on Ina's Rock. They were also active on Park Banks at about the same time. For two years another lull in climbing followed until in 1977 when the Woodwards free-climbed *Atlas* making this and its neighbour *Tactical Weapon* two of the very best routes in the valley.

In 1978 Stephen and Brian Dale took on the task of preparing a more detailed guidebook to the Churnet Valley. Steve, along with Barry Marsden, found *Northern Lights* and *Dancing Bear* behind Peakstone Inn whilst lower down the valley Brian, with Ewan Murray, found *Christopher James*. In the Autumn of 1978 the Woodwards climbed *Gentleman John* without the aid, and also the strenuous *Jack the Traverse*. They moved onto Alton Cliff and did several hard climbs including a free ascent of *Rig a Dig Dig*. Across the river on Park Banks they added the bold *Patient Weaver* amongst others. The Dale brothers climbed *Impacted Bowel* on Ousal Crag and Murray was busy on Toothill Rocks producing the awkward *Daddy Long Legs*.
The Winter of 1978/79 was a hard one and it was not until early Summer that the area came under attack again. The Dale brothers became obsessed with Dimmings Dale and added over thirty climbs including the excellent *Top Brick*, *Slippery Caramel* and *Toast Rack*. Murray, during the first ascent of *The Mexican*, had a spectacular fall from the lip of the overhang into the bushes below. On Wright's Rock Jonny Woodward was in action climbing *Soar Off*, *Thorns* and *Alternative Three*. On nearby Painter's Rock the Dale brothers produced all the present-day routes whilst the Woodwards did *Whispering Myth* on Ina's Rock.

Towards the end of the Summer the Dale brothers climbed *Desert Rat*, *Dust Storm* and *Sandbagger* in Rakes Dale and then went on to find Stony Dale Quarry. *Dance of the Flies* was ascended and the quarry was left for Jonny Woodward to move in. *Doina Da J'al*, *Robin Hood* and *Friar Muck* were produced. In the same month he climbed the desperate *Hand Jive* on Lion Rock. He then escaped from the valley to climb *5000 Volts*, *Dimetrodon* and *Time's Arrow* on the more open Peakstone Rock. At the end of a fine spell, in May 1980, Steve Dale returned to old haunts in Stony Dale Quarry and led *Cave Crack*, *Long Lankin* and *Little Nick*.
The 1980 guidebook appeared, telling all of a wealth of new climbs in the area. However it failed to be the catalyst and with Jonny Woodward losing enthusiasm and only the Dale

brothers retaining a flickering of interest, the area has been quiet ever since. Isolated ascents have occurred. Paddy Gaunt arrived for *Mental Traveller*, Ian Barker managed to free climb *Lord's Arête* and in 1987 Simon Alsop soloed *The Brazilian*.

Perhaps the passage of time, increasing interest in esoteria and the lack of virgin rock in other areas will draw more climbers to the area. Then again it may, as before, continue to return to its once-peaceful Amazonian-state.

PARK BANKS CRAG   O.S. ref. SK 082429

SITUATION, ACCESS and APPROACHES

The crag is on the south side of Alton Park just east, of Slain Hollow and 1km from the bridge below Alton.

It will be noticed that all the crags in Alton Towers rise from a convenient well-kept path — The Rock Walk. Posts describing the various flora and fauna along this path are evident as will be your presence if spotted by any of the security measures employed by the Towers! During the summer months you will probably be evicted or charged the entrance fee (expensive). In winter, attentions appear to be turned to improving the facilities for the summer visitors. The owners have not been approached — let sleeping dogs lie! From the northern side of the bridge, an old railway-track can be reached through a works yard and followed laboriously for 1km to some old crossing gates. Through the left-hand gate is the derelict Gig Cottage. A security camera will monitor your movements as you walk up the steep path behind the ruins to a broad path, The Rock Walk.

CHARACTER

The rock is Keuper Sandstone with bands of pebbles which tend to disappear when in use. It is generally quite clean and free from the more copious vegetation.

THE CLIMBS are described from RIGHT to LEFT.

As one catches one's breath after the stiff walk from Gig Cottage, a 6m roof can be seen.

1 Coelred's Crack 9m HVS 5c
The obvious crack 50m right of the roof.   (pre-1951)

2 Fast and Bulbous 10m E2 5b
The arête right of Hollybush Hell. Start on the left and traverse to a ledge at 4m (or start direct at 5c), then follow the arête on its right-hand side. (1984)

3 Hollybush Hell 9m S
Climb the wide crack to the left of the 6m roof, battling past the holly. A pleasant slab finishes the climb. (1959-63)

3a Hopeless Holly 9m E1 5b †
The upper slabby arête left of Hollybush Hell, gained by the short arête below. (1988)

4 Defiance 9m S *
The narrow slab can be gained from the corner on the left. Really pleasing. (1959-63)

5 Chilton's Superdirect 9m VS 4b
Start at the short corner to the left and climb direct to reach a small ledge at 4m, then go up the groove until a move right onto the arête of Defiance can be made. Moving left to a ledge is 4c. (1959-63)

6 Alien Wall 9m HVS 5b
Climb the depresion 1m left with difficulty to a hard landing (even harder if you fall off!) on the upper shelf. Finish up to the left. (1970)

6a Aliens 9m E3 6c †
Climbs the faint flake and thin crack between Alien Wall and Right Twin Crack avoiding hold on either route. (1988)

7 Right Twin Crack 9m S *
Interesting jamming up the crack. (1959-63)

8 Left Twin Crack 9m S
Bunter pebbles are present hereabouts. Two possible exits exist; neither are as easy as they look. (1959-63)

9 The Height Below 9m E1 5c
Reach a crack by desperate moves 2m left of Left Twin Crack. (1977)

10 The Renaissance 9m VS 4c ***
The thin crack to the left gives an excellent climb. (1970)

10a You'll Always Reap What You Sow 9m E5 6a **†
The elegant rounded arête left is taken direct by fine moves. Unprotected. (1988)

11 Anthem for a Doomed Youth 9m E3 5c
Start 3m left and climb rightwards to the arête, then move
back left to reach a sandy ledge. Go up the wall above on
terrible holds. (1975)

11a No Future 9m E6 6b *†
The centre of the wall left of Anthem for a Doomed Youth.
Start at the letters scraped 'Mark Capper' and ascend direct
using pockets, friable holds and adrenalin. Unprotected.
(1988)

*The easy chimney gives a good means of descent whilst
tree roots in the layback provide excellent holds on:*

12 Blunder 7m D
Interesting wooden holds. (1959-63)

The crack to the left is filthy; **Uchimata**, Difficult.

13 Four Horsemen 9m E2 5c
Problematical starting moves up the crack on the left lead to
a break. The nose is ascended on small holds. (1977)

*Fifty metres left is a buttress with a superb chimney. To the
right of this is a steep wall with a broken arête (it is not
known who broke it!).*

14 Honest John 18m E1 5a
Start on the right of the wall and traverse left with some
degree of strenuousness before going up to a rhododendron
runner. Above this move awkwardly right, then go straight
up past a bush to a good slab and the top. (1971)

15 Brad's Chimney 18m VD ***
The obvious magnificent chimney. (pre-1951)

16 Patient Weaver 20m E5 6a *
A very bold undertaking. Go up the small corner at the
right-hand end of the wall to the left for 1m or so, then go
out left to gain fingery ledges. Follow these, then move
leftwards up a scooped wall to a good hold (the first one!)
and finish with a long reach. Unprotected. (1978)

17 Time Flies By 20m E4 5c †
The hanging arête which starts at half-height left of Patient
Weaver. Climb the wall below the arête to a ledge, then
traverse right until just past the arête. Climb the wall on
sandy pebbles and brittle pockets to a break 3m below the
top. Move left and follow the arête to the top. (1986)

18 The Overhang 18m E1 5b
At the left-hand end of the face is a blocky overhang with a
ledge on the right. Move up and then swing onto the ledge.
Continue up the nasty crumbling wall to a tree-bound
ledge. The cracks on the right give the finish to another
poorly-protected climb. (1970)

*A pleasant stroll for 100m towards Alton Towers leads to a
'nose' with a steep groove on its right-hand side (not
visible from the path). Climbers with an arboricultural bent
(a love of trees and shrubs, for the uninitiated) will enjoy
this batch!*

19 Tre Cime 7m VS 4b
The groove is strenuous but at 3m an escape can be made
using two tree stumps. Climb the nose and wall, using a
root to good effect, to gain the top. (1971)

20 Per Rectum 9m VS 4b
The layback crack is quite good with two or tree stumps for
aid. (1971)

21 Extractum 9m HVS 5b (1 pt. aid)
The wet wall on the left has good holds but unfortunately a
hard move to gain the tree. Lasso a stump above the
overhang and use it with difficulty. (1971)

22 Mark 7m S
The corner round to the left. Once again tree stumps come
to the rescue on the overhang. (1971)

23 Stark 7m VD
Climb Mark for 3m, then go left to a ledge and finish up the
slab. (1970)

24 Stephen 7m VS 4a
The corner-crack on the left reserves its crux for the final
move. (1971)

25 Dark Star 9m E3 5c
The steep arête to the left is very hard indeed. (1975)

*The crags continue towards Alton Towers but are about as
worthwhile as they look – unpleasant and scrappy.*

INA'S ROCK

O.S. ref. SK 087429

SITUATION, ACCESS and APPROACHES
The crag is 400m from Park Banks Crag at the same level
and on the same path.
You will still be wandering around in the grounds of Alton
Towers so access is rather a delicate issue.
The best approach is by following the white chipping track
north-east from Gig Cottage for about 250m. This fine crag
will then be seen on the left standing free from the trees in
a small clearing (sounds like the jungle!). It can also be
approached from Park Banks Crag by staying on The Rock
Walk and going past Coelred's Crack.

CHARACTER
The rock is a lot firmer than that of its neighbour though
with fewer pebbles. It is generally very steep and clean,
yielding some fine climbs.

THE CLIMBS are described from LEFT to RIGHT.

1 Rawhide 7m S
A small chimney lies hidden in the trees and gives the route.
(1970)

2 Gladiator 9m VS 4b
The bulging crack is quite hard.   (1970)

3 Donor 12m S
The scoop to the right is climbed to a tree. Go right to finish
up a corner.   (1971)

The next six climbs, being on exceptionally good rock,
certainly make this crag worthy of a visit by any competent
party.

4 Amazing Grace 25m VS 4c
Go up a shallow chimney right of Donor until a traverse
right leads to a stance. Continue up the wall above, past a
peculiar hole, then traverse right to Ina's Chimney and finish
outside the chockstone.   (1971)

5 Ina's Chimney 22m S   **
An excellent expedition into the bowels of the crag.
(pre-1951)

6 Atlas 25m E2 5b,5c **
To the right is a stone pillar. Round the corner to the right a
fierce crack splits the crag from top to bottom. A fine climb.
1. 15m. The crack is climbed strenuously out of the cave to
reach a good ledge.
2. 10m. Hard climbing over the roof soon eases. (1970/1977)

7 Ground Support 24m HVS 5b ***
Climb the thin crack just right of the cave to a bush. The
wide crack above is climbed in fine position. Not as hard as
it looks. Brilliant climbing on good rock. (1970)

8 Whispering Myth 22m E2 6a,5a *
1. 12m. Climb Ground Support for 3m, then traverse right to
gain a faint line going left. Followed this with great difficulty
to a bolt, then continue right to a stance and:
2. 10m. Climb the thin crack left of Tactical Weapon. A
problem that will probably propitiate the most demanding
connoisseur of difficult moves, complicated and serious
positions, with awkward terrain. (1979)

9 Tactical Weapon 20m HVS 5b **
From the ledge on the corner of the face, climb pleasing
cracks and rugosities to reach a small tree. The crack above
is climbed to the top. (1970/1975)

10 Initiation Groove 10m VS 4b
The groove round the corner requires a tree to aid progress.
(1970)

11 Bloody Crack 6m VS 4b
The crack in the buttress 45m to the right is climbed direct
to a ledge. As the upper crack has never been climbed,
escape right. (1970)

12 Crud on the Tracks 80m HVS 5b
Taking stances as and when required, girdle the crag from
left to right with no appreciable variation in grade. (1978)

WOOTTON LODGE CRAGS O.S. ref. SK 195435

SITUATION, ACCESS and APPROACHES
The crags are on a wooded hillside overlooking a farm track
opposite the gates of Wootton Lodge. The entrance to the
lodge lies 2km along the lane from Farley to Ellastone.

Farley is just under 2km north of Alton.
No problems have ever arisen over access to these crags.
The area is probably owned by Bamfords, the earth
excavator company. Although JCBs could be used to good
effect on some of the Churnet crags, the presence of
climbers here would not go down too well. Another case of
sleeping dogs...
Opposite the lodge-gates, at an entrance to a small cave is
a space for parking. Scramble up the hillside immediately
right of the cave, then cross the ferny hill to the right of the
crag.

CHARACTER
The crag is divided into two separate buttresses by a
fern-clad slope. The left-hand buttress is undercut at its
centre and has steep walls on its extremities. The
right-hand buttress is undercut in its entirety and has a
break running across it at 6m. The rock is rather pebbly on
the left-hand buttress but very good on the more open,
right-hand buttress.

THE CLIMBS are described as one would normally reach
them – from LEFT to RIGHT.

LEFT-HAND BUTTRESS

1 Ungodly Groove 9m E1 5b
The hanging groove on the left-hand side is extremely
strenuous. (1970/1971)

2 Central Route 12m VS 4c *
Climb the steep wall diagonally rightwards to a ledge, then
traverse right to a crack. Follow this to the top. Excellent
climbing. (1970)

3 Pull John 15m E5 6a
Make horrendously difficult moves up the crumbling arête,
then move right to a ledge. Continue up the wall 5m right of
the overhanging upper arête gradually moving left near the
top. Serious. The route takes its name from a one-sided
conversation between Barry Marsden (the second) and John
Yates (the leader). (1971)

4 Quasimodo 12m E2 6a *
The desperate crack on the right. Finish up the crack above
the ledge. (1971/1973)

5 Cripple's Corner 11m VS 4b
From the extreme right-hand end of the crag, traverse
leftwards up the bulging wall to a ledge. The crack on the
right gives the finish. (1971)

6 Wootton Wanderer 25m HVS 5a
Start on the left side of the crag and traverse right below the
hard part of Ungodly Groove to the large ledge on the
corner. From the left-hand end of the ledge, go diagonally
right and finish up Quasimodo. (1971)

*Up the hill above and left of the crag is a small isolated rock
with a tree. There are two Severes up the right and left of
this (the rock not the tree!).*

Across the fern-covered bank about 100m away is:

RIGHT-HAND BUTTRESS

7 The Long Traverse 34m VD ***
A brilliant climb. Start at the left side and traverse right at
6m. (1970)

8 A Phoenix too Frequent 12m E3 6a **
Make a fingery traverse left from just left of Hanging Crack,
from where the easier upper wall can be gained. (1975)

9 Hanging Crack 9m HVS 5b **
Good strenuous climbing up the obvious crack. (1971/1975)

**ALL THE CRAGS ARE NOW ON THE SOUTH (RIGHT) SIDE
OF THE RIVER.**

CASTLE CRAG O.S. ref. SK 173425

SITUATION, ACCESS and APPROACHES
This cliff is directly below the castle in Alton, overlooking
the River Churnet.
The crag is on private land but small parties have met no
opposition in the past.
On the Alton side of the bridge opposite the entrance to the
Talbot Inn a track leads to Cliff Farm Cottage. Once inside
the gateway turn right and head straight up the hill to the
crag.

CHARACTER

An impressive cliff which is undercut for most of its length with overhangs of various sizes topping the majority of the perpendicular walls. The rock is quite pale and fairly solid. At the time of writing scaffolding on the right-hand side would seem to indicate the crag is being reconstructed (or maybe it's the wall above!). An obvious break crosses the crag at 10m.

THE CLIMBS are described from RIGHT to LEFT starting at the metal pipe running down the corner at the right-hand side of the crag. At the time of writing protection on the first five climbs could be arranged on the scaffolding.

1 Daedalus 9m VS 4a
The arête is followed direct to the top. (1970)

2 Minos 9m VS 4c
Start on the left and follow a crackline finishing just left of a tree. (1970)

3 Minotaur 15m VS 4c **
The bent crack to the left leads to a thread at 8m. From the top of the crack, go right into a chimney and finish leftwards. (1970)

4 Theseus 18m HVS 5c *
The wall 3m left of Minotaur is ascended until it is preferable to traverse right below a sloping groove. Climb the crack in the slanting groove to the top. A good effort.
(1970/1971)

5 Icarus 17m HVS 5b **
Climb the wide crack to the left by laybacking, with a desperate move onto a ledge on the right. The flake and wall above give the finish to an excellent but rather strenuous way up the cliff. (1971)

6 Zeus 17m E1 5b
Bridge up the cave on the left and swing right using a tree. The overhanging crack requires a great deal of effort to gain a dirty gully. (1971/1978)

7 Pasiphae 22m S
From the tree on Zeus, move up the groove on the right to a stomach-traverse ledge. Wriggle along this and through a slot (is this climbing?) to a junction with The Gallows. Continue left along this for 5m to a groove which is climbed to a belay. Abseil from an elder tree on the left. The route

can be climbed direct by moving left from the cave on Zeus and following a thin crack and wall on its left to reach the traverse; 4b.   (1970)

8 The Gallows 17m HVS 5b
Pain and difficulty are prominent when progressing up the vertical cracks above the opposite entrance to the keyhole cave. The steep upper crack yields to laybacking. Belay and abseil to the left.   (1970)

9 The Labyrinth 85m VS 5a   ***
The Churnet Valley's version of Chee Tor Girdle. Pitch lengths are left to the individual as belays are plentiful. The climb takes the obvious break from right to left starting at the pipe, therefore little description is required. The first and last sections will be found to be the most difficult. An abseil down The Gallows finishes the route.   (1970)

One hundred metres left of the castle is a buttress which has to be approached from the farm track below so as to cause no offence to the occupants of the castle. Left of the block overhang on the right half of the crag is a ledge at 9m.

10 The Prodigal 17m HVS 5c
Hard moves below the ledge enable a smaller ledge on the right to be gained. Climb the crack to its top, then traverse left with difficulty to another ledge. Tree roots enable progress to be made up the dirty corner.   (1971)

11 The Graduate 15m HS 4a
An interesting slab leads to a small ledge. The crack above completes the climb.   (1971)

Four hundred metres left again is **ALTON CLIFF**. *The climbs are described from* LEFT *to* RIGHT.

12 Rig a Dig Dig 11m E1 5c   ***
This climb is well worth the walk. Climb a short groove left of a large roof at the left end of the crag. Traverse strenuously right below the roof to an easier finish up the crack, grass and wall above. Superb.   (1971/1975)

13 The Brothers 12m HVS 5b
Climb anxiously up the pebbly arête 4m right to a horizontal crack. Make hard moves left to a good hold, then go up right of a tree and finish up the slab above.   (1971)

14 To Live Again 9m E3 5c   *
Move left to the undercut arête, left of the crack in the steep wall on the right, and follow it until it eases.   (1978)

15 Transit Crack 9m S
Back to normality by climbing the straightforward crack to
the top.   (1971)

16 Down to the Elbows 9m E3 6a
The ferocious overhanging off-width crack right of the
gully; demanding.   (1978)

17 Pull Jonny 9m E1 5b   **
Excellent climbing up the crack 9m to the right leads to a
step right at its top. Continue up to a tree.   (1978)

TOOTHILL ROCK   O.S. ref. SK 068425

SITUATION, ACCESS and APPROACHES
The rock occupies a position 1km west of Alton Castle.
No access problems have ever been encountered here.
From the Talbot Inn, follow The Red Road for 1km to a sharp
right-hand bend in the road. It is possible to park
hereabouts. A path climbs steeply through the wood on the
left. This leads to the top of Toothill Rock.

CHARACTER
The rock will suit the pebble enthusiast — plenty of vegetation
too!

THE CLIMBS; starting from Toothill Rock, which has a huge
overhang at its right end, the routes are described from
RIGHT to LEFT.

1 The Highwayman 18m VS 4b,4a
1. 9m. The crack left of the roof leads to a large ledge.
2. 9m. Climb the wall past a small tree to the top. Quite
pleasant.   (1970)

2 Hot Pants 18m VS 4c
Climb the wall 2m right of the arête. Awkward moves right
then lead to moves back left to gain a ledge. The groove in
the wall gives the finish.   (1970)

3 Droopy Draws 12m HS 4a
The jamming crack to the left.   (1978)

4 Tyre Pressure 10m S
To the left, on the upper tier of the crag near the centre of the face, is a short corner. Climb this, then swing right and go up the wall with awkward moves to gain the break. Escape left to ledges. (1978)

5 Parking Fine 5m VS 4b
The wall to the left, trending left over a small bulge. (1978)

6 Ant's Corner 7m VS 4a
Farther left is an obscene pebbly roof with a corner on the left. Climb the corner which is most difficult at the top. (1978)

7 Uncle's Arête 7m VS 4b
The arête on the left. The top gives the crux. (1978)

Two hundred metres to the left, past several awful buttresses, is an obvious crack:

8 Daddy Long Legs 10m HVS 5b
Climb a nasty crumbling wall to the crack. Make a hard move to gain good jams in the roof and exit awkwardly.
(1979)

RAKES DALE O.S. ref. SK 066424

SITUATION, ACCESS and APPROACHES
A small, pleasant dale 1km west of Alton Castle.
The crags on the left bank are owned by Austin Plant (a pioneer of several climbs hereabouts). He is willing to allow climbing. The crags on the right bank are on land owned by a farmer in Rakes Dale who does not appear to mind climbers on his property either, although he has not been approached.
From the sharp bend described in the approach to Toothill Rock a sandy track runs into Rakes Dale. After 180m, another track goes to the left which leads to a gate in 80m. For the crags on the left bank stay on the track for 20m, then break off left up the hill. A discreet ascent over the fence on the right of the gate and then steeply uphill, will lead to the crags on the right.

CHARACTER

The crags on the left bank have bands of Bunter pebbles alternating with quite solid rock. They are generally clean and pleasant. The right bank crags consist of several buttresses, the best of which is a long steep undercut wall of excellent rock.

THE CLIMBS are described from LEFT to RIGHT starting on the left bank.

The crag is split into two buttresses by a fern-covered bank. The left one sports no climbs due to its acute verticality. On the left of the right-hand buttress is a short dirty corner. Five metres right of this is a flake at 3m.

1 Dust Storm 9m HVS 5b   *
Climb direct to gain the flake, then traverse cautiously left for 2m. Continue over a difficult bulge past a tree and finish up a short crack. (1979)

2 Sandbagger 12m HVS 5a
Five metres of tree-filled crack-climbing leads to a delicate traverse left into shallow corner. Finish trending left at the top. (1979)

3 Austin's Chimney 9m M
The clean chimney/gully to the right. (1979)

4 Desert Rat 9m HVS 5a   *
The hanging corner in the right wall gives the route. Short but excellent. (1979)

5 White Mouse 9m VD
Start at some chipped holds 6m right and climb up to the break. Traverse left with an awkward step to reach the foot of the chimney. (1979)

The main buttress on the right bank looks impressive from a distance but closer inspection reveals an extremely steep wall devoid of any holds. At the right-hand end is a good clean chimney.

6 Rakes Dale Chimney 9m HVS 5a
Tarzan-type antics on the ivy lead to the chimney which is hard to start. (1979)

To the right are vegetated crags but 350m along the rim of the dale a steep clean crag has a slab on its left which has been left for future pioneers.

RAINROACH ROCK

O.S. ref. SK 063430

SITUATION, ACCESS and APPROACHES

The crag is situated just over 1km roughly north-west of
Alton Castle. No access problems have been encountered.
From the sharp bend in The Red Road previously described,
walk a few metres along the road to a track that runs behind
the Holm Cottage and parallel to the road. The track goes
below the crag. After 380m go uphill, fighting desperately
with dense undergrowth, to eventually arrive exhausted at
the foot of The Rock.

CHARACTER

Superbly impressive from the valley, the crag is somewhat
disappointing being split by several ledges each sporting an
abundance of bushes. The quality of the rock is excellent
and the crag is very steep.

THE CLIMBS are described from RIGHT to LEFT starting at
the obvious groove at the right-hand end of the crag.

1 Five Bar Crack 12m HVS 5b
To the right of the groove is a thin crack. Climb this and the
fierce overhanging crack above.   (1983)

2 Spreadeagle 18m S
Climb the groove to a good ledge. Go up the corner above
to a grassy ledge, then stroll along this for 2m and go up
the wall above finishing with a mantelshelf. First climbed as
a lead up to: (1969)

3 The Taxman 25m HVS 5a   *
As for Spreadeagle to the ledge. Climb the slab for 2m, then
go left for 5m to reach a bush. Swing across the corner and
mover onto a ledge. Climb up over another ledge and
stomach-traverse right to an overhanging corner. This gives
a hard finish to quite a good route.   (1969)

4 The Unveiling 17m VS 4c
Start 5m left and climb a steep wall to a ledge. Walk left to
an overhanging crack which is climbed to its top. Go right
and jam the final crack. The route can also be finished
direct.   (1969)

5 Pebble Drop 18m HVD
Start at the base of the slab in the centre of the crag and
climb to a tree at 6m. Finish up the crack at the back of the
ledge.   (1976)

6 Climb to the Lost World 28m S and A1
A vegetated crack leads to a ledge at 9m. Use aid to climb
the crack, then traverse 9m left to finish up another crack.
Aptly named.   (1976)

7 The Fly 10m E1 5b   *
This hard climb takes the overhanging wall at the extreme
left-hand side of the crag. A flake is gained with
considerable difficulty.   (1969/1975)

PEAKSTONE INN AMPHITHEATRE   O.S. ref. SK 055428

SITUATION, ACCESS and APPROACHES
A rectangular amphitheatre of crags behind the Peakstone
Inn on the southern side of Dimmings Dale.
There are no access problems. The best approach is from
the Peakstone Inn on the B5032 Cheadle-to-Ashbourne
road. The first crag on the left-hand side is below the pub
car park at the southern end of the amphitheatre. The car
park has been used for years without objectims as have the
other facilities of the inn. Perhaps the latter justifies the
former.

CHARACTER
The rock varies from excellent to terrible, some of the crags
being quite green and overgrown.

THE CLIMBS; as no circular tour exists, climbs on the
left-hand side are described as one would meet them, from
LEFT to RIGHT. On the right-hand side they are described
from RIGHT to LEFT.

LEFT-HAND SIDE OF THE AMPHITHEATRE

*From the pub follow steps down to a bridge. The first crag
is up the bank to the left as one descends.*

1 Northern Lights 14m S   *
The obvious line running from left to right is followed to an
awkward step onto a ledge. Finish up the arête on grass,
rock and beer cans!   (1978)

One hundred metres right past a 'lava flow' of rubbish and mud, and beyond a small steep buttress, is **BACK WALL**. *The main face has a horrendously overhanging wall of pebbles bedded in sand. At the right end of the crag is a solid, slabby groove:*

2 Dancing Bear 17m E1 4b,5b　　　　　　　*
1. 8m. Climb the slabby groove to a shelf, then go left to belay at a huge thread.
2. 9m. Gain a standing position on the ledge, then step left and climb a steep wall to a break. Make a precarious mantelshelf out right and finish straight up.　　(1978)

The remaining climbs are situated across a slight gully and fern-clad bank to the right, on the most northerly point of the left-hand side of the amphitheatre. The climbs are on very good rock and are worthy of attention.

3 Scoop Wall 9m HVS 5a　　　　　　　　　*
The centre of the clean wall left of the overhanging arête is climbed on small holds. Finish on the right.　　(1971)

4 Chockstone Crack 8m S　　　　　　　　　*
The obvious well-scratched crack to the right.　　(pre-1951)

5 Right Wall 13m HVS 5a　　　　　　　　　*
Start from a vegetated ledge 9m to the right and climb the wall on good holds to a flake. Ascend this to a ledge, then ascend diagonally rightwards up the steep wall to the top.
　　　　　　　　　　　　　　　　　　　　(1971)

A small buttress lies 200m to the right:

6 BJM 8m VS 4b　　　　　　　　　　　　*
Climb direct up the steep crack and narrow chimney.　　(1971)

7 Scout Wall 6m VS 4c
Climb the wall left of the crack.　　　　　　(1971)

RIGHT-HAND SIDE OF THE AMPHITHEATRE

From the far side of the bridge at the foot of the steps, walk diagonally across the bank through a pleasant wood to reach a small group of crags. The right-hand wall has several short problems on good rock. It eventually becomes very overhanging at the left-hand end, terminating in an arête.

8 Supermac 6m E4 6b　　　　　　　　　　†
The line through the overhangs right of the arête, now free. 'Short, hard and superb.'　　　　　　(pre-1951/1988)

9 One Dunne 6m VD   *
The pleasing arête to the left.   (pre-1951)

9a All Day and All of the Night 9m E5 6b   **†
Start 3m left of the huge block left of One Dunne. A hard
boulder problem start up the leaning wall leads to a
rounded break, thread runner. Step left, then power up the
wall, thread runner, to the top break. Pull up and exit right
on the rounded top. Excellent.   (1988)

10 Dead Tree Slab 9m D   *
Wonderful climbing up the slab at the left end with a dead
tree-stump at its base.   (pre-1951)

11 Dead Tree Crack 9m VD
The crack to the left is awkward at first. Finish up the arête.
                     (pre-1951)

WRIGHT'S ROCK   O.S. ref. SK 058430

SITUATION, ACCESS and APPROACHES
The crag overlooks fields high above the jungles of
Dimmingsdale.
It is quite public and no objections have ever been raised
about climbing.
Continue past Dead Tree Slab round the corner. Wright's
Rock will then be seen overlooking the fields below.

CHARACTER
The rock is far superior to most in the area being sound and
compact. It is quite clear of vegetation and is well worth a
visit despite occasional greenness.

THE CLIMBS are described from LEFT to RIGHT, starting at a
cave.

1 Stonemason's Route 14m HVD   **
From the cave, go up and left to a good ledge. The wall
above is surprisingly hard. A good climb.   (1959-63)

1a Puppet Life 11m E1 5b   †
Start at a pebbly rock 3m right of the cave between
Stonemason's Route and Sauron. Pull over the bulge, step
right and climb the wall rightwards, peg runner, to reach a
rounded break. Move left and up to finish behind a tree.
                     (1988)

2 Sauron 9m HVS 5a   **

The corner to the right is climbed by bridging and
laybacking to an awkward exit.   (1970)

3 Soar Off 9m E1 5b   *

The fine arête to the right. Frequently green.   (1979)

4 Sculptor's Wall 12m VS 4a

The wall on the right leads to a large ledge. Finish up the
wall.   (1959-63)

5 Central Crack 14m D

The obvious deep fissure to the right is quite
straightforward.   (1959-63)

6 Thorns 12m E3 5c   **

Start in a recess 5m right of the crack. The overhanging
corner is taken to ledge. Climb thin flakes with some
trepidation just right of a tree and go over a bulge to a wide
crack finish. A little friable.   (1979)

6a The Leading Fireman 11m HVS 5a   †

From the tree of Thorns, move right onto a ramp and climb
the wall above the break and traverse right to the finish of
Alternative Three.   (1988)

6b Fingers in Every Pie 8m E6 6c   †

Jump for the pocket 2m left of Alternative Three and climb
the bulge to a peg runner. Pass this with difficulty to gain
the top flake of Alternative Three and finish up this.   (1988)

7 Alternative Three 12m E4 6a   **

Overcome the 4m undercut 6m to the right of Thorns using
a thin flake on the final horizontal section. Move left onto
the overhanging wall just above the lip to a short layback
flake. Finish more easily up this and the wall above. A fine
climb.   (1979)

8 Tunnel Chimney 7m D

Either side of the slab on the right leads to a filthy chimney.
     (1959-63)

9 The Hob 7m VS 4c

The undercut sloping ledge on the right is gained from the
left by a difficult rightwards mantelshelf. Move 2m right and
finish up the bulging wall. It is possible to go left from the
ledge and up a groove at HVS 5a.   (1970)

Farther right is a fence, above which is an upper tier:

10 Tiger's Wall 6m VS 4b
Start below the highest point of the face and climb direct.
Hard to start. (1970)

11 Ugly Puss 6m VS 4b
The obvious flake to the left. (1970)

*Three hundred metres east (left) of Wright's Rock and at the
same level is* **PAINTER'S ROCK**.

The rock here is not as firm as that of its neighbour being
sandier and much more pebbly. Do not be put off by the
first of the two buttresses as one saunters across from
Wright's Rock. The upper half of this buttress sits on an
overhanging wall of horrendous pebbles, so walk swiftly
past to the better rock of the second buttress.

THE CLIMBS are described from RIGHT to LEFT as one
would normally approach them from Wright's Rock.

12 Recess Corner 6m VD
The short corner just left of the first buttress. (1979)

13 Working Hunter 16m HVS 5b
Go up the slab of the next buttress, climbing just right of
the arête to a good ledge below an overhang. Cracks then
lead through this to another ledge. Traverse left to a tree
and finish up a root-filled crack. (1979)

14 Rabbit Stew 18m E3 5c
Climb a delicate groove 3m to the left and gain a good hold
at 5m. Go left to a flake which is followed to a bulge. A hard
move over this leads to a peg runner; difficult climbing then
follows until it is possible to go left into the corner of Bright
Eyes for a finish. Steadiness is essential. (1979)

15 Bright Eyes 16m E2 5c
Start 12m left and follow a faint crack into the final corner
which is surprisingly difficult. (1979)

Left of the next vegetated section is an upper tier:

16 Glossy Finish 9m VS 4c
Start just left of centre and go strenuously up to a good
ledge on the right. The wall above involves a long reach to
finish. (1979)

17 Undercoat 11m HVS 5b
Climb to the roof on the right. Traverse right round the
corner to a difficult mantelshelf just right of the arête. The
nose has been climbed on a top-rope. (1979)

PEAKSTONE ROCK

O.S. ref. SK 052422

SITUATION, ACCESS and APPROACHES

The crag is on the side of a shallow hollow on Alton Common, 5km east of Cheadle.

Permission to visit the crag (which has so far always been granted) must be sought from either the bungalow or the farm (beware of the dog).

It is best to approach from Cheadle on the B5032. Two kilometres on the Alton side of the Highwayman Inn, a farm track leads off right. This goes past the bungalow and to the farm at the end. The crag is across the field on the right, 400m away; notably difficult to find on the first or any subsequent visit.

CHARACTER

This peculiar group of rocks is in the form of a small ridge with a fine pinnacle halfway along. The eastern side is overhanging and fairly loose, the southern side is a steep face with an obvious crack, whilst the west face is a bulging wall. The crag is in a fine setting and ideal for an evening visit.

THE CLIMBS are described from RIGHT to LEFT starting at the wall on the right of the south face.

1 Stumblehead 9m HVS 5a   *
Step off the wall and climb the face bearing slightly leftwards. A finish has been made by moving right at half-height to follow a hairline crack on poor holds; E1 5b.
(1971)

2 Peakstone Crack 9m VS 4c
The obvious crack. A bush was pruned prior to the first ascent but has subsequently grown back. Very prickly and unpleasant.   (1971)

3 Marajuander 11m VS 4c
Ascend the crack to the break, then traverse left with difficulty and go round the arête to a crack. Finish up this.
(1971)

4 Dimetrodon 9m E3 6a
Climb the shallow groove to the left of the crack to a break. Move left to the arête and climb its left wall on small holds.
(1979)

5 Plebble 9m E1 5c
The wall left of Dimetrodon is hard. Finish up a thin crack.
(1971)

6 Five Thousand Volts 8m E1 5c   *
A good climb. Start 3m right of the corner and climb direct
with difficulty.   (1979)

7 Afrodizzy Crack 8m HVS 5a   *
The corner is most awkward.   (1971)

8 Time's Arrow 9m E4 6a   *
Climb the slight scoop 3m left of the crack. Go left to a
break below the roof, then move 1m farther left and pull
over using a jug. Finish up the slab. A really trying,
desperate pitch.   (1979)

9 Back Side 5m VS 4b   **
The pinnacle is climbed up its short side on large holds to
an awkward finish. Descend either by abseil from the lone
summit tree or by precariously reversing the route. A good
expedition.   (1959-63)

The pinnacle has been girdled in both directions at an airy
Severe standard.

DIMMINGS DALE   O.S. ref. SK 062432 to 045436

SITUATION, ACCESS and CHARACTER
A beautiful wooded dale running down to the southern side
of the River Churnet at Lord's Bridge, 2km upstream from
Alton. No access problems have been encountered.
The best approach is from The Red Road. Two kilometres
from Alton Castle is a lodge that serves excellent meals and
drinks. A broad track known as Serpentine Drive follows a
stream up the southern side of the dale passing an old mill
and several ponds. Crags are scattered all over the dale so
approaches are included in the description of the individual
crags. Some of the buttresses are obscured by trees and
bushes and as such are difficult to find on first acquaintance.

CHARACTER

Most of the crags seem to be constructed from 'dry-mix concrete' making climbing on them somewhat worrying. Some are quite sound, whilst others are a botanist's paradise, disappointing except in their variety of flora. Many of the routes are lichenous.

THE CLIMBS; at the lowest point of the ponds is a gate. A small valley runs down from the left and at the top of the right bank of this valley, hidden by trees, is a vegetated buttress. *Right of this is* **FISHERMAN'S CRAG**.

1 Fisherman's Crack 7m S
The crack in the centre of the wall on the left-hand side of the buttress.   (1979)

2 Basket 10m VS 4c
The front face is steeper. Go up the short wall, then move right below a block and climb up its right side almost to the top; reach this by using roots. The crack can be climbed direct at 5a.   (1979)

Near the top end of the pool and about 180m from the gate, go up the bank fighting and cursing the rhododendrons. With much effort **SMELTING MILL BUTTRESS** *will eventually be gained. At the left-hand end of the crag is a short dirty corner with.a large tree to its right.*

3 Slip Knot 23m E1 5c
Climb the corner for 3m, then move delicately along the break to the arête. Climb this to a horizontal crack which is followed in a spectacular position across the overhanging wall.   (1979)

4 Dimmingsdale Crack 16m E1 5b   *
The huge fissure to the right has two hard sections.   (1979)

Nine metres to the right, in the centre of the wall, is a flake at 3m:

5 Iron Ore 23m E1 5b
Gain the flake and pull onto a good foot-ledge. Traverse left for 3m, then go up to gain more ledges with difficulty. Move right to a good pocket which is used to reach the break, then step left below the bulge and take it direct with an awkward mantelshelf. Difficult route finding!   (1979)

Six metres right is the 'moac block'. Up the bank right of this is a good slab:

6 Green Slab 23m HVS 5b
Climb easily up the slab to below twin cracks. Traverse left
to the bulge on Iron Ore and finish over this.   (1979)

*A scramble up a short corner leads to the upper section of
the crag. A good crack splits the overhang:*

7 The Mexican 10m E1 5b   *
Climb to the roof and, using good flakes, follow the crack
out to the lip. Hard moves over the overlap lead to a wide
finishing crack.   (1979)

8 Chocolate Orange 6m VS 4c
The delicate corner to the right is mossy.   (1979)

9 Twiggy 6m S
The steep crack in the right wall of the gully is awkward.
                                                          (1979)

10 Fagen 6m S   *
The steep crack on the front face is climbed by laybacking.
Quite worthwhile.   (1979)

*Looking left from the top of Fagen, a big fir tree is visible. A
crag near this gives a good climb. Easy to see, hard to find!*

11 Christmas Tree Crack 7m VS 4b
Start just left of the tree and step left into the steep crack.
                                                          (1979)

*On the right-hand side of the drive, 230m from the gate, is
a short section of fence, much the worse for wear. A direct
line taken up the bank, through various tunnels hacked in
the bushes, will lead (eventually) to* **LORD'S BUTTRESS**.
*Perhaps the best crag in the dale with some good rock and
climbs. It stands clear of trees but during Summer is
completely hidden from the path.*

THE CLIMBS are described from LEFT to RIGHT.

*At the left-hand end of the buttress is a 3m high wall which
gives some hard problems. Above and right is a peculiar
buttress, with a hole at half-height, to the right of which is
a steep gully.*

12 Slippery Caramel 16m E3 5c   *
1. 5m. Climb the gully to a belay at a bush.
2. 11m. The short overhanging crack leads to a shelf. At its
top move right with difficulty to a large ledge. A struggle up
the wide crack above remains. Serious.   (1979)

13 Christopher James 18m VS 4c,4b
1. 5m. The steep crack to the right of the gully leads to a ledge.
2. 13m. From the right-hand end of the ledge, traverse right to the base of Lord's Chimney. (1978)

Five metres right is an arête. Just round this is a shallow groove:

14 Lord's Arête 18m E4 6a   *
Climb the groove to a sandy ledge. Move up the wall with difficulty past a sling, staying right of the arête to reach a break; sustained. Swing left onto the arête which is then followed in a fine position. Quite a frantic lead. (1979/1986)

15 Top Brick 15m E1 5c   ***
Traverse left from the chimney to below two pockets and a good thread runner. Hard moves leftwards lead to a cave. Trend left to a second thread, then go diagonally rightwards to finish over a pocketed bulge. Superb steep climbing on excellent rock. (1979)

16 Lord's Chimney 9m VD
Climb the chimney on the outside by good bridging. (1979)

17 Mental Traveller 9m E1 5b
The arête of the chimney is climbed, initially on exploding pockets. (1981)

Nine metres right of the chimney is a green and dirty corner.

18 Reverse Charge 12m VS 4b
Follow the break leftwards from the corner to reach the arête. Pull up using a flake then step left and continue to the top. (1979)

19 Toast Rack 30m HVS 4b,4c   **
1. 12m. As for Reverse Charge to the arête. Continue across to a belay in the chimney.
2. 18m. Cross the wall strenuously on good holds to reach the front face. Traverse the delicate slab to gain a large ledge, then walk off left. A good climb with the crux on the edge of nothing. (1979)

Farther right is a small buttress:

20 Rhody Crack 8m VD
Start under a prow on the right-hand side. Swing left onto a lower prow and mantelshelf to finish. (1979)

*One hundred and forty metres up the drive from the rotting fence, another journey through jungle leads to possibly one of the most vile buttresses in the Churnet; **PEBBLE BUTTRESS**. On the right of the crag is a slab with a crack:*

21 Grott 8m D
Climb the slab and crack to trees. Quite interesting!   (1979)

*One hundred and fifty metres farther up the drive, stop at a large boulder. Directly through the trees is **LONG CRAG**. It consists of four buttresses, each being split by a gully. The left-hand crag is loose and has no climbs whilst the central part of the crag has an easy break at 5m with an excellent slab on the left.*

22 Root Slab 9m S
Climb tree roots in the gully, then follow a break right to reach the arête up which the climb finishes.   (1979)

To the right is a long 5m-high wall; steep, clean and virgin. Right of the wall and at a lower level is a small buttress.

23 Drop Leaf 7m HS 4a
Climb the groove in the roof left of the obvious boulder and gain the break. Traverse left and finish up trees in the arête.
(1979)

*On the left of the first of the upper ponds is **GENTLEMAN'S ROCK**.*

24 Gentleman John 15m E3 6a   **
The overhanging crack is difficult until huge jugs are reached. Climb the slabby crack above avoiding the final overhang on the right.   (1971/1978)

25 Jack the Traverse 30m E3 5b
A girdle along the bottom break at 5m, starting from a boulder on the left and gradually ascending to Gentleman John. Finish up this.   (1978)

The next climbs are, at the time of writing, completely overgrown.

26 Lady Jane 15m VS 5a
Start below a large birch tree above the slab on the right. Traverse 5m left and go direct via sandy ledges.   (1979)

27 Bill the Bandit 9m E1 5b
Start as for Lady Jane but continue direct to the birch tree.
(1979)

Returning to the Lodge Cafe, a broad track follows the right bank past the lower pond. Follow this keeping to the lower path where it forks. Continue past the old smelting mill cottages to a small brick outhouse on the left. Just beyond this, a path cuts up through the trees. Take this and, after 50m, go rightwards up the hill. In the trees just past the second of two large pine trees is **EARL'S ROCK**. *It is covered in ivy at the right end with a large 'hermit's cave' on the left. A wide crack above gives:*

28 Maloof 6m HVS 5b
Gain the ledge and climb the awkward crack above.   (1979)

Follow the path from Earl's Rock up through the wood to a fence. Go back from the fence along the same path at another on the left (complicated!). This leads to the left bank of **OUSAL DALE**. *150m along the path is a pleasant little crag.*

29 Bubble 8m VS 4b
Start in the middle of the pebbly wall and go diagonally right to a recess in the overhang. Finish over this.   (1979)

30 Squeak 12m VS 4b
Round the corner to the right, traverse left from a standing position on the top of the wall. Obvious.   (1979)

OUSAL DALE *is best approached from the lower pool by taking the right track at the point where the path forks. After a few hundred metres the path bears sharply right. On the bend are* **COTTAGE ROCKS**.

THE CLIMBS are described from RIGHT to LEFT starting at a small crag 10m up the path.

31 Pine Tree Wall 8m D
Climb the obvious weakness in the wall to reach the tree.
(pre-1970)

32 Footpath Climb 6m D
Tackle the flake in the centre of the buttress by the path.
(pre-1970)

33 Strenuosity 11m VS 4b
On the right of the main crag is a wide corner-crack which is climbed to its top. Go left and finish up a second wide crack.   (1979)

34 Pocket Wall 8m VS 4b
Climb the steep wall 3m left of the corner to a break. Finish
as for Strenuosity. (1979)

35 Crusty 11m VD
Ascend cracks in the slab on the left from behind a small
birch tree in the centre. Continue more easily to the top via
a prominent boulder. (1979)

Two hundred metres farther on is **LONE BUTTRESS**. *The
front face consists of a series of bulges. On the left-hand
side is a fine steep wall.*

36 Lone Wall 9m HVS 5b
Start on the right-hand side of the wall, at the foot of the
crag. Climb direct, using a thin crack near the top. (1979)

37 Even Lonelier 11m E1 5c
From a ledge 1m left of Lone Wall, traverse right to a ledge
below the overhang. Climb over this with great difficulty,
near the arête, using a ripple. (1979)

Three hundred metres along the path is **OUSAL CRAG**. *It
stands back from the path in a patch of ferns. The lower half
is steep and pebbly. There is an excellent break across the
entire buttress.*

38 Thum 8m VD
From the boulder at the left end of the crag, climb a short
wall to a crack running through the overhang. Climb this to
the top. (1979)

39 Solo Chimney 9m VD
The chimney to the right, past a good chockstone. (pre-1970)

40 Moto Perpetuo 11m E2 5c *
Difficult climbing up the scoop at the right end of the main
face, moving left to gain the break. Go leftwards finishing up
the obvious diagonal crack. (1979)

41 Impacted Bowel 40m VS 4c,4b **
An interesting climb on good rock.
1. 12m. Start left of Thum and follow the break to the
chimney. Move round the arête, then go across to a stance
below the final crack of Moto Perpetuo.
2. 18m. The break leads to a corner at the right-hand end
of the buttress. (1978)

STONY DALE QUARRY

O.S. ref. SK 048483

SITUATION, ACCESS and CHARACTER

The quarry lies high on the southern side of Stony Dale, a small dale that runs down to The Red Road, 1km from Oakamoor. The crags appear to be quite public.

There is plenty of parking space at the old station in Oakamoor. A short section of the wall runs down along the southern side of The Red Road, 200m beyond the junction with the road down Stony Dale on the Alton Side. A path goes steeply up from the right-hand (Oakamoor) end of the wall. 30m up the path, another path leads off to the right and this is followed to the quarry.

CHARACTER

The quarry has an impressive array of vertical walls, corners and arêtes. The rock is almost sound gritstone, quite green but easily brushed. The corners are frequently damp. One of the most important of the Churnet Valley crags.

THE CLIMBS are described from RIGHT to LEFT. The most obvious features are two huge unclimbed corners. Unless ledges above them are cleaned off they are destined to remain that way.

1 Pegger's Original 18m A2
The thin crack 5m right of the left-hand corner gives a poor and messy climb. (pre-1970)

2 Dance of the Flies 18m E2 5c ***
The route of the quarry. Climb the arête of the left-hand corner with hard moves to start. A poor peg runner protects the upper half of the climb. Brilliant. (1979)

3 Little Nikki 13m E1 5c *
The crack 10m left is straightforward but steep to a peg. Difficult moves enable a sandy shelf to be gained. Finish up and leftwards. (1980)

4 Longstop 10m E2 5c *
The corner to the left, usually out of condition, gives some hard climbing. (1983)

5 Doina Da J'al 9m E4 6a   ***
The superb clean arête to the left is climbed on the left wall
above the break. Difficult and serious. Climbing the arête on
its left-hand side all the way gives **The Brazilian**, E4 5c.
(1979/1987)

6 Cave Crack 12m E1 5b
A delicate mossy groove 3m left is climbed to a small cave.
Difficult climbing up the crack leads to a sandy finishing
ledge.   (1980)

7 Long Lankin 20m E1 5b
Go up the same groove to a traverse-line which is followed
left for 6m to a greasy crack. This is climbed to a ledge. The
crack can also be reached direct but this is usually very wet
and slippery.   (1980)

8 Friar Muck 9m E1 5c
Make hard moves up the wall to gain a tree 12m left of the
corner. Use the tree to gain the break and finish by
laybacking up the final crack. At the time of writing the tree
was about to desert its post.   (1979)

9 Robin Hood 9m E3 6b   *
Start below the bow-shaped crack above the break. Difficult
moves lead to the break and a finish up the crack.   (1979)

10 Maid Marion 8m E1 5c
Climb the wall to the left, diagonally leftwards to the top.
Much harder than it looks.   (1979)

*At a point 40m back along the path from the quarry, another
path goes right into a small quarry with an excellent bivvy
cave on its right-hand side. Do not remove the wooden
post....it appears to be holding up the crag!*

11 Short Ride 6m HVS 5b   *
The clean arête left of the cave is short but very good. (1979)

*Continue through the back of the quarry to a flight of steps.
Follow these down to **LION ROCK**. The rock hereabouts is
very good! The right-hand end is in the form of an upper
and lower tier split by a grassy path.*

THE CLIMBS are described from RIGHT to LEFT starting at
the obvious twin cracks on the lower tier.

12 Evensong 9m VD
Climb direct to a ledge and finish up a wide crack.   (1972)

13 Psalm 9m S
Go diagonally left from the foot of Evensong to a ledge at 3m. Ascend the slabby scoop and finish up the wall above. Variations are possible. (1972)

14 Magnificat 12m S   *
The overhanging crack to the left is taken direct. The slabby corner above is somewhat easier. (1972)

15 Hand Jive 18m E5 6b   *
Climb the overhanging wall left of the corner to a flake that crosses the roof rightwards. Follow this to the lip on the right-hand side of the nose. Precarious and difficult moves requiring bionic fingers lead up and leftwards to a short groove and the top. Strenuous and rather wild climbing.
(1979)

15a The Pride 12m E5 6b   ***†
The huge roof left of Hand Jive, gaining the upper headwall by a hand-traverse from the left. A superb route. (1988)

16 Rocking Stone Crack 7m HS 4a   **
The obvious layback-crack left of the roof. Steep. (1972)

17 Descant 6m HS 4a
Six metres left is a short corner which is climbed to its top. Step left and go up to a dead tree. (1972)

18 Canticle 6m VS 4c   *
Ten metres left is a steep arête. Climb this for 3m, then step right to a short diagonal crack. Move awkwardly up this to the top. Enjoyable. (1979)

LOWER CHURNET VALLEY LIST OF FIRST ASCENTS

Pre-1951	**Ina's Chimney, Brad's Chimney, Coelred's Crack, Chockstone Crack, Himac, One Dunne, Dead Tree Slab, Dead Tree Crack** *Himac was climbed free as Supermac by G Gibson, April 6 1988*
1959-63	**Hollybush Hell, Defiance, Chilton's Superdirect, Left Twin Crack, Right Twin Crack, Central Crack, Tunnel Chimney, Blunder** David Hudson and some members from Denstone College Climbing Club
1959-63	**Stonemason's Crack, Sculptor's Wall, Back Side**
1969	**Spreadeagle** Austin Plant, J Stubbs

1969	**The Taxman, The Unveiling** Austin Plant, Bob Hassall
1969	**The Fly** (some aid was used) Austin Plant, Bob Hassall *Climbed free by Andrew and Jonny Woodward in 1975.*
Pre-1970	**Pine Tree Wall, Footpath Climb, Solo Chimney, Pegger's Original** D. Hewitt
1970 Jan.	**Sauron, The Hob, Tiger's Wall, The Highwayman, Hot Pants** John Yates
1970 Jan.	**Ugly Puss** Barry Marsden, John Yates
1970 March	**Initiation Groove, Ground Support, Rawhide, Bloody Crack** Norman Hoskins
1970 April	**Long Traverse, Central Route** Bob Hassall
1970 April	**Tactical Weapon** (1 pt.) Bob Hassall *Climbed free by Andrew and Jonny Woodward in 1975.*
1970 April	**Gladiator** Austin Plant
1970 April	**Atlas** (1 pt.) Austin Plant, Bob Hassall, Norman Hoskins *Climbed free by Jonny and Andrew Woodward in 1977.*
1970 April	**The Renaissance** Norman Hoskins
1970 April	**Ungodly Groove** Norman Hoskins *Only a partial ascent was made.*
1970	**The Gallows** John Yates, Norman Hoskins, Bob Hassall *The route was finished by continuing up the castle walls.*
1970	**Pasiphae** John Yates
1970	**Minotaur, Labyrinth** Austin Plant, Bob Hassall
1970	**Daedalus** Norman Hoskins
1970	**Theseus** Norman Hoskins *Only the upper half was climbed, the route was started to the right.*
1970	**Alien Wall, The Overhang, Minos** North Staffordshire Mountaineering Club members
1971 Feb.	**Mark, Stephen, The Brothers, Transit Crack** Norman Hoskins
1971 Feb.	**The Prodigal, Per Rectum, The Graduate** Dave Salt
1971 Feb.	**Extractum, Honest John** John Yates
1971 Feb.	**Tre Cime** Barry Marsden
1971 April	**Peakstone Crack, Stumblehead, Plebble, Marajuander** John Yates, Barry Marsden
1971 April	**Afrodizzy Crack** Barry Marsden
1971 April	**Donor, Amazing Grace** Bob Hassall

1971 May	**Scoop Wall, Right Wall, Scout Wall** John Yates, Barry Marsden
1971 May	**B.J.M.** Barry Marsden
1971 May	**Icarus** Norman Hoskins, Dave Salt, Bob Hassall
1971 May	**Theseus** Norman Hoskins *Only the lower half was new.*
1971 May	**Zeus** (1 pt.) Norman Hoskins *Climbed free by Andrew and Jonny Woodward in July 1978.*
1971 Spring	**Ungodly Groove** John Yates *The first complete ascent.*
1971 Spring	**Gentleman John** (1 pt.) John Yates *Climbed free by Jonny and Andrew Woodward in 1978.*
1971 Spring	**Quasimodo** (some aid was used) John Yates, Barry Marsden *Climbed free by Andrew and Jonny Woodward in 1973.*
1971 Spring	**Cripple's Corner** Barry Marsden, John Yates
1971 Spring	**Wootton Wanderer** Pete Ruddle, Chris Cartlidge
1971 Spring	**Hanging Crack** (1 pt.) Pete Ruddle, Barry Marsden, Chris Cartlidge *Climbed free by Andrew Woodward in 1975.*
1971 Spring	**Rig a Dig Dig** (4 pts.) Pete Ruddle, Dave Salt, Norman Hoskins *Climbed free by Jonny Woodward in 1975.*
1971	**Pull John** John Yates, Barry Marsden
1971	**Stark** Norman Hoskins
1972 March	**Rocking Stone Crack, Magnificat, Evensong, Psalm, Descant** Bob Hassall
1973	*Staffordshire Gritstone Area guidebook, Rock Climbs in the Peak, Volume 9, published.*
1973 Feb.	**Quasimodo** Andrew Woodward, Jonny Woodward *First free ascent.*
1975 Feb.	**Hanging Crack** Andrew Woodward (solo) *First free ascent.*
1975 Feb.	**A Phoenix too Frequent** Jonny Woodward (solo)
1975 Feb.	**Rig a Dig Dig** Jonny Woodward (solo) *First free ascent.*
1975 May	**The Fly** Andrew Woodward, Jonny Woodward *First free ascent.*
1975 Summer	**Dark Star** Jonny Woodward, Andrew Woodward

1975 Oct.	**Anthem for Doomed Youth** Jonny Woodward *Top-roped first.*
1975 Oct.	**Tactical Weapon** Andrew Woodward, Jonny Woodward *First free ascent.*
1976	**Pebble Drop, Climb to the Lost World**
1977 Sept. 17	**The Height Below** Andrew Woodward, Jonny Woodward
1977 Sept. 17	**Four Horsemen** Jonny Woodward, Andrew Woodward
1977 Sept. 17	**Atlas** Jonny Woodward, Andrew Woodward *First free ascent.*
1978 May 22	**Northern Lights** Steve Dale, Barry Marsden
1978 June 10	**Dancing Bear** Steve Dale, Steve Smith
1978 July	**Zeus** Andrew Woodward, Jonny Woodward *First free ascent.*
1978 Aug. 30	**Christopher James** Brian Dale, Ewan Murray
1978 Summer	**Ant's Corner** Steve Dale, Brian Dale
1978 Summer	**Uncle's Arête** Brian Dale, Steve Dale
1978 Summer	**Droopy Draws, Tyre Pressure, Parking Fine** Ewan Murray, Sharon Tonks
1978 Sept. 2	**Impacted Bowel** Steve Dale, Brian Dale
1978 Sept.	**Crud on the Tracks** Ewan Murray
1978 Oct. 7	**Jack the Traverse** Jonny Woodward, Andrew Woodward
1978 Oct. 7	**Gentleman John** Jonny Woodward, Andrew Woodward. *First free ascent. Jonny proposed the new name of Gentleman Jonny!*
1978 Oct. 15	**To Live Again, Down to the Elbows, Pull Jonny** Jonny Woodward, Andrew Woodward
1978 Oct. 22	**Patient Weaver** Jonny Woodward, Andrew Woodward *Top-roped first.*
1978	**Jack the Traverse** Jonny Woodward, Andrew Woodward
1979 Jan. 9	**Daddy Long Legs** Ewan Murray
1979 May 22	**Rhody Crack, Lord's Chimney, Reverse Charge** Steve Dale, Brian Dale
1979 May 28	**Basket, Fisherman's Crack** Steve Dale, Brian Dale
1979 May 29	**Iron Ore, Dimmingsdale Crack** Brian Dale, Steve Dale
1979 May 29	**Slip Knot, Green Slab** Steve Dale, Brian Dale

1979 June 5	**Moto Perpetuo** Jonny Woodward, Andrew Woodward	
1979 June 12	**Whispering Myth** Jonny Woodward, Andrew Woodward	
1979 June 18	**Top Brick**, **Slippery Caramel**, **Toast Rack** Steve Dale, Brian Dale	
1979 July 3	**Lord's Arête** (1 pt.) Steve Dale, Brian Dale *Climbed free by Ian Barker in 1986.*	
1979 July 9	**Working Hunter**, **Rabbit Stew**, **Bright Eyes** Brian Dale, Steve Dale	
1979 July 9	**Recess Corner** Steve Dale, Brian Dale	
1979 July 10	**Glossy Finish**, **Undercoat** Steve Dale, Brian Dale	
1979 July 20	**Five Thousand Volts**, **Dimetrodon**, **Time's Arrow** Jonny Woodward, Andrew Woodward	
1979 July 26	**The Mexican** Ewan Murray	
1979 July 26	**Chocolate Orange**, **Twiggy**, **Fagen** T Salt	
1979 July 26	**Christmas Tree Crack** Steve Dale, Brian Dale	
1979 July 30	**Grott**, **Roof Slab**, **Drop Leaf** Steve Dale, Brian Dale	
1979 July 31	**Lady Jane**, **Bill the Bandit** Steve Dale, Brian Dale	
1979 Aug. 14	**Desert Rat**, **White Mouse** Steve Dale, Brian Dale	
1979 Aug. 14	**Dust Storm**, **Sandbagger** Brian Dale, Steve Dale	
1979 Aug. 15	**Austin's Chimney**, **Rakes Dale Chimney** Steve Dale, Brian Dale	
1979 Aug. 28	**Canticle**, **Dance of the Flies** Steve Dale, Brian Dale *Dance of the Flies was top-roped first.*	
1979 Sept. 2/3	**Strenuosity**, **Pocket Wall**, **Crusty**, **Lone Wall**, **Even Lonelier**, **Thum**, **Maloof**, **Bubble**, **Squeak** Steve Dale, Brian Dale *Some of these may have been climbed before.*	
1979 Sept. 18	**Soar Off**, **Thorns**, **Alternative Three** Jonny Woodward, Andrew Woodward	
1979 Oct. 11	**Doina Da J'al**, **Robin Hood**, **Friar Muck**, **Hand Jive**, **Short Ride** Jonny Woodward, Andrew Woodward	
1980 May 16	**Cave Crack**, **Long Lankin**, **Little Nikki** Steve Dale, Brian Dale	
1981	*Staffordshire Area guidebook, Rock Climbs in the Peak, Volume 6, published.*	
1983	**Mental Traveller** Paddy Gaunt *Incorrectly named in Peak Supplement as Reverse Charge.*	

1983 March 6   **Longstop** Steve Dale, Barry Marsden
Originally with a peg for aid but climbed free the same day by the same pair.

1983 March 27   **Five Bar Crack** Steve Dale, Barry Marsden

1984 Dec. 16   **Fast and Bulbous** Brian Davison, Richard Jones, Neil Horn

1986 July 27   **Time Flies By** Brian Davison, Richard Jones

1986 Aug. 6   **Lord's Arête** Ian Barker
First free ascent. Climbed slightly right of the original route.

1987 April 20   **The Brazilian** Simon Alsop (solo)

1988 Feb. 15   **Hopeless Holly, Aliens, You'll Always Reap What You Sow** G Gibson, solo

1988 Feb15   **No Future** G Gibson, solo after self top-rope inspection

1988 April 6   **Supermac** G Gibson, unseconded
A free version of Himac

1988 April 6   **All Day and All of the Night** G Gibson, unseconded

1988 April 23   **Fingers in Every Pie** S Nadin, unseconded

1988 April   **The Leading Fireman** J Perry, S Nadin

1988 July 22   **The Pride** M Boysen, R Carrington

1988 Sept. 10   **Puppet Life** J Nichols, R Nichols

OUTLYING CRAGS

BOSLEY CLOUD

O.S. ref. SJ 903638 to SJ 898631

by Ian Dunn

SITUATION and CHARACTER

Bosley Cloud is the most prominent hill 5km east of
Congleton, overlooking the Cheshire plain.
The climbing here lies on both natural and quarried
gritstone. The natural rock is as solid and well-weathered
as any. The quarried rock, whilst on the whole reliable,
contains friable bands requiring care. Although the crags
have been climbed on for nearly 80 years they are not as
popular as the larger Staffordshire crags such as The
Roaches and consequently a quiet day or evening can be
had hereabouts.

APPROACHES and ACCESS

The approach to this obvious feature can be surprisingly
difficult. The easiest route is from the Macclesfield-to-Leek
(A523) road. Turn off the road westwards at the signs for the
wood-treatment works 2km south of Bosley crossroads
(traffic lights at the junction with the A54). Follow the minor
road through the works and over the River Dane. After about
1km, and at the top of a steep hill, a minor crossroads is
reached, immediately below the northern end of The Cloud.
From this crossroads a path leads directly to the summit via
the North Quarry. Parking at the crossroads however is a
problem and it is best to follow the road round the eastern
slopes of The Cloud and park either just after the second
farm where a path leads round to the crags or farther up the
road.
For The Catstone, take the road skirting The Cloud on the
west side towards Timbersbrook. About 1km from the
crossroads the buttress will be seen behind a large house on
the left.
Cloud End Crags and The Catstone are owned by the
National Trust and its bye-laws should be observed. The
present owner of the large house below The Catstone is
quite happy for small parties to climb as long as access to
the rocks is from above and not through his land. Take the

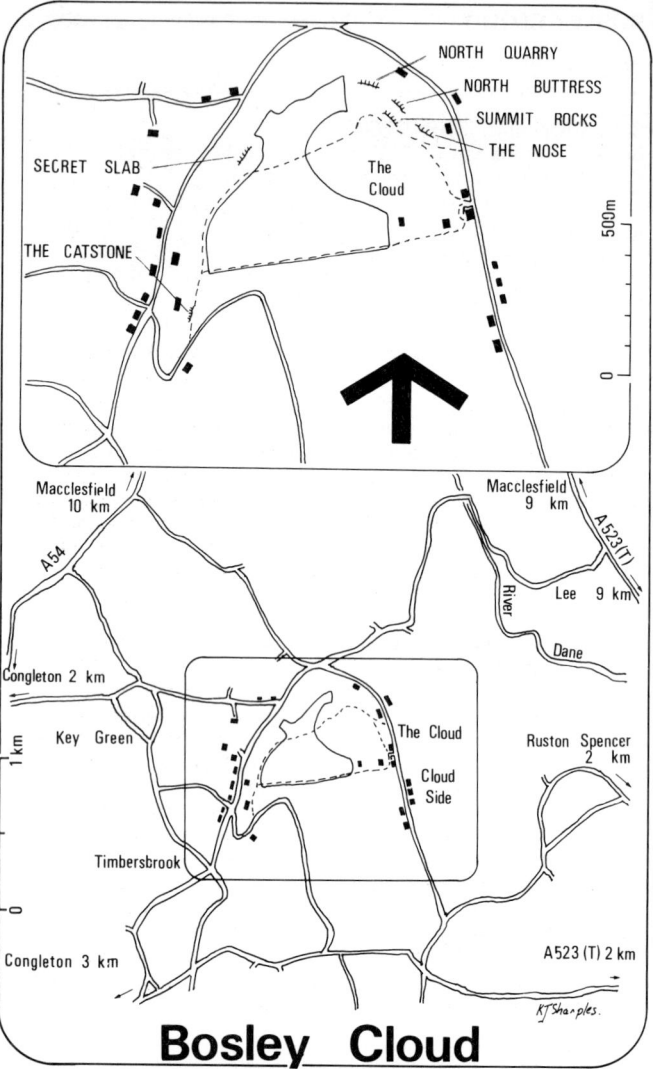

NORTH QUARRY
NORTH BUTTRESS
SUMMIT ROCKS
THE NOSE
SECRET SLAB
The Cloud
THE CATSTONE

500m

0

Macclesfield 10 km
Macclesfield 9 km
A 523(T)
A 54
River
Lee 9 km
Dane
Congleton 2 km
Key Green
The Cloud
Ruston Spencer 2 km
Cloud Side
1 km
Timbersbrook
0
Congleton 3 km
A 523 (T) 2 km

KJSharples.

Bosley Cloud

lane on the right of the large house and follow the path up towards the top of The Cloud. After a few metres descend to the foot of the climbs.

HISTORY

The first record of climbing here was that of Stanley Jeffcoat around 1908. He was later joined by Siegfried Herford and John Laycock which resulted in a short guidebook to Bosley. This was included in Laycock's book 'Some Gritstone Climbs' published in 1913. The first routes of significance, however, came in the 1920s when Morley Wood, Fred Pigott and Harry Kelly climbed *Mutiny Chimney* and *The Cat Crawl* on The Catstone. By the 1940s Eric Byne and Mike Holland had explored The Cloud and compiled a rough guidebook. *V-chimney* is believed to have been climbed in 1941 and though it is not known if it was climbed free, it was a very fine lead for the time. Byne's guidebook was given to A. Lowe of the Manchester University Mountaineering Club who compiled a complete guidebook intended for 'Climbs on Gritstone Volume 3' in 1957. Unfortunately, for reasons of space, the guidebook was seriously condensed and the full notes were lost. In 1963 Peter Bamfield, with the aid of Byne's old guide, began to write up the area for the new series 'Rock Climbs in the Peak'. *Bulldog Flake* was led by a local teacher named Drummond; an impressive effort and the first Extreme on the crag. Other new lines were climbed by Bamfield, Eric Dance and Frank Johnson. Bamfield's notes appeared in full in the Midland Association of Mountaineers Journal of 1965 but Paul Williams and his friends were unaware of this when they produced their script for the Staffordshire Gritstone guidebook of 1973. Williams, with John Amies and P. King, climbed and named routes on the Timbersbrook Quarry in 1969 which have subsequently become overgrown and the excellent *Hot Tin Roof* on The Catstone. The equally fine *Slab Wall* is also probably the result of this trio's efforts.

The publication of the 1973 guidebook led to the rediscovery of Bamfield's notes which formed the basis for the 1981 and present edition. In 1977 a young Macclesfield-based lad, Jonny Woodward, climbed the very impressive *Impact Two* up the right arête of the main wall. The following year with his brother Andrew, he proceeded to free climb *Main Wall* itself and the first E5s on the crag were born. They also added routes to the North Quarry such as *Death Wish* and in 1979 they visited the then virgin Secret Slab and climbed

Slender Thread and *Crystal Voyager*, the former route being a particularly impressive effort in the days before sticky rubber. It was thanks to Byne and Bamfield that these routes were able to be found and ascended. *Summit Arête*, long done with a point of aid, was freed by Jonny Woodward in late-1980, just before the previous guidebook was published. This was a particularly impressive ascent as the route has since repelled all attempts at a second ascent and has therefore been up-graded to 7a!

In the early 1980s two lads from the North-East moved to the area and both were to add fine routes to the crag. Nick Dixon with Andy Popp and Allen Williams started the ball rolling. Dixon found *Herbivacious*, Popp the superb *Existentialist Arête* whilst Williams came up with *Big Red Rock Eater* and the superbly named *Pretentious Moi*. Twelve months later Dunn climbed *Solitaire* which was top-roped prior to a solo ascent; the hardest route on the crag. Dixon and Dunn joined forces later in 1985 to create *Why Kill Time...*, *Kremlin Wall* and *Contraception on Demand* with Dunn also climbing *Tin Tin* with his wife Claudie. Dixon, Williams and a cast of thousands on the Stoke Manpower Services Commission scheme cleaned and climbed *Death Crack*, *Living Wall* and *Mr Magoo*. Other short routes were added in 1984 and 1985. *April Showers* and *May Day* by gritstone gurus John Allen and Mark Stokes and the four routes left of The Catstone were climbed by combinations of Keith Ashton and Malc Baxter.

THE CLIMBS are described from LEFT to RIGHT.

Two hundred metres along the path is a tiny pinnacle in a hollow in the hillside. Below and 40m to the right of this is a green buttress with two short routes of Moderate and Difficult standard. 100m farther on is a large buttress, **THE NOSE**, *on which the first climbs are to be found. It has a prominent overhang near the top and an obvious V-shaped groove in its centre.*

1 Corner Route 17m VD

Take any of several lines up the ledgy wall left of 'the nostrils' to finish up the slabby corner left of the Left Nostril's final chimney. A harder finish is up the steep right wall of the corner at Severe. (pre-1951)

The rock to the left contains one or two poor rambling routes.

2 Left Nostril 15m VD
Start below the broken chimney. Pull awkwardly out left onto a slab and climb a crack to a ledge on the right, below the chimney. Climb this and go over the chockstone to finish.
(pre-1951)

3 Right Nostril 15m S
Climb the steep jamming crack just to the right of the Left Nostril to gain the ledge and a common finish. (pre-1951)

4 V-chimney 15m E1 5b *
Climb the steep green groove on small holds and exit right to a small ledge. Move up then go leftwards across the overhanging wall to the top. (1940s)

5 Why Kill Time When You Can Kill a Friend?
14m E5 6a **
Climb the arête immediately right of V-chimney on its right-hand side. The crux is below the obvious protection crack. Serious. (1985)

6 Green Gully Direct 11m HS 4a
Climb the corner 6m to the right to reach a large grassy ledge on the right. Go back left, then move up the corner to a mantelshelf on the right at the top. (pre-1951)

Sixty metres to the right is a good natural buttress, **NORTH BUTTRESS**. *Twenty-five metres to its left is a small wall:*

7 Envy Face 8m S
Climb the thin crack in the wall with an awkward start. Finish on the left arête. (pre-1965)

8 Mr Magoo 14m HVS 6a.5a
Start at the small wall 5m right of Envy Face.
1. 6m. Climb the obvious brushed wall to a grassy ledge.
2. 8m. Continue up the centre of the wall above to the overhang and surmount this to gain the top. The only two pitch climb at Bosley Cloud and quite a good route. (1986)

There are two obvious flakes on the front face of North Buttress. Round the arête, and to the left, is a shallow undercut corner.

9 Contraception on Demand 7m E1 5c
The very left-most slab of North Buttress gives fine delicate climbing. (1985)

10 Fertility Rite Left-hand 8m E1 5c
Just right of the previous route is an obvious 'blind' crack
which provides the route. (1977)

11 Fertility Rite 8m HVS 5a
Climb the corner; the section above the overhang is delicate.
A good route. (pre-1973)

12 Slab Wall 8m HVS 4c   **
Climb the wall on the right, close to the arête . (1973)

13 Kremlin Wall 8m E4 6a
Ascend directly up the wall, immediately right of the arête.
(1985)

14 Bulldog Flake 8m E1 5b   *
The fierce overhanging flake round to the right is climbed by
slippery laybacking. Strenuous and poorly-protected. (1963)

15 White House Crack 8m VD   *
The flake in the centre of the face. An old classic. (pre-1973)

16 Solitaire 8m E6 6b   **
Start just left of Deception and climb diagonally leftwards
across the wall to finish with some desperate moves right of
White House Crack. Protection in White House Crack greatly
reduces the E grade. (1985)

17 Deception 8m HS 4b
The obvious undercut crack, 5m to the right, is rounded and
hard to finish. (pre-1973)

18 Tin Tin 7m HVS 6a
Climb directly up the wall right of the crack of Deception.
(1985)

Above this buttress, on the top of The Cloud, are **SUMMIT
ROCKS**. *There are many boulder problems hereabouts,
particularly in the lower grades. However, two routes on the
main buttress are rather longer and deserve special mention.*

19 Summit Arête 8m E5 7a   †
The main arête of the buttress has a 3m overhanging base.
Desperate, dynamic moves lead to easier climbing. The
pre-placing of a wire helps avoid the awful landing and
reduces the E grade. (1980)

20 Dry-stone Wall 9m E1 5a
Climb the thin crack 3m right of the arête for 5m, then move
1m left and finish up the centre of the wall. (pre-1965)

Fifty metres right of North Buttress, and at the same level, is
NORTH QUARRY. *The path from the crossroads below
arrives steeply at this point. At the left-hand end of the
quarry is a wall with an obvious crack:*

21 Living Wall 6m E3 6a
Climb the wall left of the obvious crack. (1986)

22 Death Crack 6m E2 6a *
The obvious crack is much harder than it looks. (1986)

*Twenty metres right of this wall is an obvious square-cut
arête:*

23 Big Red Rock Eater 7m E1 5c *
Climb the obvious arête on its right-hand side with
assistance from the large pocket. (1984)

*Twenty metres right of this buttress is a narrow acute corner.
Just left is a shallower corner and left again a
blank-looking, slabby wall.*

24 Everdance 8m VS 4b
Climb the wall on surprisingly good holds. (pre-1965)

25 Death Wish 8m E3 6a
The shallower corner on the right proves very fingery and
leads to holds on the right wall where the angle eases.
Continue easily to the top. Quite serious despite the ledge.
(1978)

26 Thin Finger Corner 8m VS 4b *
The acute corner. Climb over ledges to the corner proper.
Use the left arête to begin some thin fingery moves up the
corner. Belay up and to the left. (pre-1965)

27 Existentialist Arête 8m E3 6a **
Climb the arête right of Thin Finger Corner whilst reading
Jean Paul Sartre. Cultural. (1984)

*Approximately 15m to the right of the previous climb, the
rock becomes higher and forms a corner on the left of an
overhanging wall:*

28 The Lubricant 14m VS 4b
Climb the broken corner until the crack forks. Follow the
left-hand line boldly, then go over broken rock to the top.
(pre-1965)

29 Wet and Warm 13m VS 4c
The rather inferior, right-hand fork of the crack. (pre-1973)

To the right is the highest buttress in the quarry. Both routes on it are serious and difficult undertakings. The thin leftward-slanting crack in the overhanging wall was originally pegged. There was a rock-fall here in 1986. Above and to the right of the main buttress care should be exercised with belays.

30 Main Wall 15m E5 6a
The crack direct is strenuous and sustained. Peg runners exist at 7m and 12m but they are old and not too trustworthy. The crux is at the top and friable rock just below makes protection suspect. (pre-1973/1978)

31 Impact Two 13m E5 5c
This route takes the right-hand side of the arête right of Main Wall. Gain the arête at half-height from ledges on the right. Step left into the void, wait for your heart to start working again, then layback the smooth final arête. (1977)

Ten metres right is a short smooth slab. A 5a problem takes its right-hand side.

The remaining climbs are on buttresses on the north-western side of the hill.

*About 450m from the quarry are two buttresses 30m apart; hidden by trees they are rather awkward to find, but are just beyond a junction on the road below. The left buttress, **THE SECRET SLAB**, contains four good routes, the original two being of exceptional quality.*

32 Herbivacious 9m E4 6a
Start below the obvious central crackline. Move up and leftwards to follow the blunt arête to the top. Bold. (1984)

33 Slender Thread 9m E5 6b   **
The very thin finger-crack in the centre of the slab. Climb this with increasing difficulty until it ends. Make a long reach for an indefinite horizontal break, then move left to finish just right of Herbivacious. A serious pitch on which protection is both suspect and hard to place. (1979)

34 Crystal Voyager 9m E3 6a   **
A delicate and sustained climb with good protection for the final, difficult groove. Right of Slender Thread is a thinner crack system. Climb on small holds in the line of the crack to a good hold just to the left of a large grassy ledge.

Escape is possible here for those not capable of continuing.
The final groove is hard to enter and awkward to climb. A
superb route. (1979)

35 Pretentious Moi 8m E1 6a *
The wall below the grassy ledge of Crystal Voyager provides
a technical test-piece, fortunately with a good landing. (1984)

Thirty metres farther right is the next buttress:

36 Birch Tree Climb 8m S
At the left-hand side of the buttress is a corner. Climb this
to an old tree stump near the top. Make an exposed swing
right to to finish on the arête. Inferior finishes exist.
(pre-1965)

37 Sirloin 8m HS 4b
From the overhang on the right, swing right onto the face
and go up cracks. (pre-1965)

38 Anticlimax 8m VS 5a
Climb the wall right of Sirloin to a big ledge. Finish up the
crack just right of the finish of Sirloin. (1973-1981)

39 Bottle Crack 8m D
To the right is a gully containing the 'bottle' boulder. Above
this, climb the crack on the left wall. (pre-1965)

*About 250m right again is a small face split down the front
by a crack with a protruding chockstone.*

40 Minute Wall 6m HVD
Start 5m left of the crack and go up with a mantelshelf,
beginning at the cutaway. (pre-1965)

41 Key Green Crack 6m VD
Climb the chockstone-filled crack direct. (pre-1965)

42 April Showers 8m HVS 5a
Climb the wall right of Key Green Crack using good pockets.
(1984)

43 May Day 8m HVS 5c
Climb the wall right of April Showers by some awkward
moves. (1984)

Four hundred metres farther right is **THE CATSTONE**, *a fine
tower-like buttress. 10m to the left is a small buttress giving
the next four climbs.*

44 The Crafty Cockney 8m HVS 5b   *
At the left-hand side of the buttress is an obvious slabby
wall. Climb the wall finishing on the arête. A good route.
(1985)

45 Cool in a Crisis 9m HVS 5c   *
The prominent arête, about 3m right of The Crafty Cockney,
gives good climbing.   (1985)

46 Crying Wolf 9m VS 4c
The central crackline just right of Cool in a Crisis.   (1985)

47 Prescription for the Poor 8m VS 4c
Start about 4m right of Crying Wolf. Climb the bulge and
short slab above the cutaway on the right of the buttress.
(1985)

48 Termination Crack 18m S 4a
The overgrown corner-crack, on the left-hand side of the
large buttress, 10m right again.   (pre-1973)

49 The Cat Crawl 18m S 4a   *
The left arête of the tower. 5m of easy rock leads to the
arête. Climb this awkwardly at first then on better holds to
the top. Alternatively take the upward-curving ledge right of
the upper section.   (1920s)

50 Hot Tin Roof 18m E1 5a   ***
A bold route though good Friends now make runners in the
chimney somewhat redundant. Climb the crack at the
left-hand side of the main face, then move rightwards along
ledges to a point overlooking the obvious chimney. Follow a
line of pockets, crux, to the fine upper wall. An excellent
pitch, one of the best of its grade in Staffordshire.
(1973)

51 Mutiny Chimney 18m VS 5a
Climb the difficult short wall to gain the chimney which is
taken to a hard and unpleasant exit onto the hollybush
ledge. Step left onto the face and finish pleasantly up the
arête.   (1920s)

52 Hollybush Wall 10m VS 4c
Climb the wall below the hollybush ledge using thin
indefinite cracks and the arête to the right at the top. A good
finish can be made up the final arête of Mutiny Crack.
(pre-1973)

TIMBERSBROOK QUARRY

Owing to frequent landslides, creeping vegetation and restricted access, this quarry is not considered worthy of climbers' attention at present and is therefore not included in this guidebook.

BOSLEY CLOUD LIST OF FIRST ASCENTS

by Gary Gibson

1920s	**Mutiny Chimney, The Cat Crawl** Morley Wood, Fred Pigott, Harry Kelly	
1940s	**V-chimney** Eric Byne, M. Holland	
Pre-1951	**Green Gully Direct, Left Nostril, Right Nostril, Corner Route** *Mentioned briefly in the 1951 guidebook.*	
1963	**Bulldog Flake** Ed Drummond	
Pre-1965	**Envy Face, Dry-stone Wall, Thin Finger Corner, Everdance, The Lubricant, Birch Tree Climb, Bottle Crack, Minute Wall, Key Green Crack** *All appeared in Peter Bamfield's notes in the Midland Association of Mountaineers club journal but were lost for the 1973 guide.*	
1973	**Hot Tin Roof, Slab Wall** Paul Williams, John Amies, P. King	
Pre-1973	**Fertility Rite, White House Flake, Deception, Wet and Warm, Main Wall** (aided), **Hollybush Wall, Termination Crack** *The first free ascent of Main Wall fell to Jonny Woodward in 1978.*	
1973	*Staffordshire Gritstone guidebook published outlining only a few routes on the crag. Peter Bamfield's notes were, at that time, not available.*	
1977 Aug.	**Death Wish** Jonny Woodward *Top-roped first.*	
1977 Oct. 8	**Impact Two** Jonny Woodward *Top-roped first.*	
1977 Oct.	**Fertility Rite Left-hand** Jonny Woodward (solo)	
1978	**Main Wall** Jonny Woodward, Andrew Woodward *First free ascent.*	

1979 Spring	**Slender Thread, Crystal Voyager** Jonny Woodward, Andrew Woodward

1980	**Summit Arête** Jonny Woodward

First free ascent. Probably the first 7a route in Great Britain and still unrepeated!

1973-1981	**Anticlimax** probably Jonny Woodward (solo)

1981	*Staffordshire guidebook published detailing all the routes on Bosley Cloud for the first time.*

1984 April 30	**April Showers** Mark Stokes, John Allen

1984 April 30	**May Day** John Allen, Mark Stokes

1984 May 31	**Big Red Rock Eater, Prententious Moi** Allen Williams (solo)

1984 May 31	**Existentialist Arête** Andy Popp (on sight solo)

1984 May 31	**Herbivacious** Nick Dixon (solo)

1985 May 30	**Solitaire** Ian 'Squawk' Dunn (solo)

Top-roped first and climbed over two days, then given the joke grade of E3/4!

1985 June 20	**Tin Tin** Ian Dunn, Claudie Dunn

1985 Oct. 13	**Why Kill Time.....** Nick Dixon, Ian Dunn

1985 Oct. 13	**Contraception on Demand, Kremlin Wall** Ian Dunn (solo)

1985 Dec. 21	**Prescription for the Poor, The Crafty Cockney** Keith Ashton, Malc Baxter

1985 Dec. 21	**Crying Wolf** Keith Ashton, Malc Baxter

1985 Dec. 21	**Cool in a Crisis** Malc Baxter, Keith Ashton

1986 April	**Death Crack** Nick Dixon, Mark 'Face' McGowan, Simon Oaker, Denise Arkless, Allen Williams

1986 April	**Living Wall** Nick Dixon, Allen Williams

1986 April	**Mr Magoo** Simon Oaker, Nick Dixon, Mark McGowan

MOW COP

by Gary Gibson

SITUATION and CHARACTER

This craggy outcrop is a prominent feature on the Cheshire – Staffordshire border and is clearly visible from miles around. The Folly Castle is a well-known landmark some 11km north of Stoke-on-Trent.

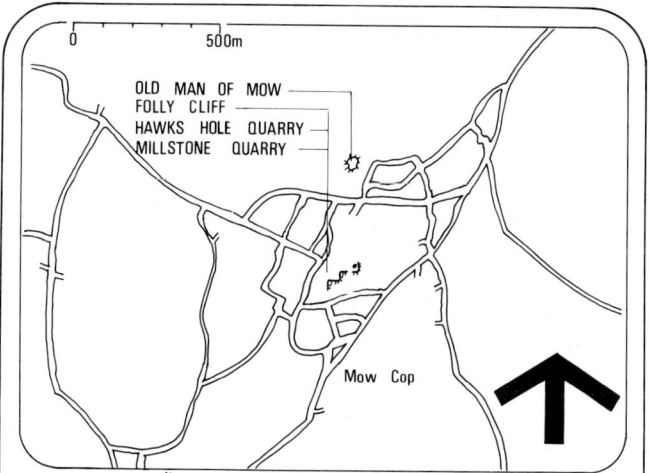

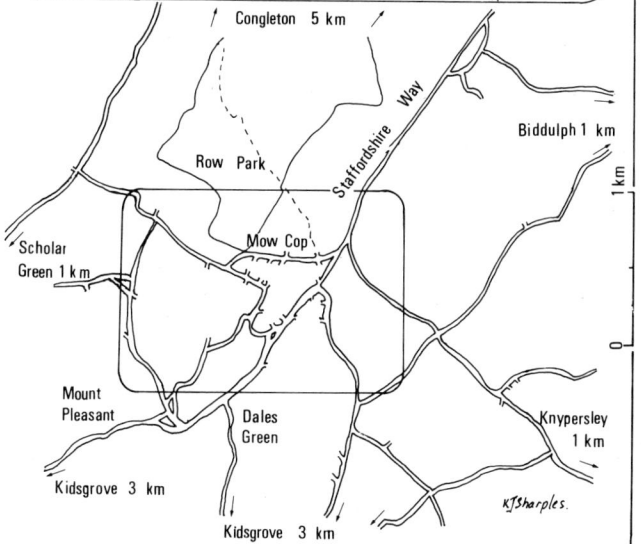

0 500m

OLD MAN OF MOW
FOLLY CLIFF
HAWKS HOLE QUARRY
MILLSTONE QUARRY

Mow Cop

Congleton 5 km

Row Park

Staffordshire Way

Biddulph 1 km

1 km

Scholar
Green 1 km

Mow Cop

0

Mount
Pleasant

Dales
Green

Knypersley
1 km

Kidsgrove 3 km

Kidsgrove 3 km

K.J.Sharples.

Mow Cop

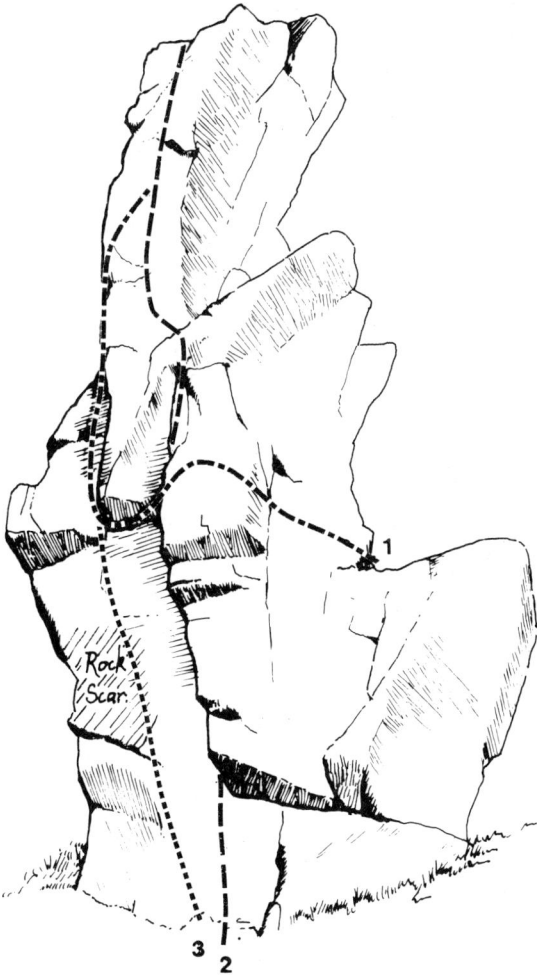

Rock
Scar.

1

3 2

Philip Gibson.

Old Man of Mow

All of the routes lie on quarried rock which has a very brittle nature. The climbs on The Old Man are worthy of attention, especially The Spiral Route which is quite unique. Otherwise, the cliffs have little of note to tempt those from farther afield than the neighbouring villages.

APPROACHES and ACCESS

The best approach is by car, because bus services have recently been reduced and are very irregular. Mow Cop is well-signposted from Biddulph and Kidsgrove and there is adequate parking at the foot of the castle on its western side. The Folly Cliff and nearby quarries lie on the eastern side of the castle whilst The Old Man lies 200m to the north-west. Follow the ridge northwards, then pass between some bungalows to find the pinnacle nestling in a small quarry.

Though the land hereabouts appears quite public, it is owned by The National Trust who have expressed a certain amount of concern about the nature of the rock. At the time of writing (Winter 1987/88) the stability of the cliffs is under scrutiny and The Old Man is being monitored on a regular basis. By the time of publication, fences around the base of the Folly Cliff may have been erected; under no circumstances should such fences be damaged or removed and climbers crossing them do so at their own risk. Stabilisation work may continue and it is advisable to consult the climbing magazines for future information. It should also be remembered that climbers should not encourage local youngsters to climb alongside them; they rarely have a rope!

HISTORY

The first route to be recorded was K. Maskery's first ascent of The Old Man by *The Spiral Route*, which remains the best route hereabouts. Various other people have visited the crags and contributed over the years. Harold Drasdo and friends added four more routes to the pinnacle; *Cambridge Crack*, *Piton Route*, *Alsager Route* and *The Direct Route*. Since, then records of activity are poor. Routes certainly became established such as *Castle Crack* but who did them first is unclear. Several, including *Carbonel*, were added by A. Taylor and Paul Williams around 1960. A little later P. Kenway, John Amies and John Lockett found *Hawk's Hell*, *Left Eliminate*, *Folly Berger*, *Man Mow* and *Right Tot* to suit their tastes. John Amies then described all the known routes in the 1973 Staffordshire Gritstone guidebook.

Following this the Woodward brothers, Jonny and Andrew, stepped in to tidy up a few loose ends by free climbing *The Arête* and *B.S. Mow* whilst also creating *Silent Scream* and *Captain Skyhook*. John Holt appeared on the scene in 1978 to climb *Special Branch* whilst a year later Gary Gibson added a few morsels.

Despite the controversial placing of a bolt on The Old Man, little has happened since and this situation doesn't look like changing. However, stabilisation work may yet bring the downfall of some routes altogether.

THE OLD MAN OF MOW   O.S. ref. SJ 858576

THE CLIMBS on this unique and contorted pinnacle are described in a CLOCKWISE fashion starting at the step just right of the fence below a rock-fall on the front face. It should be noted that descent from this pinnacle is by a very precarious abseil; not advised for the inexperienced. However, quite recently, a bolt has appeared and may make this a safer proposition.

1 The Spiral Route 20m VS 4a   ***
A unique outing. From the left-hand end of the steps, climb up left to gain a ledge at the base of a slab. Move left and down, go round the corner and move up another slab to the left shoulder (possible belay). Step up, then move out right onto the forehead and finish direct.   (pre-1960)

2 The Direct Route 17m HVS 5a   *
Start just inside the fence guarding the front face. Climb the left-facing groove, carefully at first, then go through an overhang to the initial slab of The Spiral Route. Step up and move out left onto the forehead and climb delicately at first, then more easily to the top.   (pre-1960)

3 Alsager Route 17m HVS 5a
From the foot of The Direct Route trend left across the rock scar, then climb direct up to the left shoulder and the belay of The Spiral Route. Finish up the tight groove in the arête above.   (pre-1960)

The back of the pinnacle sports three routes:

4 The Lee Side 20m E1 5a
Climb the right-hand side of the small pedestal to its top, then move out rightwards across the leaning wall and go round the arête onto the shoulder. Finish diagonally back leftwards. (1973)

5 Cambridge Crack 11m VS 4c *
Climb the obvious leaning fissure. Finish up any route from the small slab.

(pre-1960)

6 Piton Route 17m E1 5b
A series of steps on the left leads all the way to the top. The final step is the most difficult. (pre-1960/1970s)

THE OLD MAN'S QUARRY

Numerous problems and routes of varying grades are possible in the adjacent quarry. None has any particular merit though in the past, two climbs of Very Difficult standard have been recorded up the left-hand side of the face.

THE FOLLY CLIFF   O.S. ref. SJ 858573

This double-faced quarry is divided centrally by the obvious arête, lying directly beneath the castle.

THE CLIMBS are described from RIGHT to LEFT.

7 Cioch Groove 9m VD
An obvious leaning chimney/groove at the right-hand end of the cliff. (pre-1973)

8 Crystal Voyager 9m HVS 5a
The slabby wall just left of the groove is climbed direct to its conclusion. (1979)

9 Initiation Wall 10m VS 4b
The loose overhanging wall 3m left. (pre-1973)

10 B.S. Mow 18m E1 5c
The once-pegged crack 3m left again is started with difficulty but soon relents for a rightwards finish up the wall above. An easier but loose start can be made just to the right. (1960s/1975)

11 The Arête 18m E3 5c
The sandy peg-scarred cracks in the obvious arête.

(1960s/19760)

FOLLY CLIFF

TO OLD MAN OF MOW folly

FOLLY CLIFF

HAWK'S HOLE QUARRY

MILLSTONE QUARRY

MOW COP RIDGE

0   10   25 metres

Way Down

Folly Cliff

9

7

14

13

11

10

29

31

26

25

Way Down

Millstone Quarry

19   18

Way Down

23

21   20

17

16

15

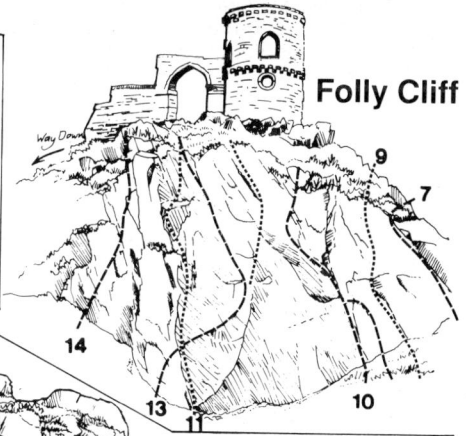

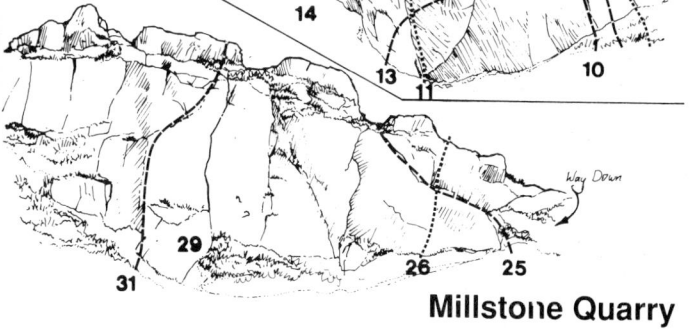

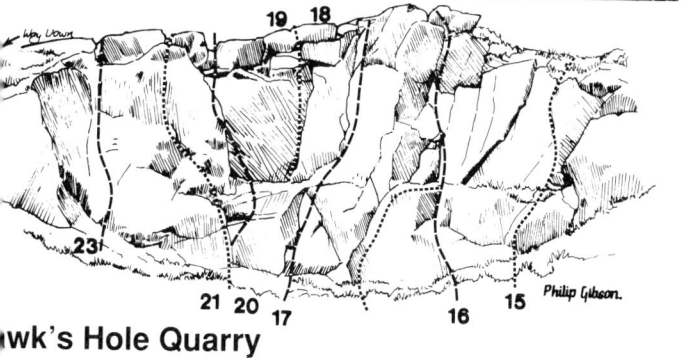

Philip Gibson.

wk's Hole Quarry

12 Man Mow 20m E1 5a
Start just left of The Arete and gain it, then swing right to a
ledge in the centre of the face. Continue directly above past
a Damoclean spike. (1960s)

13 Folly Berger 20m HVS 5a
From the ledge of Man Mow move diagonally leftwards to
The Arête, then step back right and finish direct. (1960s)

14 Right Tot HVS 4c
To the left of The Arête is a scoop. Climb the wall to its
right, move 3m left to a rotten flake and finish up this and
the wall above. (1960s)

Rot and **Tot** lie up the wall to the left. Both should delight
the connoisseur of loose rock and poor climbing. A girdle
traverse is of equally fine quality.

HAWK'S HOLE QUARRY O.S. ref. SJ 858573

The large hole slightly to the south of the castle. Its upper
right wall sports two V-shaped notches.

15 Double Vee 12m HS 4a
Climb through the two notches to reach the top. (pre-1973)

16 Three Steps 14m S
Gain the stepped, broken corner left of Double Vee from that
route. A harder start lies below, up the obvious short ramp;
HVS 5a. (pre-1973)

The overhanging prow just to the left sports the dynamic
aid-climbing duo, **Batman** and **Robin**. Both are A2.

17 Hawk's Hell 18m VS 4c
The back right-hand corner of the quarry, gaining the
half-height ledge via a large flake. (1960s)

*Two cracks spring from the half-height ledge of Hawk's
Hell:*

18 Right Eliminate 9m A1 (pre-1973)

19 Left Eliminate 9m VS 5a (1960s)

20 Vee Diff 15m S! *
Start just left of Hawk's Hell. Climb leftwards to reach a
large ledge and continue up the arête or the slab above.
(pre-1973)

21 Square Buttress 9m HS 4a
The centre of the square buttress 5m to the left. (pre-1973)

To the left is an obvious scooped face:

22 The Captain's Blood 8m E2 6a
The blank-looking right-hand side of the scoop gives a good problem.
(1979)

23 Captain Skyhook 8m E1 5c *
The centre of the scoop gives good climbing to a step right to finish.
(1976)

The largest quarry lies round to the left again.

MILLSTONE QUARRY O.S. ref. SJ 858573

24 The Reach 11m HS 4a
Climb the right arête until a step left leads to a groove and the top.
(pre-1973)

25 Carbonel 18m VS 4c
From 5m up The Reach, move left and follow the obvious diagonal rampline across the wall to the top.
(1960)

26 Silent Scream 13m E3 6a
Start below the mid-point of the traverse of Carbonel. Climb directly up the crystalline wall by difficult moves to reach Carbonel and a finish up the shallow groove above.
(1979)

27 Bow and Arrow 15m VS 4c †
The disgusting bird-limed crack 10m to the left.
(1960)

28 Special Branch 16m E1 5b
The vague crackline just left of the obvious appalling gully.
(1978)

29 Castle Crack 18m VS 4b *
Climb the conspicuous wide crack in the face to the left, gained from a small rib below. Very worthwhile.
(1960s)

30 Crystine 18m E2 5b
Climb the wall just to the left to a good ledge. Climb the wall 3m left of Castle Crack to easy ground and finish up the arête directly above.
(1979)

31 Arête and Slab Climb 25m S
Follow a vague line 3m left again, by-passing a tricky section to the left. Move rightwards on the obvious line and finish as for the upper section of Castle Crack.
(pre-1973)

Numerous problems exist on the smaller walls of the quarry. A short slab gives pleasant climbing for beginners but otherwise there is little of worth.

NICK I' TH' HILL O.S. ref. SJ 881607

There are several quarries along the crest of this ridge, 4km north-east of Mow Cop. Many overlook gardens (or are gardens themselves!) and are therefore not worthy of attention.

MOW COP LIST OF FIRST ASCENTS

Pre-1960	**Spiral Route** K Maskery
Pre-1960	**Piton Route** Harold Drasdo *At least one peg was used for aid but it was probably fully aided. Climbed free be persons unknown in the 1970s.*
Pre-1960	**Alsager Route** Harold Drasdo, K. Finlay
Pre-1960	**Cambridge Crack, Direct Route** J. Sutton, Harold Drasdo, Bob Downes, Tony Moulam
1960	**Carbonel, Bow and Arrow** A. Taylor, Paul Williams
1960s	**Hawks Hell, Left Eliminate** (aid), **Folly Berger, Man Mow, Right Tot** P Kenway, John Amies, John Lockett
1960s	**Castle Crack**
1960s	**B.S. Mow** (some aid) *Climbed free by Jonny and Andrew Woodward in 1975.*
1960s	**The Arête** (some aid) *Climbed free by Jonny and Andrew Woodward in 1976.*
1973	**The Lee Side**
Pre-1973	**Cioch Groove, Initiation Wall, Double Vee, Three Steps, Right Eliminate, Vee Diff, Square Buttress, The Reach**
1975 June	**B.S. Mow** Jonny Woodward, Andrew Woodward (both solo) *First free ascent.*
1976 June	**The Arête** Jonny Woodward, Andrew Woodward *First free ascent.*
1976 June	**Captain Skyhook** Andrew Woodward (solo)
1978	**Special Branch** John Holt
1979	**Silent Scream** Andrew Woodward
1979 Sept.	**Crystal Voyager, The Captain's Blood, Crystine** Gary Gibson (solo)

KNYPERSLEY ROCKS

O.S. ref. SJ 901558

by Simon Whalley

SITUATION and CHARACTER

These crags are situated 2km south-east of Biddulph, in the woods on the eastern side of Knypersley Reservoir.

The rock is gritstone, tends to be sandy in places and unfortunately, due to the proximity of the trees, is also very green with an abundance of lichen. The crag has a few good routes and its situation may make it worth an evening's exploration.

APPROACHES and ACCESS

The rocks are best approached from the A527 crossroads at Knypersley. Follow the Biddulph Moor road (Park Lane) for almost 2km and turn right along Lodge Barn Road and follow its unmade surface for 300m until it forks. Park here or farther along the right-hand fork. From the fork, a path runs down the right-hand side of a dry-stone wall. Follow this past a stile on the left to the point where the path leads rightwards through the wall. The first buttress is at the extreme right-hand end of this wall. This is Green Slab.

The rocks have been climbed upon sporadically. Please seek permission to climb at the first house (note: this does not mean to climb ON the house) in the row of houses on the left, otherwise access problems may arise.

THE CLIMBS are described from RIGHT to LEFT.

1 Twinkletoes 11m VD   *

Start at the left-hand side of the slab and tiptoe delicately rightwards to reach the right arête. Climb this to the top, past a large ledge at half-height. Exciting.

2 Two Step 9m S

Start as for Twinkletoes but continue directly to the top.

One hundred and fifty metres left of Green Slab is **THE PINNACLE**, *the front face of which is split by a chimney through a large overhang.*

3 Cold Shoulder 11m HVS 5b

Gain the right arête by a diagonal weakness, then continue until the short finishing crack on the left can be reached.

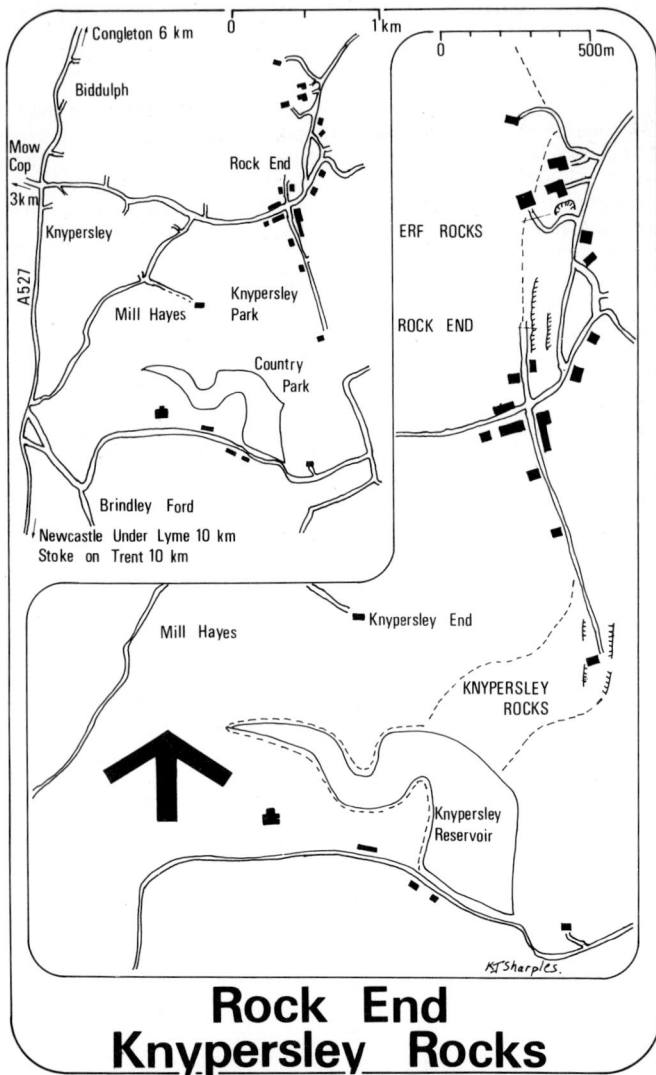

Congleton 6 km
Biddulph
Mow Cop
3 km
Knypersley
A527
Mill Hayes
Rock End
Knypersley Park
Country Park
Brindley Ford
Newcastle Under Lyme 10 km
Stoke on Trent 10 km

0   1 km

0   500m

ERF ROCKS
ROCK END

Mill Hayes
Knypersley End
KNYPERSLEY ROCKS
Knypersley Reservoir

KJSharples.

Rock End
Knypersley Rocks

4 The Jug Jam 12m VD **

Scramble up the leftward-facing corner below the chimney. Climb the twin cracks and make a hard move at a bulge to gain the chimney then the top. The best route on the crag.

5 Scorpion 11m VS 4c

Start round the left arête and partway up the grassy bank. Make a stinging traverse right to gain the arête and teeter up this to gain the top. Poorly-protected.

6 Logos 9m VS 4c

The shallow groove left of Scorpion is climbed to a bold swing onto the arête. Move slightly right and finish direct.

The broken slab to the left of The Pinnacle has been climbed at Very Difficult.

Fifty metres down the valley, and on the left, is a large boulder perched on top of several blocks. Right of this is the largest crag, a natural arch bounding its right-hand side.

THE CLIMBS are described from LEFT to RIGHT.

From the boulder, scramble up the grassy bank to its highest point against the crag. The crack on the right is:

7 Keep Left 8m VS 4c

The slanting crack. Hard if the holds on the next route are avoided.

8 Danera 9m VD

Start up the narrow ramp and gain a crack which is followed to the top.

9 The Common Good 8m VS 4b *

Layback through the overhang to a scary move onto a rounded ledge. Finish easily to a tree belay.

10 Prometheus 8m M

The wide crack to the right.

11 Northern Lights 8m D

The corner and dirty crack right again.

12 Misogynist 9m VD

The obvious chimney is climbed direct.

13 Christmas Cracker 9m HVS 5b

Climb the broken lower wall to reach a narrow crack via a worrying move past the black central section.

14 Briar 9m VS 4c
The cracks left of the arch are gained by slippery moves up
the green and greasy wall.

ROCK END   O.S. ref. SJ 898570
by Simon Whalley

SITUATION and CHARACTER
These excellent gritstone outcrops lie along the left-hand
side of the Knypersley-to-Biddulph Moor road, 2km east of
Biddulph.
Composed of excellent gritstone these small buttresses give
fine, though rarely-frequented, bouldering to tempt the
connoisseur.

APPROACHES and ACCESS
There are two main outcrops. The first, visible in a field at
the left-hand end of the small escarpment, is approached
through the back garden of the house at the extreme
left-hand end of the crag. Permission to climb must be
sought at the house.
The second outcrop of any size is situated in a field behind
and to the left of the ERF Plastics factory. Discreet parking in
the lay-by partway down the factory access road is
advisable and climbing does not appear to be prohibited.

THE CLIMBS are described from LEFT to RIGHT starting with
the outcrop situated at the left-hand side of the crag.

GARDEN BUTTRESS

1 Tube Snake 9m VS 4c
The obvious jutting prow on the left arête may be gained
from the left by a series of sandy pockets. Squirm painfully
along the prow until it is possible to gain a standing
position, then layback the huge flake above to finish. The
final flake can also be gained direct at 5a.

2 Joshua 9m HVS 5b   *
Four metres right is a shallow water-worn runnel below a
'whitish' flake. Hard starting moves enable some
extraordinary holds to be reached at the top of the runnel.
Continue direct past the flake to an awkward move to gain
the headwall. Finish straight up.

3 Cherry Hill 9m E1 5b
The ramp 2m right is followed until it is possible to swing left under the roof. Tackle this direct using a long reach for hidden holds.

4 Brick Bank Crack 9m VD
The wide central crack is climbed using holds on the right past a difficult section at mid-height.

5 The Friends of Eddie Coil 9m E3 6b *
The undercut slab right of Brick Bank Crack. Start just left of centre and move up then right to make desperate moves over the overlap, small wires, to gain easy ground above a poor pocket. Continue, stunned, to the top.

6 Hot Digital Dog 8m HVS 5c
The right arête. Use pockets in the right wall to gain the arête proper. Balance up this to reach the top. Short and sharp.

The crag continues farther right, but decreases in height, to give some entertaining boulder problems.

The vandalised slab in the field 200m right again yields many excellent and hard friction test-pieces. The two large outcrops, which can be seen 200m farther along the ridge, are on private land and the owners have made it clear that they DO NOT WISH CLIMBING TO TAKE PLACE.

ERF ROCKS

7 Enterprise 5m 5b
Climb the scoop just right of the left arête on brushed flakes. Don't be tempted to pull on the heather!

8 Titan 6m E2 6a
Victory over the thin roof crack is only gained by those with a 'take no prisoners' attitude.

9 Up to the Elbows 6m HS
Easy laybacking, awkward bridging and a complete body-jam are needed to overcome the central crack.

10 The Fruit Palace 6m VS 4b
The pocketed slab on the right. Hard starting moves enable the centre of the easier-than-it-looks slab to be gained and climbed direct. Poorly-protected.

11 Harvest Moon 6m HS
The obvious groove 2m to the right is hardest at the top.

12 Sickle Moon 6m HVS 5a
An eliminate line up the brushed wall between Harvest Moon and:

13 The Blackpool Trip 6m HS
Easy moves up the leftward-facing corner allow the crack above to be gained. This succumbs to classic gritstone jamming.

14 Bilberry Slab 6m VD
Amble up the centre of the large slab to the right.

Seven metres left of the gate, and at the right-hand end of the crag, is:

15 Desert Head 6m HS
The vertical crack which bends sharply leftwards at the top, past two natural threads.

HEIGHLEY CASTLE QUARRIES   O.S. ref. SJ 470773

by Gary Gibson

SITUATION and CHARACTER
A group of small sandstone quarries lying roughly 2km north of Madeley, a small village 6km west of Newcastle-under-Lyme.
Whilst only known to a handful of climbers, in ideal conditions, these quarries offer very good training facilities. A rope is not really needed except for a couple of top-rope problems and the quarries main attributes are their excellent traverse-lines and numerous boulder problems. Ideal climbing time is either Autumn or Spring, preferably after a short dry spell. Summer is not particularly advisable due to greenness and swarms of midges. The rock is sound but a little sandy and green in places — take a brush (but not a wire one).

APPROACHES and ACCESS
From Newcastle-under-Lyme, follow the A521 Newcastle-to-Crewe road until, after 7km, the road passes underneath a motorway bridge. Take the first right turn after the bridge (less than 1km farther on) and follow the minor road down the hill past a farm and go up the other side to the first forestry track leading off to the left. There is parking space available here or a little farther on. The quarries are

up the hill in the trees to the left. From Nantwich and Crewe, the junction is somewhat harder to indentify; it is better to locate the motorway bridge and back-track from there.

Climbers have been known to be confronted by a local farmer who claims the land to be his. His protestations never amount to ejection.

THE CLIMBS are described as they are most often approached; from LEFT to RIGHT.

FIRST QUARRY

This offers a 30m-long wall with an obvious corner at its right-hand end and a shorter wall right again.

The Traverse 36m 5c
A superb exercise taking the obvious half-height break, usually from left to right. A short sustained section halfway along proves most difficult and an extension can be made to the right edge of the wall. Continuing back and forth keeps the 'pump' going.

Low Traverse 36m 6b
Keep as low as possible for maximum effect. Very, very fingery, like putting your fingers through a mangle! Again best done from left to right but this time reversal is unheard of?

The Corner 8m 5a
The angle of the bay. A good bridging exercise with an adequate finish.

Numerous upward problems, throughout the entire length of the wall, are possible. However, due to the nature of the upper part of the wall as well as the awful finishes, these are best not extended beyond the half-height break.

10m to the right and at a lower level is:

SECOND QUARRY

Punch Arête 5m 6b
The left-hand arête of the wall has been completed only a few times. The finish can be dirty. Sustained and technical but with a good landing.

The long wall to the right sports two lines of chipped holds. Both are 5a but only if you are the same height as the chipper!

Right again the section of crag has copious finishing vegetation. Arêtes, walls and corners give good boulder problems and a left-to-right traverse at a low-level, from the first corner to just right of the right arête, has one move of 6a and some sustained 5b climbing.

Second, But Last, Arête 5m 6a
The right-most arête can be finished but is best reversed for maximum effect.

Continuing right for 40m one encounters the poorest of the four quarries.

THIRD QUARRY

Interesting problems are few and far between. The arête at the right-hand end and the wall to its left are worthwhile 5b routes, but they are rarely climbed.

The biggest and best quarry is 50m farther on, down a large bank.

FOURTH QUARRY – THE PIT

This is often dank and dismal though it is always the driest of the four quarries.

Slim Corner 9m 5c
The first slim corner has an awkward start on the right arête and an amenable exit.

Suicide Arête 13m 6b (not led)
The massive dominating arête. A brilliant problem top-roped only a couple of times. Very hard and sustained.

Hilti-gunner 13m 6b (not led)
Start up the slim groove 2m right of the arête and continue direct up a short vicious headwall. Very fingery.

A traverse right, from the foot of Suicide Arête to just before the main angle of the bay, with fingers at 3m or 2m, gives superb training. There is one 6a move when traversing at 3m height, with plenty of 5b and 5c climbing, whilst at 2m height there are plenty of 6a moves with one 6c stretch. The 3m height traverse can be done in reverse.

The large angle gives a good 6b problem for bridging training; how high can you get?

To the right, the crag deteriorates into the grassy hillside. Boulder problems as well as a short low-level traverse, of lesser value, can be found here.

Windgather and Castle Naze Supplement

As these two fine training crags are as close to the Roaches Area as they are to the Kinder area, particularly for those approaching from the west, a strategic transfer of route descriptions only has been made for this interim reprint while their proper guidebook home is reassessed. The climbs are not indexed and their histories are in the Kinder guide.

WINDGATHER ROCKS   O.S.ref.995785

SITUATION and ACCESS
The rocks are in Derbyshire, close to the Cheshire border, and lie at a height of 1300 feet above sea level. They are two miles south-south-west of Whaley Bridge on a ridge leading south to Cat's Tor and Shining Tor.

Two lanes lead south-east from Kettleshulme on the A5002 Macclesfield to Whaley Bridge road. They join just short of the crag and there is a layby below the cliff. Windgather can also be approached from the Goyt Valley or from the Buxton/Macclesfield road by more devious routes. The crag is owned by the Peak Park Planning Board, and must only be approached from the layby via the two stiles and the fenced alley. Climbers have access to the area within the fences above and below the crag, and they are asked not to damage them or the walls *which limit* the access area at either end of the crag. The lower fence, denoting the boundary, runs to the right (south) under the crag towards the quarry to meet one of these transverse walls. **Please do not climb over this.** There is a stile giving access to the quarry hidden higher up the slope. It is better to approach the Quarry along the cliff top or by the road – 140 yards uphill from the layby. The quarry face is quite low but gives many possibilities for soloing and other problems.

The climbs on the main cliff are described from RIGHT to LEFT. Route length averages 8 –10m. The quality is good where the crag architecture allows. One star indicates the climbs of better quality than the norm.

Forty yards to the right of the entrance is a large undercut buttress with a 'cave' at the right-hand end and a pulpit under its left hand end. This is SOUTH BUTTRESS. The crack immediately on its right is South Crack. Four yards to its right are three cracks through small overhangs.

1   Overlapping Wall   HS 4b
Climb the small bulging buttress just to the right of the third crack.

The three cracks: **Right Triplet** MS, **Middle Triplet** S, **Left Triplet** D.

2   South Crack   D   The wide corner crack right of the first big buttress.

3   Route 1   HS 4a   From South Crack, shuffle leftwards round the arête onto the ledge above the cave. From the left-hand end of this, pull up past some blocks and continue to the top.   *Variations:* The right-hand side of the arête followed direct is HVS 5a The left-hand side of the arête, from the right-hand side of the ledge, is VS 4c.

4   Arête Direct   E1 5b   From the right-hand side of the cave, pull direct onto the nose of the arête and follow it direct.

5   Editor's Note   HVS 5b
From left of the cave, pull out and up to join and follow Route 1.

6   Route 1.5   HVS 4c
From 6 feet to the right of the pulpit, climb direct. Strenuous.

7   Route 2   VS 4b   From the pulpit, step right and climb the crack through the overhang. Finish direct.

8   Leg Up   HVS 5a   From the pulpit, pull over the nose directly below the arête. Continue up the arête above.

9   Overhanging Arête   VD   From the gully left of the buttress, move out rightwards to join and follow the arête of Leg Up.

The small walls within the next 30 yards offer many problems. The next buttress, with a small holly on the right wall, is **BUTTRESS 1.**

10   Side Face   S   Climb directly up the right flank left of the holly.
11   First's Arête   D   Follow the right-hand side of the arête.
12   Face Route 1   D   Start 3 yards to the left of the arete. Pull over the small overhang, then more easily up the face .

13   Face Route 2   M   Follow the broken cracks just to the left.
Ten yards to the left, past some small faces, is **BUTTRESS 2.** *This is directly opposite the fenced entry to the crag.*

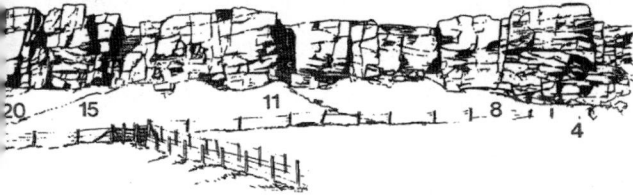

14 Cheek HVS 5a   Start from a block below the right-hand side wall and climb up to meet the arête at the top.

15   The Broken Groove in the Arête D

16   Traditional HS 4a Step to the right off the block below the face and climb directly past the blunt flake.

17 Aged Crack S   Step off the left side of the block and climb direct to the crack. Gaining this from Corner Crack on the left gives a VD climb.

18 Corner Crack VD   The crack in the corner gives the line.

19 Struggle HS 4b   Just to the left, the crack through the nose.

20 Squashed Finger VD   The crack 3 feet to the left.

21 Centre VD   Climb the centre of the small face to the left.

22 Middle and Leg D   The chimney crack just to the left again.

23 Leg Stamp M   Take the easiest line up the slab just to the left.

24 Gully M   The couloir just to the left.

The next 10 yards of small walls lead to **HIGH BUTTRESS**:

25   Heather Face HS   Start at the bilberry-filled niche in the centre of the right-hand side-face and climb almost direct.

26   High Buttress Arête D
Start at the foot of the arête and follow it almost direct.

27   Nose Direct VD   Start at the small recess just left of the arête, and climb direct to the nose. Pull over it, step left, and continue direct. Straight over the nose is **Director,** VS 4c,

28 Footprint VD   Start 2 yards to the left of the recess. Climb direct between a bulge on the right and the heel of a large 'footprint' on the left.

29 **Too Nail** D Start below the toe of the footprint and climb direct.

For the **Zigzag**, D start at Toe Nail and climb diagonally right to a position above the nose, then finish direct. **The Corner** to the left of the face is D. **The Bulging Arête** of the block just to the left is S.

Ignoring scrappy rocks move 10 yards left to a buttress with a broad platform on its upper right-hand aide, **MIDDLE BUTTRESS**:

30 **M.B. Arête** D
Climb up just to the left of the right-hand arête of the buttress to an awkward move into a corner. This leads to the broad platform. Step left and climb the right-hand edge of the face above.

31 **The Medicine*** HS
Start 6 feet to the left of the arête and climb direct over two bulges.

32 **Mississippi*** (or **Straight Crack**) VD
Climb to, and up, the obvious bottomless crack 3 feet to the left.

33 **Chockstone Chimney** D Follow the ragged crack, using the wall on its left, to the final wider crack.

34 **Centre Route** VD Start below a thin crack in the crag top and climb direct to it. The crux is at mid-height. For **Slant Start** VD, climb diagonally to the top crack from the start of Chockstone Chimney. The crux is then the top crack.

35 **Wall Climb** HD Climb parallel cracks to the final chimney.
An easier (HS) twin to Portfolio goes up the headwall, right of Wall Climb.

36 **Portfolio*** HVS 5a Avoiding the holds on Wall Climb, ascend direct to the overhang. This is surmounted via a series of strenuous pulls. This route has seen accidents so be careful, especially if soloing.

The corner to the left is Moderate. Stepping left out of it onto the platform gives an easy way up (or down). Just to the left, and at a lower level, is a **Small Wall**, 4b. The problem over the **Taller Overhang,** on the left is 5b.

37 **Heather Buttress** HD Fifteen yards left of Portfolio take a broken arête to a gap below an overhang, climb it and the wall above.

Twelve Yards to the left is the start of NORTH BUTTRESS. *Just to the right of this buttress, broken rocks provide an easy way down.*

38   Chimney and Crack   HD   Climb to the first platform on the right-hand side of the buttress. Move up leftwards into the chimney and finish up the wide crack on the left.

39   Arête Indirect   S   Start in the small groove below the left-hand end of the first platform. Follow the arête on its right-hand side, pulling round left onto the front face near the top.

40   Arête Direct   VS   4c   Surmount the undercut left side of the arête (crux), then continue up its left-hand side.

41   Green Crack*   HVD   Six feet to the left of the arête, a groove leads to the wide, awkward, upper crack.

42   Black Slab   VD   Three feet to the left of the groove, start at the blunt nose. Climb over the bulge, then go up a flake to finish 3 feet left of Green Crack. Hardest at the start.

43   Green Slab   S   Start just to the left of the wide flake-crack. Make an awkward move off the flake-top and go up the wall above.

44   Staircase   M   The corner just to the left.

45   The Rib   VS   5b
To the left, the front face of a rib stands forward. Climb directly up the centre or, more easily, up the right-hand arête at VS 4c.

The rocks continue leftwards (north) to the boundary wall (and in fact well beyond), offering a variety of small problems not meriting description except for a cluster of climbs almost opposite a stone wall running up to the road on its other side. They are grouped round two grassy bays.

46   Christmas Arête   HS   4b
Climb a short wall on the right-hand side of the first grassy bay to a grassy ledge. Climb the sharp arête above.

47   Red Nose Route   D   Go up the 'angle' on the left.

48   Christmas Nose   VS 5a
Easy moves up the staircase on the left, then move over the nose.

49   Bay Wall*   S
To the left, there is a concave wall above a second grassy bay. Climb the shallow angle at its centre, moving left at the bulge.

CASTLE NAZE

O.S. ref 054785

SITUATION and CHARACTER

The edge is on the 1400-foot contour at the north-western corner of Combs Moss above Combs. In its exposed position it can be cold in windy conditions but it does at least face west and catches the evening sun. Although it can become very green after wet weather, it dries fairly quickly. Most of the crag is of sound, well-weathered gritstone. However, the southerly (right-hand) end of the main crag has been quarried and is less sound. The top of the crag, particularly above Scoop Face, is friable and care should be taken when emerging from climbs to avoid triggering stonefalls onto those below. Care is also needed in belaying using the odd in-situ stake combined with cracks and boulders for belays of length to allow a cliff edge position so that the rope does not trigger rockfalls. Because of these dangers, sections of the cliff are not suitable for group training of novice. The cliff, though small, is packed with interesting climbs, many of which are not immediately obvious. A place that rewards curiousity in seeking out obscure problems. The crag also has great historical significance in gritstone development (see *Kinder* guide).

APPROACHES and ACCESS

Turn off the A6 Buxton / Chapel-en-le-Frith road at Doveholes, heading west to the station. Cross the railway bridge and, 200 yards later, turn left along Cowlow Lane. After a mile, and before the road drops down a hill, there is a small lay-by on the left. The path to the cliff crosses a stile just east of this and climbs steeply right to the northern end of the edge. The crag can also be reached from the west direction via the Combs turn off the B5470 Whalley Bridge/Chapel road. At Combs a steep winding lane leads up below the crag to the layby.

THE CLIMBS are described from LEFT to RIGHT:

A dry-stone wall runs up towards the edge. In line with this on the cliff a short face with a crack split in two by a small fin.

1   Double Crack   5m D.

2   The Arête   5m HS   The bounding right-hand arête of the face.

Just right is a large fin of rock and between it and the sadly violated pinnacle is a short wall with three cracks; all are Difficult.

3   Pinnacle Crack   6m VD   Start at the centre of the left-hand face of the pinnacle, and finish up the back wall behind the pinnacle.

4   Pinnacle Arête   6m   VD   The outer arête of the pinnacle. The present top block rocks, handle it with care.

5   Sheltered Crack*   6m   D   The crack just right of the pinnacle.

6   Bow Crack   6m   S   Start as for Sheltered Crack and follow the rightward-trending crack to a perched block. Finish direct.

7   Slanting Crack   8m   S   Climb the crack into the bay, finishing leftwards up a small corner.

8   Overhanging Chockstone Crack   8m   VD   Start up the gully and, using footholds on the arête to the right, pull over the chockstone. Finish up the cracks behind. The through route is D.

9   The Fifth Horseman*   8m   HVS   5a   Just to the right, climb up the narrow wall to an awkward move at the level of the chockstone.

Just right is a short steep wall with a broken ledge above it. Five routes start up this wall. **V Corner,** S; **Thin Crack** VS 4c, *just to the right;* **Muscle Crack** VD, *is the blocky crack;* **The Bloody Crack** S. *and the left-hand and right-hand* **Block Cracks,** S, *lead up to a blocky sentry-box. From the broken ledge, finish up either the wide left-hand crack or, to the right, another behind a flake (both Severe).*

10   The Nose   13m   HS   Bridge up the square recess just to the right, then move left under the nose into the blocky sentry-box. Move back right over the nose and follow the arête above.

11   The Nithin   13m   S   Climb the right-hand crack in the back of the recess, using the arête, to the ledge. The arête can also be climbed direct. Finish up the left-hand chimney crack.

12   Flake Crack   13m   HS   Start at the left-hand wall of the large corner to the right. Climb the crack to the ledge of Nithin. Tenderly layback the two propped flakes above, then move left to finish.

The next two routes are hardly independent but **Main Corner,** S, *is the angle just to the right. In its upper reaches one is forced right to:*

13   The Fly Walk*   11m   S   The well-worn crack just to the right.

14   The Niche**   11m   S   The crack to the right. The niche itself is left via a pull on a jam beside the jammed block.

15   Niche Arete**   12m   MVS   4b   Start just to the right and make progress by two long reaches and a hefty pull-up.

16   Orm and Cheep   11m   E1   6a   Climb the shallow rightward slanting groove between Niche Arête and Studio until a desperate move left gains the pocketed wall above. Go direct up the centre of the wall via three pockets.

17   Studio   11m   S   Two metres to the right, climb the crack and finish up either (or both) of the cracks above.

18   A.P. (Absolutely Perpendicular) Chimney   11m   S
The obvious wide corner-crack is a delicious thrutch.

19   Pod Crack   9m   E1   5c   Two metres to the right of A.P. Chimney, climb the crack past a small pod to the corner at the top.

20   Pitoned Crack   10m   HVS   5b   Start up Pilgrim's Progress and move left and up the obvious thin crack.

21   Pilgrim's Progress*   10m   HS   The crack at the right-hand edge of the wall, using holds on the right arête. *'Interesting but steep,* as Huckleberry Finn observed of Bunyan's book.'

22   Little Pillar   10m   HS   One yard to the right, climb the crack in the right-hand side of a rib. From the platform follow the continuation crack to the top.

23   Ledgeway   11m   HVS   5a   Climb Problem Corner (the small right-angled corner just to the right) to The Platform. Alternatively, make it **Short but Sweet**, 6a up the left arête of Problem Corner. On the right

side of the back wall, use a flake to gain a central hold below a slanting crack. Pull up to a ledge and a short wall below the top.

24   No Name 11m HVD   Two metres to the right, climb the crack to reach the right end of The Platform. Follow the corner crack above.

25   Keep Buttress 11m HVS 5a   Just to the right is a narrow rib. Climb the crack below this to finish up the right side of the rib.

On the right, a buttress sticks out from the crag. This is **KEEP BUT-TRESS** *with its famous, now worn, glacis* (The Scoop) *rising across the front face from left to right.*

26   Keep Corner* 11m HVD   Follow the corner to the left of Keep Buttress. The rock is very shiny. A midway rest can be taken on a ledge to the right.

27   Keep Arete* 11m VS 4b   The left-hand arête of the buttress is followed as closely as possible. Exposed (but at least there is a thread runner at four metres).

28   Scoop Direct 11m HVS 5a   Climb Scoop Face into The Scoop. Go straight up a blind crack and finish with a rightward-slanting crack. One can finish direct at the same grade.

29   Scoop Face*** 11m HVS 5a   A route steeped in history. Start three metres to the right of Keep Arête and climb with difficulty into The Scoop. Traverse right and go up a thin crack to a ledge and pocket. Move up and left to a steep finish. The start is becoming harder with wear otherwise the crux is near the top.

The **Direct Start,** HVS 5b . Begin two metres to the right of the usual start on a small ledge. Under the edge of the centre of The Scoop there is a small pocket. Any means may be used to get both hands in the pocket. Muscling-up, a hold for the left toe is obtained at hand-level and a press-up made into The Scoop'. Other 6a superdirects have been done and one can go straight up the upper wall via the obvious pocket.

30 Scoop Wall 9m E1 5b Climb the Keep Buttress's right wall just to the left of Footstool Left. Spaced holds lead to the right end of The Scoop. Move left and up, then move right at the bulge.

31 Footstool Left 8m VD Climb the wide crack on the side of the semi-detached pillar (holds on the main face), then the corner above.

32 Piano Stool 11m HVS 5a Force a way directly up the overhanging arête, and the short arête above.

33 Footstool Right 8m VD The corner on the right of the pillar, then the groove above.
The layback crack to the right, if climbed independently, is HVD
34 Combs Climb S A finger-crack then cracks in the summit blocks.

A staircase on the right leads to the final cracks of Comb's Climb (HVD), or an easier groove. The broken gully on the right is the way down.

35 The Twostep 6m D On the right, climb the ridge on its left.

36 Fat Man's Chimney 8m M The sturdy thrutch to the right.

37 Plankton 10m E3 5c A difficult and serious problem wall between Fat Man's Chimney and Deep Chimney.

38 Deep Crack 9m VD A crack just left of Deep Chimney.

39 Deep Chimney 9m VD A taxing thrutch. Aren't they all?

The next route begins at a lower level on the front of the tall buttress which is almost cut off from the rest of the crag by Deep Chimney. *It has a large sentry-box at half-height.*

40 Birthday Climb 16m HVS 5b Climb the crack in the centre of the lower wall into the sentry-box. Cross its left wall, and the narrow face just left, to make a long reach leftwards to the bottom of a layaway flake. With scarcely enough breath to puff candles out, follow this to the top.

41   The Crack** 15m VS 4b   Start as for Birthday Climb into the sentry-box. Present arms, then follow the crack through the overhang. Well into the 1920s, this was a local test-piece.

42   Nozag* 14m VS 4c   Two metres to the right, follow the crack to the sentry-box. Continue up the crack in the same line. Where it goes rightwards, move left onto the face and climb it by a thin crack.

43   Zigzag Crack 16m HS   Start as for Nozag but continue along the crack as it goes right and finish up the wide crack (Black Chimney).

44   Zig-a-Zag-a 15m D   Start two metres to the right and climb the corner groove to the terrace. Finish up the wall right of Black Chimney.

45   Long Climb 15m VD   Start three metres to the right and climb the broken pillar to the terrace. Take any finish above.

On top of the tall tower to the right are two iron stakes, about 10 metres back, suitable as belays for the next six routes.

46   Central Tower * 15m VD   Follow the often green corner on the right to a move leftwards onto a terrace. Move back right to a good ledge and climb the groove on the left to finish

47   Atropine** 15m HS 4b   A 1977 classic. Start three metres right of Central Tower's corner and step up onto a projecting flake into a bay. Go up a thin crack near the left arête of the bay (crux) to a ledge. Take the right sloping crack to one of the two final cracks.

48   Belladonna* 15m E1 5c   Start as for Atropine but, after the thin crack, continue up the arête to an overlap. Move right under an overlap and move up using a layaway crack and a downward-pointing flake to another overlap. Move left past a horizontal creaky lump to the arête, then finish wildly up this. Exhilarating, if deadly.

49   Green Crack* 15m S   Start as for Atropine and move up into the back of the bay. Climb the obvious corner crack to the top. It is possible to belay in the bay below the final cracks.

Below and to the right is a section of quarried rock across which runs a rough terrace at two-thirds height. The first four metres of the quarried section, which contains loose blocks, is potentially lethal and best ignored. However the following unpleasant lines do exist:

50 The Blusher 15m VS 4b Start 2m right of the left corner of the lowest tier. Follow blocks and cracks for 6m. Move left and go up to a left-facing crack splitting a short arête above. Worrying.

Other dead-end lines run up to the rough terrace. Just to the right of a left-facing overhanging corner is a steep slab with an obvious thin rightward-slanting crack. This is:

51 Morocc'n Roll 15m E1 5c Make a hard start and follow the crack until a step right can be made into Syringe Benefit. Step left into the middle of the wall and go direct past a dodgy fin of rock to the terrace and an *in situ* peg belay. Finish up the wall or arête behind. Satisfying climbing.

52 Syringe Benefit 17m E1 5c The crack 2m to the right has an awkward start. Follow it direct to finish as for the previous route.

53 Columbal Convenience 15m S The chimney to the right has jammed blocks, in situ pigeons, and much guano. Above these attractions is a zone of shattered rock.

The slab to the right contains three thin cracks. The first ends halfway up the wall. The centre one is:

54 Peg Crack 17m E1 5c Follow the crack, then a loose finish.

The third crack is known to have been top-roped (6a). There are two chimney cracks to the right, both pleasant and both VD, which sadly lead to the shattered zone. Belays could be contrived with expertise and courage. Every gritstone crag should have a Hollybush Crack and there is a fine hollybush in a crack just to the right.
    About 20m to the right **SOUTH BUTTRESS** *is across the rough ground of the descent route and higher up the slope – a long stepped buttress of natural rock.*

55 Hodgkinson's Chimney 5m M On the upper left wall.

56 South Crack 5m D A pleasant rightward-slanting crack.

57 South Buttress 15m D Follow the steps of the buttress and finish up the broken V in the final steepening.

58 V-Chimney 7m D The groove to the right, with two flakes

59 Southern Arête 7m HS On the right wall of V-Chimney.

Across the gully is another buttress, marked by horizontal ripples,

60 Bubbly Wall 6m HVS 5a Just left of its right arête, climb the side-wall of the buttress direct. Small, good, but unprotected.

61 Vanishing Crack* 8m HS   Start up the V-shaped corner at the foot of the buttress and follow the crack.

62 The Vice 8m D   The broken crack on the right to a V-cleft.

63 Struggle 5m HS   The short chimney and twin cracks above.

Ten yards right is the start of a small cluster of ribs and grooves.

64 Boomerang 5m M   The wide crack left of the first rib.

65 Boomerang Buttress 6m VS 4b   The blunt arête to the right.

66 Overhanging Chimney 6m HVD   The slightly leaning crack is the other side of the Boomerang fissure

The ribs and grooves farther to the right also give pleasant problems in the lower grades and are left to the individual explorer.

67 Herford's Girdle Traverse 76m S
A fine expedition. Start at the dry-stone wall at the left-hand end of the rocks, pass the Pinnacle, Sheltered Crack and make a high or low traverse to the overhanging Chockstone. Descend the Arête to a platform and move rightwards to the shelf of The Nithin. A crack leads to The Fly Walk which is climbed before an airy traverse to the top of A.P. Chimney. Traverse awkwardly to Paradise Corner.
Descend Little Pillar to a large platform. Cross this and ascend No Name until the ledge on Keep Corner can be reached. Descend Keep Arête and cross The Scoop to Footstool. Cross Fat Man's Chimney to a ledge to Deep Chimney and up to the top of the crag.
Harder variations include: 1. Descend The Fly Walk and reach across to The Niche. Continue the traverse to the mantelshelf on Studio. Regain the ordinary traverse by ascending A.P. Chimney.
2. From the ledge on Keep Corner traverse round to the ledge on Scoop Face. Descend Scoop Face to rejoin the ordinary traverse.

Index